Freya Stark (1893–1993), 'the poet of travel', was the doyenne of Middle East travel writers and one of the most courageous and adventurous women travellers of her generation. She travelled extensively throughout Syria, Palestine, Lebanon, Iran, Iraq and Southern Arabia, where she became the first western woman to travel through the Hadhramaut. Usually alone, she ventured to places few Europeans had visited. Her travels earned her the title of Dame and huge public acclaim. Her many, now  classic, books include *Traveller's Prelude*, *Ionia*, *The Southern Gates of Arabia*, *Alexander's Path*, *Dust in the Lion's Paw*, *East is West* and *Valleys of the Assassins*.

'It was rare to leave her company without feeling that the world was somehow larger and more promising. Her life was something of a work of art... The books in which she recorded her journeys were seductively individual... Nomad and social lioness, public servant and private essayist, emotional victim and mythmaker.'

Colin Thubron, *The New York Times*

'Few writers have the capacity to do with words what Faberge could do with gems – to fashion them, without violating their quality. It is this extraordinary talent which sets Freya Stark apart from her fellow craftsman in the construction of books on travel.'

The Daily Telegraph

'Freya Stark remains unexcelled as an interpreter of brief encounters in wild regions against the backdrop of history.' *The Observer*

'It is... as the writer of beautiful, measured prose rather than as a traveller or as an exotic 'character' who wore Dior in the wilder reaches of Asia and Arabian dress in London, that Freya Stark will ultimately be remembered.' *The Independent*

'One of the finest travel writers of our century.' *The New Yorker*

'A Middle East traveler, an explorer and, above all, a writer, Freya Stark has, with an incomparably clear eye, looked toward the horizon of the past without ever losing sight of the present. Her books are route plans of a perceptive intelligence, traversing time and space with ease.' *Saudi Aramco World*

Tauris Parke Paperbacks is an imprint of I.B.Tauris. It is dedicated to publishing books in accessible paperback editions for the serious general reader within a wide range of categories, including biography, history, travel and the ancient world. The list includes select, critically acclaimed works of top quality writing by distinguished authors that continue to challenge, to inform and to inspire. These are books that possess those subtle but intrinsic elements that mark them out as something exceptional.

The Colophon of Tauris Parke Paperbacks is a representation of the ancient Egyptian ibis, sacred to the god Thoth, who was himself often depicted in the form of this most elegant of birds. Thoth was credited in antiquity as the scribe of the ancient Egyptian gods and as the inventor of writing and was associated with many aspects of wisdom and learning.

THE SOUTHERN GATES OF ARABIA

A Journey in the Hadhramaut

Freya Stark

TPP

TAURIS PARKE
PAPERBACKS

New paperback edition published in 2011 by Tauris Parke Paperbacks
An imprint of I.B.Tauris and Co Ltd
6 Salem Road, London W2 4BU
175 Fifth Avenue, New York NY 10010
www.ibtauris.com

First published in 1936 by John Murray (Publishers) Limited

Cover image: 'Yemen – Wadi Dawan' © Lucie Debelkova

ISBN: 978 1 84885 315 7

A full CIP record for this book is available from the British Library
A full CIP record is available from the Library of Congress

Library of Congress Catalog Card Number: available

Printed and bound in Great Britain by CPI Cox & Wyman, Reading, RG1 8EX

THIS BOOK IS DEDICATED TO

The Royal Air Force,
And especially to those in Aden
Who made the writing of it possible
By carrying me to safety from Shibam

Contents

Map

Author's Note

The reader will find, scattered in the pages of this book, the names of many to whom I owe a debt of gratitude: Lord Halifax, Sir Akbar Hydari, Mr. Marmaduke Pickthall, H.H. The Sultan of Makalla – by whose assistance I was enabled to find a welcome when first I landed in the Hadhramaut.

The Emir Salim ibn Ahmad ibn 'Abdullah al Qe'eti, Governor of Makalla: Their Highnesses the Sultans 'Ali ibn Mansur al-Kathiri of Sewun and 'Ali ibn Salah al Qe'eti of Qatn: the Sayyids of the House of al-Kaf in Sewun and Tarim: Husain and Sa'id al-A'jam of Shibam: the Governors Muhammad and Ahmad Ba Surra of Do'an: and the Sayyids of the House of 'Attas in 'Amd and in Meshed: through their combined assistance and friendship my journeys were made possible and pleasant. In Aden I must thank the Resident, Sir Bernard Reilly, Colonel Lake and Air Commodore Portal for their kind encouragement at the beginning and their prompt and generous assistance at the end of my journey: Mr. A. Besse for valuable help and even more valuable advice of every sort; Squadron-Leader Haythorne Thwaite and Flight-Lieutenant Guest for their devoted care in the rescue from Shibam: and the Doctors, Matron and Nurses of the European General Hospital afterwards.

I must thank the Royal Geographical Society and the Percy Sladen Trustees in London for their help and encouragement: and Mr. Rhuvon Guest for his invaluable assistance during the writing of my book – an assistance to which such Islamic learning as appears within its pages is chiefly due.

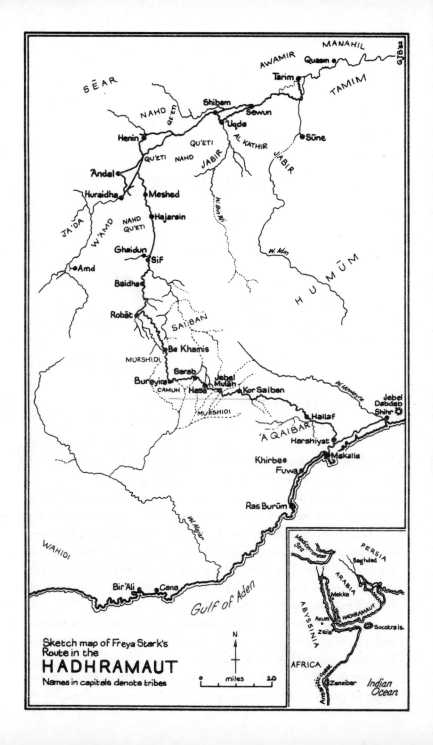

Sketch map of Freya Stark's
Route in the
HADHRAMAUT
Names in capitals denote tribes

Introduction

The Incense Road

> "Who is this that cometh out of the wilderness like pillars of smoke, perfumed with myrrh and frankincense, with all powders of the merchant?"
>
> (Song of Solomon.)

> "Centumque Sabaeo
> Ture calent arae sertisque recentibus halent."
>
> (Aeneid I, 416.)

In the first century of our era an anonymous Greek sea captain wrote the *Periplus of the Erythræan Sea*. He was neither educated not literary, but he wrote for the information of sailors and merchants, taking one by one the Red Sea ports of his time, their markets and exports, and following first the western, then the eastern coast, to the regions near Zanzibar whence "the unexplored Ocean curves around towards the West" and eastward to Malacca, "the last part of the inhabited world . . . under the rising sun."

Few books are more beguiling than this of the old captain – for elderly I think he must have been to have had so intimate a knowledge of voyages behind him.

After his African journey to the frankincense lands that lie by the Cape of Spices which is now Cape Guardafui, he starts from Egypt eastward. He passes the trader's road from Petra where the King of the Nabatæans collected dues, and, sailing along the coast of Arabia, tells how "the land next the sea is dotted here and there with caves of the Fish Eaters," and "the country inland is peopled by rascally men who live in villages and nomadic camps, by whom those sailing off the middle course are plundered, and those surviving shipwrecks are taken for slaves. Therefore we hold our course down the middle of the Gulf, and pass on as fast as possible by the country of Arabia, until we come to the Burnt Island. (Jebel Tair 15°35′N. 41°40′E.) directly below which there are regions of peaceful people, nomadic, pasturers of cattle, sheep and camels."

Here he reaches the Himyaritic kingdom of Yemen, the last of the ancient independent empires of Arabia, and its port Muza [which is now Mokha or Mauza'], "crowded with Arab ship owners and seafaring men, and busy with the affairs of commerce. . . . "

Here are the high-shouldered mountains of Yemen, dark with abysses and overhanging summits, beyond a yellow foreground of sand a two days' journey. Their multitudinous flat heads are massed in distance to one heavy range, so that, as Hamdani says, "they are not many mountains, but one mountain, called Sarrat, which goes from Yemen to Mekka." Their colour, seen from the sea, is not that of the temperate mountains of earth, but is smouldering and dusky, as if the black volcanic points were coated with desert sand, and the red sandstones subdued by ashes of volcanoes – like embers of coal dying in a crust of cinders.

From here the old navigator sailed southward between converging coasts. Where the sun-darkened waves grow more frequent, he entered the channel of Bab el Mandeb, which "forces the sea together and shuts it into a narrow strait, the passage which the island Diodorus [now Perim] divides." Close above it, "directly on the strait by the shore," was a "village of Arabs called Ocelis . . . an anchorage and a watering place, and the first landing for those sailing into the gulf from the south." This was the most convenient port from India, and north of it no Indian ships were allowed, for the Arabs guarded the secrets of their trade for centuries before the Romans came. The anchorage of Perim and Shell tanks have now taken the place of Ocelis; but the smooth ridges, the treeless snouts of land, the current racing round the sharp corner, are there unchanged; and beyond, "the sea widening again toward the east and soon giving a view of the open ocean," we still follow, as did the old sailor, the south Yemen coast, and drop anchor in "Eudaemon Arabia, a village by the shore, of the kingdom of Caribael (the Himyaritic king in Yemen) and having convenient anchorages and watering places, sweeter and better than those at Ocelis." This was Aden, the meeting place of East and West.

Beyond it, eastward, "is a continuous length of coast and a bay extending two hundred miles or more, along which there are Nomads and Fish Eaters living in villages; and just beyond the cape projecting from this bay, another market town by the shore, Cana of the Frankincense country. Inland from this place lies the Metropolis Sabbatha [now Shabwa] in which the king lives. All the frankincense produced in the country is brought by camels to that place to be stored, and to Cana on rafts held up by inflated skins after the manner of the country and in boats. . . . The place has a trade also with the African ports, with Barygaza [Broach in India] and Oman and Persia."

Thus the old sailor wrote – a newcomer into what was once the richest and most rigidly guarded and perhaps the oldest of all the trade routes of the ancient world.

Its secret had been revealed only a few years before his time. In A.D. 45, Hippalus, a Greek, was the first Western navigator to discover the use of the monsoon. He led Mediterranean commerce across the Indian Ocean. After him the Romans, conquerors of the northern caravan routes and of Egypt, and tired of paying Arabian dues, gradually fought for a sea-way of their own, and pushed into the forbidden waters in new and larger vessels garrisoned with bowmen.

But no one knows how long before them, in what morning light of history this trade began, nor when Dravidian boats first set their single sail, and with high carved stern and rudder at the quarter, and sun and wind behind them in the favourable season, first crossed the Indian Ocean and dumped their cargoes on its Arabian shore.

Here "the Frankincense country, mountainous and forbidding, wrapped in thick clouds and fog, yields frankincense from the trees," and Arab camelmen waited under the dust of their camps as they do now, and in their bales, together with the incense of Arabia and Africa, tied pearls and muslins from Ceylon and silks from China, Malacca tortoiseshell and spikenard from the Ganges, Himalayan cinnamon leaves, called Malabathrum,

> "*coronatus nitentes*
> *malobathro syrio capillos.*"

And from India, diamonds and sapphires, ivory and cotton, indigo, lapis lazuli, and cinnamon and pepper above all. And dates and wine, gold and slaves from the Persian Gulf; and from the eastern coast of Africa, long subject to Arabian traders, frankincense, gold and myrrh, ivory and ostrich feathers and oil.

From the sandy coastal strip, relays of beduin and camels took the bales through defiles of the hills, over the plateau steppe to inland valleys and the eastern lands of Yemen, till they reached their markets through the deserts north of Mekka, and the Arabian incense smoked on altars of Damascus, Jerusalem, Thebes, Nineveh or Rome.

This was the great frankincense road whose faint remembrance still gives to South Arabia the name of Happy: whose existence prepared and made possible the later exploits of Islam. On its stream of padding feet the riches of Asia travelled: along its slow continuous thread the Arabian empires rose and fell – Minean, Sabæan, Katabanian, Hadhramaut and Himyar. One after another they grew rich on their strip of the great highway; their policy was urged by the desire to control more of it, to control especially the incense regions of the south and the outlets to the sea: they became imperial and aristocratic, builders of tall cities; they colonized Somaliland and Ethiopia and made themselves masters of the African as well as the Arabian forests.

We can scarcely realize what riches their monopoly gave them in days when every altar and every funeral was sweetened with frankincense. Sacred rooms were kept to store it in the Temple of Jerusalem. To the Temple of Amon, in the early twelfth century B.C., 2,159 jars and 304,093 measures were delivered in one year: and the Chaldean priests burnt ten thousand talents' weight annually on the altar of Bel in Babylon alone. A thousand talents' weight used to be paid as tribute by the Arabs to Darius. Alexander the Great, after the taking of Gaza, sent five hundred to his tutor, who had reproached him in Macedon for extravagance to the gods.

"Let us only take into account the vast number of funerals that are celebrated throughout the whole world each year, and the heaps of odours that are piled up in honour of the bodies of the dead." So Pliny wrote (VII, 42), and concluded: "It is the luxury of man, which is displayed even in the paraphernalia of death, that has rendered Arabia thus 'happy.'" He describes the precautions which were taken for the safeguarding of the precious merchandise; the penalty of death imposed on its carriers if they deviated from the highroad between the sea and Shabwa; the "single gate left open for its admission" into that city; the rule in Alexandrian shops where workmen were stripped before leaving, their aprons sealed and a mask or net put over their head. All proves the value of this cargo, which merchants sent two thousand miles from sea to sea across Arabia, and sold eventually in Rome "at one hundred times its cost."

To the magnitude of this commerce must also be added the riches of accumulated time, for the earliest days of the traffic are quite unknown. The Minean nation, the first we hear of, "through whose country is the sole transit for the frankincense, along a single narrow road" has king lists which probably go back to the thirteenth century B.C. at latest. Inscriptions show it emerging like Minerva, fully armed, civilized and prosperous already from the uninvestigated background of Arabia, and with an alphabet whose ancestor is our own. What pre-historic adventures brought it to this emergence, what migrations lie behind, where and by whom the alphabet was invented, is all undiscovered: nor has anyone except Joseph

Halévy, disguised as a Yemen Jew, ever visited Ma'in, the Minean capital in Najran.

South of it and later, the Sabæan kingdom flourished – the Sheba of Solomon – with capital at Marib, also on the incense road and visited by Arnaud, Halévy and Glaser. The centre of power continually shifts to the South. As the Sabæans increased they absorbed their Katabanian neighbours, whose city of Tamna' – yet unknown – must have been near their mint at Harib, also on the incense road; for Pliny declares that "the incense can only be imported through the country of the Gebanitae," who were successors of the Katabanians in Tamna.' After the Sabæan, the Himyarite – last of the ancient Arab kingdoms – ruled from Tzafar near Yerim and survived into Christian times: the Imam of Yemen to this day sprinkles red dust on his letters to show his descendance from Himyar.

But the key of the trade lay east of all these nations in the cliff-bordered valley and narrow defiles of Hadhramaut, whose "people alone . . . and no other people among the Arabians behold the incense tree"; who ruled over the port of Cana and the coastlands to Dhufar; and whose capital Shabwa, the Sabota of Pliny "situate in a lofty mountain" and with sixty temples within its walls, could open or lock from its single gateway the sluices that fed the great commercial road.

Shabwa, last year, was still unvisited. It is marked on the maps about sixty miles west of Shibam. In some early invasion, the Banu Kinda descended and the inhabitants, according to Yaqut, abandoned Shabwa and founded Shibam. However this may be, a few diminished tribes still dwell there round brackish wells, though at some distance, it is said, from the ancient site; they live by quarrying salt and have been doing so since the tenth century at least when the geographer Hamdani found them at it.

Yielding to a passion I have always had for roads or rivers, I thought last year to try to reach Shabwa by way of the Hadhramaut. Thence I would follow either the main route by Harib and Marib to Ma'in in Najran – the "single narrow road" which led, as we have seen, through the capitals of the four Arabian empires; or if this proved to be impossible, I would do what I could round Shabwa and return to the ancient port of Cana – somewhere near Bir Ali on the coast – along what must once have been the main thoroughfare through the hills.

Neither of these plans was realized. Shabwa, scarcely three days away and with no barrier to prevent approach, was yet, through the unkindness of fate, to be unattainable as the moon: I have trodden in dreams only the emptiness of its imperial road. But the valleys of Hadhramaut which lead up to it, and the inland cities, though they have been visited several times since 1843 when Von Wrede first ventured there disguised, still tempt one by the strangeness of their beauty to some record, even if it is mostly a record of failure.

NOTE. – I very much regret that the names of plants found in the Hadhramaut have not been correlated with their English equivalents. This is owing to the fact that the press in which the plants were collected for later identification, was damaged by salt water on its voyage home, and the specimens spoiled. For this, as for so much other exact information, the reader is referred to Mr. Ingrams's forthcoming book on the country.

1

The Arabian Coast

"I have seen
Pointing her shapely shadows from the dawn
And image tumbled on a rose-swept bay,
A drowsy ship of some yet older day."

("The Old Ships," FLECKER).

I have often wondered why a ship appears to be on the whole a more satisfactory possession than a woman. It is probably because, being so frail an object, precariously and visibly balanced between the elements, even the most obtuse of men realize the necessity of attention and tact at the helm. But women, though quite as fragile, perched on edges more razor-like, though intangible, amid eternities even more momentous, must evidently give a false impression of stability, since belated and absent-minded jerks so often take the place of that gentle hand upon the tiller which keeps both ships and human beings along their course. Hence the natural but unreasonable preference of peace-loving men for ships.

In the Indian Ocean this phenomenon should be more noticeable than elsewhere, for here the monsoon adds to the general reliability of things by blowing steadily in the same direction for the same

number of months in every year; which is more than can be said for
whatever breeze compels the average domestic craft. In comparative
certainty therefore the little fleets put out from African and South
Arabian harbours, laden, as they have been through the centuries,
with frankincense and myrrh; and about Christmas time they dump
their spicy cargoes in the sheds of Aden.

In 1934 about 1,200 tons of incense were exported from Dhufar
and 800 from Somaliland. All the frankincense in the world is grown
in these two regions. British Somaliland produces an average of 400
to 500 tons and Italian Somaliland of 500 to 600. But the Arabian
quality is better and the Dhufar coast, which exports about 1,000
tons, is the only district where crops are still collected twice a year,
as when in Pliny's day the white "summer" and the red "spring"
incense were differentiated in a general way.

The chief ports and villages of the Dhufar coast are: Saudah,
which sends out about 250 tons of incense; Mirbāt, 150 to 200 tons;
Rakhiūt, 200 tons; Jadib, 100 to 150 tons; Hadhbarm, Damghāt,
Dhabūt, each 100 tons; Al Ghaidha, 50 tons and Qishn, 200 to 250
tons. The best of it comes from Saudah, Hadhbarm and Mirbāt, and
the worst from Qishn.

The trees from which this ancient harvest is collected are varieties
of the *Burseraceæ* family, *Boswellia Carteri* and *Boswellia Bhuadajiana*,
and the Arabs divide them into four kinds, of which Hoja'i, produces
the best gum, and Shehri, Samhali and Rasmi the inferior qualities.
"These incense trees," says the old sea captain, "are not of great
height or thickness. They bear the frankincense sticking in drops on
the bark, just as the trees among us in Egypt weep their gum." The
most excellent incense grows a three days' camel journey from the
coast; the medium qualities come from the slopes and hill summits,
and the inferior kind is collected near the sea shore.

But other conditions also determine the value of the gum: its
colour, noted already in the inventories of Rameses III, which varies
from clouded tears of amber, or jade green pale and luminous as
moonlight, to a pebbly mixture brown as the bed of a Dartmoor
stream; its size; and the percentage of small glistening gravel with

which the Arab has tried unobtrusively to increase the weight of his merchandise: all these determine the value of the frankincense, which varies between £80 and £10 per ton.

From March to August the Arabs tap their trees with small incisions cut into the bark: the milky juice takes three to five days to dry according to the weather; if the sun is not hot enough, the gum has to finish its drying on the ground. In Pliny's time, the gathering of it was reserved to a small class; "not over three thousand families have a right to that privilege by hereditary succession. For this reason these persons are called sacred, and are not allowed, while pruning the trees or gathering the harvest, to receive any pollution, either by intercourse with women or contact with the dead; by these religious observances it is that the price of the commodity is so enhanced." At present this right of harvesting is often rented out to Somalis who cross over from Africa for this purpose. The ancient sacred character of the tree itself is found in many writers: Herodotus mentions winged serpents that guard it and fly to Egypt every spring – tree spirits following, along the caravan route, the precious drops cut from their living sides.

But the caravan route is dead now, and the incense region has dwindled from its western boundaries, owing rather to a decrease in demand than to any natural compulsion. The trees still grow and are harvested locally in secluded valleys of Hadhramaut, but the most western point of export appears to be al. Ghaidha; and the old port of Cana, 160 miles or so to the west, is hidden and lost in sand. The Arab sailing fleets, whose shapes are as ancient as those invisible buried ruins, pass unwittingly by the market of ghosts, hugging the twisted volcanic shore when the monsoon drops to winter quiet, on their way to the wharves of Aden.

Here in sheds dim with aromatic dust and impalpable spicy perfume, where pale bars of sunlight lie on the half-transparent gums, women bend their veiled heads over the shallow baskets, and with small hennaed fingers sort out the various grades: while the sailing fleets, making for home, load up their antique holds with drums of petrol.

One of these boats, a dhow from Kuwait, was cast away last January just beyond the headland of Bir Ali. Most of the petrol had been salvaged, but the Sultan of Bir Ali, whose beduin had dragged the stuff ashore, naturally looked upon it as a gift from Allah, not to be parted with except for cash. We in Aden have no treaty with Bir Ali on the subject of wrecks but we have a treaty with the neighbouring Sultan who pockets one-third the value of whatever the high seas send him. The Bir Ali Sultan had not yet acquired this civilized standard of piracy, and demanded a quarter. Under the circumstances, A.B., who owned the cargo, came to the conclusion that private negotiation might prove less costly than government assistance, and he told me that his little steamer, the *Amīn*, would take me on to Makalla on its way to Shihr, after depositing his Ambassador on the forgotten sands of Cana, there to do the best he could.

On the evening of January 12th I went on board. A.B. and Meryem took me out: the lights of boats swung like planets in the wide shallow arms of Aden bay. The warm friendship I was leaving, the night around, gave a sharpness to this short journey, as of leave-taking from home. Aden had been kind. Her evil report among early Hadhramaut travellers is not endorsed by me for, from the Resident downwards, I found friendliness and help on every hand. In my comfortable cabin, unlike the dhow in which I had first meant to round the southern coast, I thought of these things, and woke at 2 a.m. to realize that we were away, that the wind was rising, the eastern lighthouse glaring at us, with baleful intermittent eye across sloping waters, and that the *Amīn,* her poop rearing like a sea horse and the cabins on the very crest of it, was going to have a most unpleasant time with the Indian Ocean.

All that day we breasted a short swell, and everyone more or less felt ill. I reached the deck at intervals and saw the same flat desert shore and mountain line behind it – the bay of the Fish-eaters, though their huts were not to be seen. The Ambassador from next door came staggering along against the wind, his shawls and turban billowing in circles round an equally circular face, cheerful and placid and decorated with a gold tooth; a twitter of female conversation had been rising from his cabin and he explained that it was a widowed aunt returning to Makalla. I called on her, and found a woman singularly beautiful for an aunt, swathed in thin veils of flowered chiffon, crouched on the narrow sofa which she evidently found much less comfortable than an Arabian floor. She had the type of face one comes to know in Hadhramaut, very long and narrow, with a mouth large but sensitive and easily smiling, and brown eyes, brilliant, large and dark: a long neck and a necklace of gold beads. She welcomed my presence as that of a sister in this wild and unpleasant world of waters, whose effects she was trying to mitigate with buttery pastry; she felt the need, she said, of something heavy inside to keep things from going round and round. The pastry I felt sure would soon be going round too with the force of an animated tombstone, and I left before the catastrophe, after inducing her to risk decorum by opening an inch of porthole. In the clean, buffeting openness of outer air, I walked about reflecting on this extraordinary female ideal of travel in shut boxes through the world, to see and be seen by as little of it as possible. It seems to be an almost universal prejudice, only differing here and there in degree: Mrs. X, afraid to step for one moment out of her own circle, which comprises less than the tenth of a millionth part of the fascinating population of our globe, really acts on the very same principle as the Arabian aunt, alone in her dark and stuffy cabin.

Next morning a sudden quietness and silence suggested that we were at anchor. Close ahead was the eastern arm of a wide and lonely bay, supposed by some to be the ancient bay of Cana. Its dunes and benty grasses shone in the quiet sunshine of the morning. They wrapped the feet of volcanic knolls, dusty black, which rose to flat-topped buttresses and faded into a broad valley going north, the highway to Shabwa, and hiding-place no doubt of invisible oases, for no sign of cultivation showed in all the wide and varied land in sight. Only three ruined pillars and a square fort or tower gave the loneliness an accent, as it were; and a solitary dhow, companion and guardian of the wreck we came to visit, rode at anchor, her spars and delicate tracery tremulously reflected, the flower garlands carved on her high stern, the drooping red and white flag of Kuwait clear as an etching in the luminous air.

There is something more poignant than mere natural loneliness in the deserted vestiges of man: and the most solitary object on that shore was A.B.'s cargo, a derelict mound covered with tarpaulin and ropes, drawn up on to a sandy rise away from danger of the sea, and looking as little like a commercial venture worth two thousand pounds as one can well imagine.

We saw no human being, nor anything at all but the silent morning gaiety of an uninhabited world: but there were eyes upon us, and the top of the square tower presently began to heave like an ant-hill with figures and black shawls waved over the parapet in sign of peace. By the time we had our boat down, and the Captain and officer, Ambassador and clerk, three Arabs, travelling with bedsteads and children overweighted with ear-rings, bound for Habban in the interior, and myself – by the time all this was under way, the guardians of the wreck were already coming to meet us in a boat scooped out of a log and in a long huri in which five or six of them were standing. The huri has two pointed ends so that it can travel equally either way, and rises to the waves like a bride, while the crew stands aft, and scoops at the water with wooden discs nailed on to poles, ancestors of oars. It skimmed about us like a swallow round a fly and presently, when we reached shallow water, pounced: each Arab chose his passenger, seized him without waste of words, and pressing legs and arms into an expert compact bundle against the indigo and oil of his breast, deposited the Negotiating Party on the sand.

The Bir Ali Sultan belongs to the Al Wahidi tribe, descendants of Qoraish according to their own obviously inaccurate account. Wyman Bury numbers them among the aboriginal South Arabians, unadulterated by northern immigrants, and such they appear to look at. They are about four thousand in number, I was told: they have only recently and possibly not conclusively decided that commerce is more profitable than murder, and the way up through their country, the direct highway to Shabwa, travelled in its lower reaches by Von Wrede in 1843, is still largely unknown, dangerous, and unhealthy.

They themselves looked dangerous, if put to it, but handsome. Three or four of the chief among them came from their group to shake hands with grave unsmiling courtesy. Only a few wore turbans; but most wore loin-cloths and a cartridge belt, well filled – an amulet round the neck, a greasy fillet to hold back the hair in the latest débutante fashion, and a twist of silver bracelet above the right elbow. They had old guns inlaid with silver, and one or two of the fine Hadhramaut daggers, with sheath turned up almost in the shape of a U, embossed with rough cornelians, and stuck into the loin-cloth at an angle so as to be ready to their hand. Their beauty was in the bare torso, the muscles rippling in freedom under a skin to which a perpetual treatment of indigo, sun and oil gives a bloom neither brown nor blue, but something like a dark plum. They looked very much the masters of the situation, for our Captain was in a hurry and they were not, and that is always a strong position in diplomacy. Their Sultan, they said when questioned, was in Bir Ali across the bay, inland. Our Captain cast his eyes, blue and round in dismay, over that wide, dazzling expanse with no means of locomotion upon it. One of our hosts, with the nonchalant ease of a human being independent of machinery, girt up his loins by hitching up the loin-cloth, and started to walk.

"How long will it take him to reach the Sultan?" asked the Captain.

The Wahidis, interrupted by his irrelevant brusqueness in their polite beginnings of gossip with the Ambassador, turned to look at their landscape with new eyes. It is doubtful if they had ever thought how long it took them to walk across their bay.

"Two hours possibly," one of them suggested with no great conviction. "To-day the Sultan will come."

This seemed to be all that mattered and they turned back to more interesting topics, leaving the Captain to look with baffled European eyes at the disobliging landscape and to explain how the *Amīn* costs £75 a day when she stands still.

I should have liked to examine the fort, and the three pillars which belong to a ruined mosque used before water vanished from the promontory and drove the last inhabitants inland. In fact, I should have liked to descend altogether and take the ancient highway, in spite of the grim words of the *Periplus*, borne out by later travellers: "for these places are very unhealthy, and pestilential even to those sailing along the coast: but almost always fatal to those working there, who also perish often from want of food."

My letters, however, were to Makalla, and the Captain was not disposed to listen to suggestions for lingering by the way. We would go back, he said, to the *Amīn*, and hope to see the Sultan emerge from behind a sand-dune in fullness of time.

This we did, and bracketed our glasses for hours on that silent bay, while its folds and hills and scrub-coated hollows grew dimmer and whiter in the climbing heat of the morning. Three or four of the Wahidis had come on board and strolled gingerly about the decks, touching the white paint with suspicious wonder, as if it might come alive under their hands. One of them stepped through the open door of my cabin and, squatting down with the natural Arab freedom, let his eyes wander in silence round the strange appointments, electric fans, washstand and mirror, light and curtains, of the room: finally they rested with relief on the comparatively comprehensible white counterpane of my bunk; he began to stroke it with admiring fingers. He was a tall creature, nearly black, with some mixture of Africa in him – small regular features and a short curly beard, and hair, well oiled, tied behind his ears. "*In the way of a woman he snooded his locks in a fillet,*" like the Gilgamesh hero. The beautiful proportion of all his limbs was spoilt by two enormous thumbs. After a minute or so, he saw my jug of water, reached out to lift it, and began to drink.

"Good water," I remarked.

"Praise God, I have never tasted such. It is sweet."

"Have your wells salt in them?" I asked.

"Yes."

To drink all one's life from brackish wells: we can hardly imagine what that means. I have never suffered from extremity of thirst myself, and yet I have, ever since I can remember, a natural joy and gratitude for clear and running streams. "There is no drink like good water," I said.

Five or six of the Wahidis, who had gathered round their companion and were squatting by the open door, turned their faces suddenly with enthusiastic agreement; the charm of the beduin is his grasp of realities, his genuine aloofness from the trappings of existence: in spite of the strange and civilized world in which we met, the Wahidis and I had found a common ground. My first friend, now comfortably settled on the white counterpane, which would be blue with indigo when he got up, smiled.

"Why do you not come and stay at Bir Ali?" he suggested.

"Perhaps I may do so on my way back."

"But you are a Nasrani," said one of them – a lighter-complexioned man with the luxury of a yellow cashmere turban on his head. "You are going to burn in hell."

The gathering, it was evident, could not but agree with the accuracy of this statement, but deplored so brutal a way of putting it. I was not ready to agree, and remarked that the Nasara are people of the Book. "Before the day of Judgement," I said, "they will be gathered together by their Prophet, the Presence Jesus; and the Jews will be gathered by Moses: and the Messenger of God, God bless and save him, will gather the Believers, and all will go to Paradise. It is true that your traditions say that our prophet will enter a little later than the Messenger of God – but Eternity is very long, I see no great objection if my enjoyment of it begins a little later than yours."

This reasonable apology had just been received with relief by all except the yellow-turbaned one, who continued to mutter in a low voice to himself, when a horrified steward shooed my guest off the counterpane as if he had been a beetle, and scattered the assembly to a lower deck in a manner which, no doubt, strengthened their opinion as to our ultimate fate. The Captain, at the same time, came along and told me that the Sultan had sent messengers: scouts had told him of our arrival and he was hastening to us on a camel; but there was still no sign of any moving object, and if we waited longer we should reach Makalla too late to land that night. He was going to deposit the Ambassador on shore, leave him to do the best he could, and pick him up on his way back in two days' time.

The Ambassador accordingly was lowered down into the boat, together with the chief officer, a keg of water, a keg of whisky, a roll of bedding and some bags of food. The Wahidi beduin, surprised at this impatience, but silent, settled in their huri to escort him back to the fort: and as the *Amīn* pulled up her anchor and made for the island of Baraka in the East, the last we saw of the bay of Cana was our Negotiating Party marooned on its shore, the square fort silent, lifeless and windowless behind them, and the great bay, with its half-buried volcanoes, its buried markets and dead histories, no more to outward seeming than one among the many reaches of loneliness along the Arabian shore.

2

Landing

*"As when to them who sail
Beyond the Cape of Hope, and now are past
Mozambic, off at sea north-east winds blow
Sabæan odours from the spicy shore
Of Araby the Blest."*

("Paradise Lost," iv. 156.)

We now had before us, on our left, the wild mountain coast of the incense land, that very "deep bay which is called Sachalites" – the same word as Shihr and Sawahil, and a form of the Arabic Sahl, or coastland. The coastal incense is still called Shehri and the town of Shihr perpetuates the name which seems to have been used all through the Middle Ages for the coastal strip west of 'Oman as distinct from inland Hadhramaut to the north of it.

All this country between Cana and "the great promontory facing the east called Syagrus" (Ras Fartak, 15°36′N. 52°12′E.) was once part of the incense land. On the promontory itself was a fort, harbour and storehouse, and from here the incense was probably carried to Cana on "rafts held up by inflated skins and in boats," or taken by the Wadi 'Adm, or from Saihut by the Wadi Hadhramaut, to Terim and eventually to Shabwa – the natural thoroughfare to this day. Shihr as a town, however, is not mentioned by any of the ancients, but came to replace Cana later on, and is recorded by Marco Polo as Escier, and by Yaqut, etc. Makalla is not on any natural easy outlet to the north, and seems to have come into existence much later. The first contemporary mention of it is by Ibn Mujawir in the fourteenth century, and it remains in almost unbroken obscurity until 1829, when the British came after abandoning Aden, and until 1834 when Haines, looking for a naval base, examined both Makalla and Sokotra.

Few and vague references to this country show how much it was left to itself during all the centuries of Islam. The kings and sultans of Yemen held a nominal suzerainty at intervals, but only once do we get a vivid glimpse, when Sultan Muzaffar moved with three armies, from the West, to invade it in the twelfth century. The cause or pretext of the war, like that of the British seizure of Aden later, was the looting of a ship which the men of Dhufar held up as it travelled along their inhospitable shore. Sultan Muzaffar, one of the few strong rulers of Yemen, decided to conquer the country and gave a rendezvous to his three armies at Raisut in Dhufar. It is a pity that so few details of the march are given, for their stations no doubt were those of the old incense road and an account of them might have solved the uncertainty which still envelopes the tract between Hadhramaut and Dhufar. All we are told is that the northern army took five months to march from San'a in Yemen to Raisut, fighting all the way with the Habudhis, the people of the land.

The second army marched along the coast, finding great natural obstacles, but keeping in touch with the fleet, which constituted the third invading force, and acted as commissiarat on just the same principle as that adopted by Ibn Sa'ud on his recent descent from Hejaz to Yemen. Every day provisions were landed and a market set up on shore: until at last the objective was reached, the three armies met in the plain of Dhufar, and established the Muzaffarid sovereignty there. Muzaffar's general was left to command the difficult and gradual conquest of the Hadhramaut. It took him a month to reach Shibam from Dhufar, but here again the route is not given, though until further evidence appears to the contrary, I am inclined to think that the normal way must have lain inland by the Wadi Hadhramaut either from Saihut or Shihr and that the piece between Saihut and Dhufar was done by sea. It is a fact that the incense, so strongly guarded in storehouses at Cana and Syagrus, where land routes debouched, was left, according to the *Periplus* "in heaps all over the Sachalitic country (of Dhufar), open and unguarded, as if the place were under the protection of the gods; for neither openly nor by stealth can it be loaded on board ship without the king's permission; if a single grain were loaded without this, the ship could not clear from the harbour." This system, easy enough to work at a sea port in which every outgoing craft can be examined, would be almost impossible on an overland route where, any dark night, a few camel loads could be filched away unseen.

We, on this our first day, having left the region of Cana, travelled eastward still tossing violently, and looked out through the afternoon on the volcanic fringes of the Sachalitic bay. There, in my mind, I could see the medieval army, barefooted, dark-skinned and bright-turbaned, loosely scattered about those pathless heights of rock that overhang the sea. No grimmer coast can be imagined. The mountains are sharp – naked apparently as when they hissed in black coils from the darkness of earth, lonely and hard as death, and with a derelict and twisted beauty. Their cliff faces press one behind the other towards the sea, whose luminous moving waves seemed to repeat in gentler and more living form the chaos of their desolate chasms and ridges.

The Captain grew anxious as the afternoon wore on and the prospect of making Makalla before night grew less hopeful. Sunset came and threw a pink glitter on the western slopes of sea and shore, and cast the *Amīn's* shadow before us on the water. My female neighbour, still swathed in veils in her cabin, banged on her wall at frequent intervals to ask for company, and I sat with her as long as I could stand the atmosphere, admiring the gold beads round her neck. The beads were made in Do'an and she wore in the centre a striped sort of stone which she told me the beduin bring "from the desert"; it is called Sawwama, and every woman of these valleys likes to wear one, and will pay as much as 100 rupees for it, looking upon it as a sort of talisman.

Like a peacock's tail opening, night filled the sky. The green western light, fan-shaped from the sunset, transparent as water, died into the cold blue upper dome; the coastline turned to a silhouette, and so did the Indian helmsman at the wheel. These small, dark, round-headed people from Surat are found in most steam vessels of the coast; aloof and cheerful, they move about in blue tunics made by themselves, with flowers and flags embroidered and seams worked traditionally in a white wave pattern, and a red sash at their waist. I bought one for a rupee, as I lay on deck in languid discomfort, until at last at about 8 p.m. a few dim lights in the black wall of the coast showed us Makalla.

We stole upon it almost unawares and anchored in an uneasy swell, for there is no harbour here for anything larger than a dhow; the town, indeed, seemed in that dimness to cling like a barnacle to its cliff. Above it, two bald unequal shoulders of hill pushed into moonlight, with a ledge below, whether of vegetation or mere darkness I could not see: four small square towers, now abandoned, guarded the ledge. Below, in deep shadow, lights glimmered here and there; not the open welcoming lights of our cities, but furtive things, half hidden, one could see, by shutters and high walls; their diversity gave the city its mystery, a bright flare here, a little rushlight there, no street lamps in rows, but round the minaret a subdued glimmer to show its slender tracery from below. A drum was beating; a lamp moved at intervals, carried by some slave before his master through uneven streets. Outside the walls lay the unbroken night: a valley pale and bare in moonlight on the left; a shining beach of sand. We swung tethered in lapping water. More than the alien harbour and its secret and unconscious life before us, the feeling of its solitary surrounding spaces impressed itself upon one, an unconfined remoteness in the quiet night.

The Captain's sentiments took another form.

"They are wild men," he said over and over again, as he stood waiting to be taken ashore. He had to find dhows to salvage A.B's wrecked cargo when the Bir Ali Sultan could be induced to part with it: and the owners of the dhows, knowing themselves for once indispensable, were going to drive as hard a bargain as they could. The Captain's eyes were rounder and bluer than ever as he foresaw what lay before him. "They jabber at you in their Arabic," he complained, unreasonably, I thought, since after all Arabic is the language of an Arabian dhow. The thought of dropping me alone on that un-British shore was almost more than he could bear: but he promised to do his best to get me off that night against all sunset regulations, and he splashed off in his boat from our moonlit ship into the shadow of the town.

He stayed away for hours. The lights of Makalla went out one by one. The night grew late and the moon strengthened; the ghostlike shape of the city appeared – tall, straight walls clustered together, built like white fortifications from the water. Through the exquisite stillness a clanking noise of wood came from the shadow of the harbour; a dhow unfurled her sail. Scarce visible against the illuminated water, the beautiful pale triangle bellied out between us and the town: and moved noiselessly into the darkness of the sea.

Then the police approached in a huri, swishing like a black shark in the path of the moonlight, and introduced themselves – a passport clerk in khaki and four negroes in blue uniforms with wine-coloured collars, tarbush on their head, and rifle at their shoulder. They asked if I wished to land. I said that I did, and caused evident consternation. They would get me a boat. The police huri, I suggested, was good enough. But this was out of the question. A nobler boat, they said, must be provided. It was a polite fiction, but there was nothing for it but acquiescence; the police disappeared: and Makalla bay settled back into its moonlit peace, until a flurry of lights and voices brought the exhausted Captain home.

"Wild men, all talking Arabic," was still the burden of his woes. The dhow masters were asking enormous sums; the Emir of the Sea, in other words the harbour master, would not let me land so late at night; the Governor was out of reach in his palace; and we were going straightway down the coast to Shihr, and would leave Makalla and its problems for our return to-morrow.

I was so demoralized by the Indian Ocean that I did not undress that night, and was able to stroll out more or less steadily next morning and see the *Amīn* unloading rice in the early sunshine. The coast had changed to a sandy flat, with far and hazy hills, and Shihr, a wide-stretched town, sand-coloured and white, with four minarets and five domes and the solid square of the Sultan's palace in the middle of it, was visible beyond a line of surf and a beach of boats. Jebel Dabdab stands east of it, and has, they told me, an old Portuguese (?) town with towers and a cavern where, as in most eastern caves, adventurers are still supposed to die.

We were not landing, and the boats plied to and fro: they are sewn together with coco fibre without the use of nails, in the manner told of by Ibn Batuta and Marco Polo, who describe them as having no deck, but only a cover of hides on which horses used to be carried to India. Such are the boats of Shihr to-day, broad, pointed both at bow and stern, with the bow very undercut: with green, black and white patterns, and designs of fishes, and what looked like a mask and cross-bones painted on them: and rowed by an African slave population whose brawny bodies and flat faces were less pleasant to look at than the slender Wahidis of Bir Ali.

It took four hours to steam back from Shihr to Makalla, and we were back at our old anchorage in the early afternoon, opposite houses now dazzling in light against the red cliff wall and four white forts above. The white of Makalla has a peculiarly lovely quality, dovelike and cool against its hot background: it has a stucco splendour about it, magnificent from the sea, but rather dilapidated at close quarters.

It was now buzzing with our arrival, and presently out of an ant-like chaos the harbour boat materialized, with A.B's agent and the Governor's representative in the stern, in tarbushes under a black umbrella. The agent's tarbush was red; an ample gown of blue serge showed below: heavy cheeks designed on the same profuse and stratified scale, gold teeth, and a silver-headed cane held like a wand: he is an Indian, and lives with a divan of clerks around him near the harbour. 'Ali Hakīm, the Governor's envoy, I came to know better and became attached to during my stay: he was once a chemist in Aden, but has now settled as a sort of A.D.C. in Makalla and waddles about the Governor's business carrying his portly front before him inadequately buttoned into a brown overcoat over a striped cotton gown, with as much difficulty as might the elephant god if he were made to walk. His eyes had suffered some illness which made them nearly white; he had a deep husky voice in which he spoke Arabic very fast; and he was the kindest, plainest, and most solicitous overseer of one's comfort that anybody could desire. He now apologised five times without an interval for the delays of the night before. The doctor was introduced, a young Indian in topee with university behind him: then the police inspector, in smart khaki, who had learnt military neatness with the Aden levies: he saw to my twelve packages on one hand while on the other he dealt with the Emir of the Sea, the harbour master, who in a green gown and yellow turban, was demanding precedence of some sort. The argument took place on the gangway, among brown arms and legs in whose snaky tangle my goods were rapidly descending. The water was green as paint below: little wooden huris ran in and out with round oars: I sat in a shallow boat between my new protectors, carefully shaded under the black umbrella, with a delightful feeling of being at home and happy in all this clamour: while the Captain, leaning over his bulwarks, his face a picture of distress and pity, said to me: "God keep you safely," in a voice cloquent with forebodings which would have surprised no one so much as the friendly and hospitable crowd of "wild men" whose brown bodies, shouting and bending over their oars, were landing me on the steps of Arabia.

3

The Beduin Camp at the Gate of Makalla

"Sweet to ride forth at evening from the wells
When shadows pass gigantic on the sand
And softly through the silence beat the bells
Along the Golden Road to Samarkand."

("Hasan," FLECKER.)

The Sultan of Makalla's palace is at the west end of the town, near the battlemented gate by which all traffic, whether from Shihr or the north, must enter. The palace itself is on the sea, white and new, with coloured glass like a Brighton pavilion, and best seen by moonlight. The Governor's palace, the barracks, and various buildings, are all behind it enclosed in a walled space where a few palm trees grow – the only green in Makalla: in the same enclosure, and built on to the city wall, is the guest house; a few Yafa'i soldiers, lounging and smoking in the guard house at the entrance, keep watch on all the compound.

Here I spent five days, and looked from the windows of my room on the city wall to the camping place of caravans outside the gate.

The coast stretches beyond to a sweep of hills, where Ras Burum pushes out to sea. The sunset catches the ripples of the bay; they lap in two long curves of turning waves. A "raised beach" of white sand lies huddled by old monsoons against the hill: its dunes are pale in the evening light like the clouds, and the smoke that rises from the huts, and the farther hills from which the sunset shines in rays like the markings on a shell: the water has the same dove colour, only luminous. All else is brown and dun: the block of hill; the cane huts in front of it with mosque and minaret like a village church in England; three heaps of small dried fish as high as a man, called 'Aid or Wuzif, and sold by the basketful for camel fodder; and the wide sand foreground of the estuary, whose sober colours gather themselves discreetly to a climax in the living browns and fawns of camels couched in circles.

There are about six of these resting caravans, each of twenty or more camels and human beings. Their loads (chiefly brushwood it seems) are in among them, and people here and there; donkeys with drooping heads make an outer circle; inside, among its animals great and small, the family life goes on. The whole of the estuary is as full of people as Highgate Heath on a sunny morning; and always, when one looks towards the sea, some figure is outlined dark as ebony against the shining water, the freedom of its walk a joy to look at, its curly hair tied with a band round the forehead, and the scanty cotton loin-cloth so soaked with the indigo with which itself is dyed that no break of colour destroys that grace of movement.

I spent many hours at my window on the wall watching this picture of life below; so much so, that the little beduin girls who fill their goatskins at the fountain, waved and smiled, and hid their faces as they turned away with the load on their backs, their gowns, yellow or black, high to the knee in front and trailing behind them. Through the gate one could watch a continual stream of people, especially towards evening, when the tribesmen brought their supper from the town; they looked, as they came one after the other through the gate, with their provisions in their hand, like those tomb processions in Egypt, bearers of food for the dead: three fish on a string, or a slice of red shark with black fins, or baskets that dangled at each end of a yoke of wood they held across their shoulders. Even a small parcel looks conspicuous when you wear nothing in the way of clothes but a loin-cloth, a silver armlet, and a wisp of wool tied for luck under one or both knees.

There were more elaborate costumes for, when fully dressed, the young men of the town throw a cashmere shawl jauntily over one shoulder, the two ends down behind: and when they came to play football beyond the pool where the camels drank, or to stroll hand in hand along the valley road in the cool of the evening, they wore their futahs (loin-coths) as long as a kilt or even a skirt, coloured, with contrasting hem, and above it a European pattern of coat, some other colour equally gay – or a stockinette vest, of the kind we classify as underwear. Now and then a lorry might lumber up from Shihr, or a donkey trot under brushwood, some old naked man behind it completely blue with indigo, even to his ancient beard. Women carried their parcels on their heads, and walked, like Delilah

> "With all her bravery on, and tackle trim,
> Sails filled, and streamers waving"

in billowing draperies, but with a freedom of movement still felt beneath the volume of their folds. For no one in all that busy moving world wore either shoes or corsets; and it was this, I concluded, which gave them that grace and swallow-like motion, and living Hellenic loveliness.

One man particularly I remember. After squatting on the sand beside his camels to wash his arms and legs and head and mouth, he stood to pray. One could not see in the late light that he had anything on at all (though in the middle of the prayer he did as a matter of fact loosen and hitch up his futah). He stood there with a pose graceful and sure, his beard and hair and lean unpampered limbs outlined against the sand and sea – just a Man, with an indescribable dignity of mere Manhood about him. And when he had stooped to place his forehead on the ground, he came upright again with one spring of his body, as if it were made of steel.

Meanwhile darkness stole down; the last sunset red and first camp fire burned with the same colour; the straying parties by valley and shore grew fewer; the tribes gathered into the circles of their camels for the night. I had sat so long and so silently at my window that 'Awiz came in with the lamp without seeing me, and was concerned because the Emir had called and been told chat I was out.

'Awiz had been given me as a servant. He had a face like ebony, with a fierce expression – chiefly due to smallpox; a tuft under his chin and two slits of eyes gave it the shape of a triangle, which broadened and became suddenly charming when he smiled: he did this rarely, usually only when I asked him things about the inland valleys from which he came: he had been over twenty years a servant in the royal household, and had only once revisited them, when the Sultan rode up to Wadi Hadhramaut last autumn.

European women who live in the East and often complain of Arab servants would be surprised to hear of the devoted lifetimes given by these people to their native masters. They enter a household and become part of it, and think of no private life beyond; and if they happen to be bad at things like valeting or waiting, this is taken as a dispensation of Providence, is borne as one bears the unfortunate deficiencies of a son or daughter, and does not interfere with the natural kindliness of the relationship. I have never heard an Arab speak roughly to his servant, even under severe trials of patience. The Queen of Iraq, when I was there, had a particularly bad cook, so much so that King Faisal offered to send her his own excellent one instead; but the queen, a gentle and charming woman, was attached to the cook's wife and used to go with her to the cinema now and then, and refused the exchange. In the Hadhramaut, a small slave or servant is given to every infant member of any well-to-do family, and they grow up devotedly together.

Besides 'Awiz, I had a sort of major-domo, a bearded patriarch from Huraidha who used to come every morning, look kindly down at me with proud old eyes under a red and white turban, settle his crimson plaid royally over his shoulder, and ask what I would like for lunch.

I was charmingly looked after in the Sultan's guest house. Water, brought in conduits from the western wadi, flowed into a European bathroom. I had a bed with a mosquito net, and a dressing-table with a mirror. The dining-room had a long table, six varnished chairs, and two best ones at the bottom upholstered with pink plush roses. Opening out from this apartment, the reception-room grew quite a forest of red and yellow striped upholstery, with padded crescents of the same cheerful colour to catch the small of one's back when one sat down. Mother-of-pearl ash-trays, a bronze equestrian figure, photographs of royal parties – the German ex-Kron-prinz in one foreground – beautified the walls or sprouted about on small occasional tables. Over all this the happy-go-lucky East had spread its casual veil; dust and cigarette ends lay there, left by former guests; bats flicked in and out; mice ate one's clothes in the chest of drawers: the East is vast, such small untidiness sinks into its ample bosom, and worries no one except the fussy European.

When the evening came, and the sweet shrill cry of the kites, that fills the daylight, stopped, 'Awiz appeared with three paraffin lanterns, which he dotted about the floor in various places, and, having given me my supper, departed to his home. The compound with its dim walls, its squares of moist earth planted with vegetables and few trees, grew infinite and lovely under the silence of the moon. The gate of the city was closed now; a dim glow showed where the sentries beguiled their watch with a hookah in the guard house; at more or less hourly intervals they struck a gong suspended between poles, and so proclaimed the hour. And when I felt tired, I would withdraw from my verandah, collect and blow out the superfluous lanterns, and retire to my room. None of the doors shut easily, so I did not bother to lock them; I had refused the offer of a guard to sleep at my threshold, the precaution was so obviously unnecessary. As I closed my eyes in this security and silence, I thought of the Arabian coasts stretching on either hand: – three hundred miles to Aden; how many hundred to Muscat in the other direction? the

Indian Ocean in front of me, the inland deserts behind: within these titanic barriers I was the only European at that moment. A dim little feeling came curling up through my sleepy senses; I wondered for a second what it might be before I recognized it: it was Happiness, pure and immaterial; independent of affections and emotions, the aetherial essence of happiness, a delight so rare and so impersonal that it seems scarcely terrestrial when it comes.

4

Life in the City

"The merchants of Sheba and Raamah, they were thy merchants: they occupied in thy fairs with chief of all spices, and with all precious stones, and gold. . . . "

(Ezekiel 27, v. 22.)

The Indian agent to whom I was recommended did not do very much on my behalf. I met him near his office by the custom house a day or two after my arrival, and he excused himself for not having called.

"A baby of mine died," said he.

I was sorry to hear this, but he brushed the subject aside with his silver-headed cane.

"It does not matter," he said. "It was a small one, and I have lots more. The women make a fuss about it."

Condolence seemed out of place. I left him and continued to explore the city with an Afghan chauffeur whom the Governor had kindly placed at my service together with his car. He used to drive slowly along the High Street, stopping to let me look into dark doors of shops, their wares exposed against the outer wall. There is not much to be bought in Makalla, and most of it is food of some sort set out in open baskets and made invisible by flies. There is no local manufacture except that of the curved daggers and of baskets large and vividly dyed. The drying of fish, of sea-slugs (*Holothuria edulis*) and of sharks' fins for China, the dyeing with indigo, and pressing of sesame oil, comprise the industry of the town: the Indian Ocean is a good highway, and most things come by sea; and the little business there is centres round the harbour, where dhows show their rigging and high sterns against the background of cliff, and black slaves with huge naked limbs lie asleep on the bales of the custom house, waiting for a load.

The whole town is one crowded street parallel with the sea: its western end is going to be a boulevard, but is still no more than an obstacle course of holes and blocks of stone along the sea front. The side streets climb at right angles to this main thoroughfare and end almost immediately against the cliff. The houses cling there one above the other, white and grey, with carved doors and windows, but often ruinous on a nearer view. Here are the oil presses, about twelve open sheds built for shade, where blindfolded camels – a little basket covering each eye – walk slowly in circles for ten hours every day and pull a pole weighted with boulders, by which the upper millstone grinds the seed. The seed is in a sort of funnel in the centre, which holds about 36 lb. and is filled five times a day. The camel carries on his dreary circular task with his usual slow and pompous step and head poised superciliously, as if it were a ritual affair above the comprehension of the vulgar; and no doubt he comforts himself for the dullness of life by a sense of virtue, like many other formalists beside him.

The Sultan's old palace is near the harbour, and is now a public building where the Governor holds his divan, the Qadhis give judgment, and the Treasury and such offices are lodged. The revenue comes from customs and land tax in the interior: Makalla itself has no taxable land. The law is the Muhammedan shari'a, and the Sultan is its ultimate appeal.

To the east, where the town opens out on a little headland beyond the cemetery, I visited the prison. It was an ordinary whitewashed house on the outside, with a carved and sunbleached door: a toothless old guard opened when my Afghan knocked, his thin face shaded by an immense green turban, and a key in his sash. He was pleased to show us his prison, though he could not remembered how many prisoners there were: no one went among them, he told me. Their food was pushed through a hole under the door, and one might see them from the roof above. We climbed, and looked over a low parapet into a sort of pit, pillared and dark, where ten or twelve tribesmen and as many children squatted among heaps of refuse. They leaped up when they saw us outlined against their blue square of sky.

"Peace be upon you," we said.

They replied in chorus and, seeing the camera in my hand, began to argue blusteringly among themselves for and against a photograph. Their black figures scarce showed against the dusky background and the children danced about like imps of darkness crying: "Take, take a picture!" Some stretched out their arms and pretended to point rifles at us. "Now shoot," said they, and I took my picture without waiting further. All the children and most of the men were hostages, taken from tribes who misbehave; they are changed every month or two. Cases of illness (which one would imagine to be constant under the circumstances) are put in hospital, and once a week the whole establishment is led to bathe in the sea before it says its Friday prayer. Makalla is not one of the states that send delegates to International Prison Conferences: and perhaps it is as well, for I feel sure that these beduin prefer their unhygienic misery in common, to solitary comfort in a model cell.

As for the system of hostages, it is not easy to suggest an alternative in countries where the writ of government has to run over wildernesses. Forty years ago, when Hirsch travelled in the Hadhramaut, the beduin used to levy toll to the gate of Makalla itself and make about 550 dollars a year; the contrast of order and peaceful commerce now is very great. But I was haunted for the rest of the day by that vision of darkness and squalor and sent an offering to be distributed next morning – an effort greeted with approval by my friends in Makalla, who hold that the sufferings of the poor are part of the necessary furniture of the world, a sort of perpetual gymnasium where the rich can practise virtue when they feel so inclined.

By the end of my stay in the town, the mixed people of the High Street, Beduin, Arab and Negro, had begun to grow accustomed to the sight of me, but even then their excitement was great enough to gather a crowd whenever I left the defences of the car: they were friendly, but I am only five foot two, and a way had to be cleared whenever I wished to see anything beyond their hot tumultuous faces. Only once did I make for the town on foot and then gave it up as a bad job and turned to the cliff in search of solitude; about fifty children pursued, calling "Nasrani" in a monotonous but not insulting way, till the climb took their breath. The cliff was very steep; when we reached the ledge where the four forts are, the weaklings had dropped off, and those that remained had developed the friendliness of sharers in an exploit.

We came to one of the little forts, with a small and useless gun beside it. A carved door opened half-way up, and its pyramid sloping walls were finished off with a battlement flourish at each corner. These watch-towers are called Kuts. They are all aligned on a plateau ledge which must have been quite recently inhabited, as it still has plain traces of square fields, and the top of the hill above is covered with untidy graves, not very ancient. It took some tact and persuasion to make the Somali slave who was attending me reach this hill top, and of the eleven small boys who still clung to us not one had ever been so far before; and yet the whole ascent only took an hour and a half. The truth is that mountaineering is not looked upon as a treat along the coast of South Arabia, – there are too many empty hill tops all about.

From the top we had a fine but barren view over inland rust-coloured waves of landscape, to small villages north of us in palms, where Makalla goes for summer coolness, and to the valleys that lead by long ridges to Do'an. East of us was the mound-like hill of Shihr, and Wadis Buwash and Rukub between; west of us, Fuwa, where the R.A.F. have a landing-ground, and below us the sea, with porpoises playing in it. Our hill had a wide rounded top; the pinkish veined surface of its rock looked as if it had been smoothed with a giant plane, so sharp were the edges of its honeycombed cavities; I am no geologist, but I imagine that this peculiar surface is the work of strong sand-whirling winds that scoop and wear the rock like emery. It is at all events of a most unyielding hardness; my barefoot troop grew tired as we followed a naked little gulley down the northern slope, and came out on the inland road where two forts guard the approaches to the sea and look well in the wrinkled passage of the hills, their walls the same hill-colour.

Above them is the town's water supply and the Sultan's garden, a green enclosure with a raised tank in the middle of it and a dilapidated summer palace. I drove here on my first day in Makalla, and wandered under the trees among squares of vegetables – aubergines, ladies' fingers, peppers, bidan trees with big leaves and nut-like fruit of which they eat the red pulp, pomegranates, bananas, vines and other things unrecognized – but no mere flowers. Two small dark gardeners followed me about, like ghosts still plying their prehistoric craft, which the earliest dwellers in this land must have practised – probably in exactly the same way, making with bare feet the small ridges of earth that separate one water runnel from the next.

As we came away we picked up a lanky young sheikh out for a walk and glad of a lift: he had been praying for a car, he said.

"Allah must have sent us," I remarked.

He agreed dubiously, not very sure of an unbelieving woman as an instrument of Allah. But he relaxed gradually, and told me that he would like to travel, but was poor.

"That," said I, "is because you are learned. All the learned are poor. If they were not poor, they would stop being learned."

To this he also agreed, reluctantly and sadly. He was not cut out for books, and would have been much happier as a soldier. I mentioned that I had visited the al-Azhar university in Cairo and that the term of study there is thirteen years – to which he remarked very sensibly that this was too long.

"You have studied, and your life – where is it?" he asked.

We were distracted from this rather sad review of the student's lot by the sight of a fine bushy fox under a rock; he did not move, but waited, and watched us as we passed, ready to run, his body alert and intelligent – a lucky creature, not made to be religious against his will. The young sheikh drew his cotton shawl close round his shoulders in the slight chill of evening: he was anæmic and pale. He left me at the gate of the town, anxious not to compromise himself by such doubtful company: the little human flicker disappeared; his sheikhly manner returned; and he strode away with a formal word and sudden mask-like face, a religious model in all but his walk, which was still that of a free and wild young animal under the clumsy gown.

One day my Afghan took me to Fuwa to see the R.A.F. landing-ground. It is one of many which we have dotted about the Arabian coasts, and it is in a wide open landscape leading to Wadis Khirbe and Hajar in the north. The cairns of loose stones that mark it are whitewashed to make them conspicuous in the general red and brown of the landscape, and by the natural development of history they will no doubt eventually become shrines to commemorate celestial visitations, long after the actual aeroplanes are forgotten. The place is thirteen miles from Makalla and the way lies partly by the water's edge on the sands and partly inland in stony valleys, naked and red, where fan-shaped samr trees grow in the flat places, grey as lichen or granite, and decorative in a barren way. Euphorbias, too, grow there, and dry and dusty statice, and straggling clumps of thorns, but nothing human except one little house and dying garden, and women who come out from Makalla – eight miles or so – to gather the thorns with naked thighs and kilted gowns, and eyes shining above a thick face cloth which veils them.

Between Makalla and Bir Ali – a distance of some 70 miles – there is nothing but this and the village of Barūm on the coast. It is a poor little place with no good houses, and a population disposed to kindness by the friendly influence of the R.A.F. They seemed much mixed with African, and gathered round us, and could not think of anything to show us in their small township except the school – a windowless earthen basement where twelve small boys sat in semi-darkness reading at random out of red Qurans. Some read, and some pretended to read, with a droning noise and swaying body: their negro teacher in the doorway aired his naked torso and short white beard, benevolent and pleased with the hum of learning. When I asked him which was his best pupil, he pointed at once to the ugliest of all.

As we drove back by the sea, along the strip of wet sand at the edge of the waves, gulls rose like a fluttering grey ribbon before us and sank again behind. They live here in countless numbers. They seem black and white as raindrops when they fly against the water. On the white sands they look like white pearls, and like grey pearls on the brown, and they swim strung out like pearls upon the waves. Now, as their barrage rose and fell, they made a canopy of shadow with their wings. They rose only just high enough to clear us, wheeling and almost touching; and one misjudged his distance and hit me and fell stunned in my lap. I picked him up, stiff with fear; only his eyes moved, surrounded by a delicate black beading like the glass of a miniature; his beak was red, its upper point curved over the lower; his feet were webbed and pale; and as I let his body slip away to freedom, the grey feathers felt cool and smooth as the sea they live on.

I visited three other schools in Makalla before I left. The new and handsome one, only five years old, is paid for by the Sultan and provides six years of education free to all who want it; but the teachers told me that they can very rarely persuade a boy's parents to leave him for more than four years, for there is no material advantage in education.

The teachers were young and eager, with that love of learning for its own sake of which the East is not yet ashamed. There were thirteen of them, to about 300 boys in six classes. The two smallest classes sat cross-legged on the floor; the older ones had benches, and all – from the tiniest – could produce a welcoming poem, uttered with appropriate gestures and more or less acute signs of misery, but with an obvious feeling for social obligations behind it. The children were ragged, and unintelligent to look at, as is the way of insanitary towns: and books, that come from Egypt, were few. The great treasure was a globe on a stand, kept in a bag for great occasions; two big maps, a few readers, and many Qurans provided the pasture; and five of the subjects taught were various aspects of the Quran: the rest were reading, grammar, dictation, composition, drawing, arithmetic, geometry, geography, history, and signalling with flags – the culminating point of education, and kept for the last and most advanced class as a climax to be looked forward to across the arid spaces of five preliminary years. Sayyid 'Omar, the assistant head, who took me round, was kind and gentle and fond of his children: he had the long face, little chin beard, almond-shaped eyes and large and well-cut mouth which is typical in Hadhramaut – an aristocratic type Van Dyck might have painted: and his enthusiasm and that of Shaikh 'Abdullah, who kept the school register, gave a pleasant feeling to the place in spite of the poverty of the scholars and the gigantic task undertaken with means so inadequately slender.

The old government school was on the same lines, but the third was a private venture conducted by an Indian Christian missionary, who had fifty-five pupils, much cleaner and better dressed than Sayyid 'Omar's flock, but all more or less fatally affected by that disease of smugness which oriental Christians often seem to take over inadvertently from the Pharisees. No one had wanted the Missionary in Makalla, which prides itself on admitting no Jews and hardly any Christians, and he had had to wait many months before being allowed to settle there at all; and now here he was with kind conscientious face and yellow teeth and spectacles, getting sixty rupees a month from the Sultan to run his school, provide his scholars with stationery and all they might require, and keep himself and his family alive. In his lodging upstairs he had two rows of books well thumbed to guide him on his way, a thin little wife who tried to make the best of things and not to regret Aden too deeply, and small girls whose mission lessons in embroidery were, said the wife, being all forgotten. I saw the embroidery, and did not think this an unmixed evil: some things are better forgotten. But I admired the heroism that fed the struggling spirit, wrestling alone to impart an unassimilated civilization in an unwilling land. The assembled classes sang me "God Save the King," in English and then in Arabic: I listened with some misgiving, wondering if this might not be misinterpreted as one of these subtle British arts of propaganda which we are always hearing about – but I afterwards learned that "God Save the King" is an accomplishment of which all Makalla is proud, and has no territorial implications.

The most amusing performance in the school was an English dialogue between two of the younger scholars, about a chair.

"I have bought a chair," said one.

"What is it like?" asked the other.

"It is made of wood," . . . etc. etc.

It sounds a peaceful and amicable conversation. But the two lads pitched into it as if it were a battle, at the top of their voices and with incredible fury, leaning towards each other as if the physical interposition of thirty odd fellow scholars alone kept them from each other's throats. It was only by listening carefully that I felt reassured as to its being merely the description of a chair.

I came away from these oases of western influence a little sadly, feeling as some indifferent lover may feel who sees the poverty of his own second-rate sentiments being taken for pure gold and can do nothing about it, and I was glad when my Afghan stopped outside a sort of marquee made of reed matting and asked if I would like to look at a wedding inside. He took me to the door and left me, and I slipped in through a fold and found myself in a chaos of women, packed in hot and dense twilight, and as far removed from anything to do with modern education as it is possible to be.

Slave women stood in an outer crowd, while the ladies in the centre squatted knee to knee on their heels and someone beat a drum. I was pushed into the middle, and a tumult arose: I found myself opposite an indignant lady with blue lips and a yellow veil who asked to right and left why the Nasrani was there. I spoke volubly and directly to her, with all the politeness in my vocabulary. Things hung in the balance for a few seconds; but the situation was more than she could deal with, for she was trying to talk politely *to* me and angrily *about* me, and she subsided suffocated: I squatted down: one or two, between curiosity and kindness, began to look more friendly; and I was able to examine the strangeness of the gathering.

It was a dense female parterre, glittering and gorgeous, ringed by a black slave crowd. The dresses were brocade or tinsel, stiff with embroidered silver breastplates and necklaces in rows; and heavy anklets, bracelets and girdles, and five or six ear-rings in each ear. The ladies came in with a yellow kerchief tied over their head, but this was soon taken off, and then they showed the elaborate works of art – their face and hands and hair. They wore about a hundred tiny plaits tight to the head from a smooth straight parting painted orange with henna; on their forehead the hair was plastered to a point shining with grease; their chins were bright yellow; the palms of their hands reddish brown with heavily scented henna and oil and painted outside in a brown lacework pattern, like a mitten. Their eyebrows were painted brown and a curling brown pattern darted from each temple; a brown line ran down the forehead and chin. Some were very pretty, with pointed faces and long small chins; but they were inhuman, hieratic and sacrificial; not women, but a terrifying, uncompromising embodiment of Woman, primæval and unchanging. And more so when they stood up to dance, one or two at a time. They did not move their feet, but threw dieir heads and upper bodies stiffly about, and made patterns like wheels in the air with their pigtails. A clinging scent came from their bodies; the drums beat; the bracelets and girdles jingled; the heat was almost unbearable. When one arose, it was like a flower, some many-coloured tulip, opening as she slipped from her dark street wrapping and stood to let her finery be seen, nonchalant but not without an ear for the murmur of discriminating praise. The bride was, of course, invisible in an upper room. More guests kept on arriving: space was made for them, impossible as it seemed: the drum went on beating with its subtle excitement of monotony;

more and more dancers stood up knee deep in the female sea: and I slipped out as quietly as I could, oppressed with a mystery so ancient and fundamental, so far more tenacious in its dim, universal roots than the transitory efforts of that incurably educational creature, Man.

5

I Leave for the Interior

"I will get me to the mountain of myrrh, and to the hill of frankincensc."

(Song of Solomon.)

The Sultan of Makalla's army is divided into his own bodyguard of slaves called the Nizam, and the 'Askar, who are paid troops, enlisted from the Yafa'i tribes to which the Qe'eti dynasty belonged when first it descended on its conquering way to the coast some hundred years ago. These tribesmen are paid ten to fifteen thalers a month (fifteen to twenty-two shillings), and are supposed to provide their own food; there are three to four thousand of them scattered in the sultanate.

They are fine-looking men, as muscular as snakes, with long thin faces, and dressed in whatever colour and with whatever headgear pleases them best, the essential uniform being a cartridge belt and rifle. This made their morning drill, which took place twice a week beyond the beduin camp in the wadi, as gay as a zinnia bed in summer. The bare legs marked time; the short petticoats fluttered like ballet skirts in bright variety: and the band, which had played them down from the gate with European tunes on eight brass instruments, hastened to deposit these on the ground near the camel ponds and joined in the fun; while four officers, trained in the Aden levies and very smart in khaki, directed operations with a riding switch held in their hands and the words "Lef Ry, Lef Ry," which puzzled me till I located them. The black Nizam were marching and counter-marching in other groups and not with quite the same dash and exactitude. They are the Sultan's private property, slave families from Africa, but settled for generations in the royal palace, and are an institution in Arabian palaces older than Islam, for they were known in pagan Mekka under the name of Ahabis. Their youngest members, small boys of ten or twelve, made a little corps of their own with a red flag in each hand, and did what looked like morris dancing in one corner. Across the parade ground, among these manoeuvring groups of vivid colour, camels and their indigo blue drivers moved slowly in and out on their morning way towards the hills; and the acrid smell of the camp and its tainted water rose in the damp early hour. I made my way back to the city gate so as to watch the army marching home. There I found the Sultan's cannon, two guns and four padded camel saddles to carry them, brought out to air. They were being dusted under the eye of a portly old officer in a green woollen turban, with a watch-chain decorating his very circular front. When the dusting was finished, the artillery rested here and there: the garrison hens, full of curiosity, pretended to find interesting grains as close as possible to the two muzzles heating in the sun; and presently the eight brass instruments, blowing hard, led the troops back to barracks through their battlemented gateway, with bobbing curls, tarbushes, or turbans, and sloping rifles, and with so much obvious enjoyment to all concerned that even a pacifist might have been carried away in that innocuous atmosphere of military glory.

This was my last morning in Makalla. Two wild little men of some earlier world than ours had been brought to me the day before as guides and carriers. They looked caged, like creatures that might beat themselves against the furniture to get out. They were both completely indigo, and the little wisp round their loins had taken on the same colour, whatever it may once have been: from it, almost at right angles, a curved dagger thrust out its handle, so that no time need be lost in drawing it. Some of these daggers are beautiful, with old Venetian gold coins nailed on to the hilt and cornelians beaten into the silver, and the crook of the sheath turned up again almost as high as the hilt, with a carved knob at the tip. But these two men seemed to be rather poor, though their daggers were serviceable, with a finishing-off knife stuck in behind and a packing needle beside it. They had their silver armlet over the right elbow, and a cornelian set in silver strung by a black cord round their neck by which they stop, they say, the bleeding of a wound; a strand of dark wool was tied under each knee. Their lips, like their faces, were blue with indigo, and they strolled about my room on bare dancing feet, lifting my boxes silently and gently to judge of their weight.

Three donkeys, they said, would be necessary, and one for me to ride on. They asked me to lighten one case and to shorten my bedding roll, and then they seized the small tin boxes I find convenient to travel with, bought in Aden bazaar and made in Bavaria, and shoved them into saddle-bags of sackcloth. We agreed to start the morrow afternoon on the week's journey to Wadi Do'an, for the sum of fifty rupees and five extra for their food. As they left, one of them stroked the red and yellow crescents of my drawing-room upholstery: he did it with gentle, wondering fingers – as you touch the brittle phenomena of some unfamiliar world.

Next morning I called to thank the Emir Salim ibn Ahmed ibn 'Abdallah al Qe'eti, Governor for his cousin the Sultan who was then in Hyderabad. It was through the Sultan's letters, obtained by the kindness of Lord Halifax through Sir Akbar Hydari and Mr. Marmaduke Pickthall that my journey was first made possible: and the Emir's generous hospitality in Makalla made my stay there and my progress inland easy and pleasant. He had come to call on me, disguising with urbanity the surprise he must have felt at my servantless way of travel; for the Qe'eti family is almost completely Indianized and has lost that understanding of independent poverty which almost always finds an echo in the heart of an Arab, however sophisticated.

The Qe'eti Sultans command the Nizam of Hyderabad's body-guard, which for many generations now has been recruited from the Hadhramaut. Their time is chiefly spent, and their marriages are mostly contracted, in India: and the Emir Salim was no exception, for his looks and manner, his small slim hands and narrow fingers that played with an ivory twisted cane, his waxed moustache which so took my eye that the rest of the face passed unnoticed, were all more Indian than Arab. But he had kept the pleasant simplicity of his race; he told me that he preferred Makalla to Hyderabad, because of the less formal life here; and talked agreeably about my future journey, with symptoms of surprise and pain only when I confessed that I liked to walk a few hours every day. The Sultan, he told me, had ridden up to the Wadi Hadhramaut for the first time in his life last autumn; and the fatigues of the ride were still making him ill. I explained apologetically that we are brought up to painful efforts from our childhood. The Emir's wife, pretty and round and soft as a dormouse, and too shy to say a word in her husband's presence, contemplated me with velvety eyes full of pity; she had never, I suppose, been physically uncomfortable in her short life: across that gulf impossible to bridge or to explain we looked at each other kindly.

Next day, at three in the afternoon, my luggage went trotting off on the three donkeys. I was to follow by car to the first halting place. My old patriarch from Huraidha had seen to provisions:

3 lb. of rice	—	—	—	4	annas
4 loaves of bread	—	—	—	4	"
5 lb. of dates	—	—	—	5	"
1½ lb. of sugar	—	—	—	2	"
4 lb. of tea	—	—	—	8	"
2 dozen eggs	—	—	—	9	"
2 dozen bananas	—	—	—	8	"
18 limes	—	—	—	4	"
4 live fowls	—	—	—	24	"

a total of three and a half rupees, to which 'Awiz added a cooking-pot and kettle. All this was to last me a week, until I reached Do'an.

Various people came to say good-bye. The Emir stood at the foot of the steps and gave me his hand under a cotton shawl not necessarily because of the particular undesirability of my sex, but possibly because he had already washed for the afternoon prayer, and a casual handshake would make him have to do it all over again. I left him and the white guest house on the wall with grateful feelings, and thought that, if ever I were to have a honeymoon, it would be pleasant to spend it on the curving beaches of Makalla, where the rolling of the world is scarcely felt, with a small log boat to carry me and whomsoever it might be out all day among the porpoises and sea-gulls.

6

The Mansab of Thilē

"*A highway and a way, they are not hard to win;*
The fond wayfaring man, he shall not err therein."

(W. P. KER.)

The Makalla government was pained by my desire to travel without either a servant or an escort. The reason I gave, that peace and happiness with the beduin depend on being alone with them, carried no conviction. I was the third European woman to visit the interior, and the first to go there alone – any eccentricity was possible and even probable, but, because of a lack of precedent, difficult to deal with. In the matter of the escort, however, I was not to have my way: they handed me over to a black Nizami slave soldier, whom they made responsible for my life, safety and general comfort.

He was just as dubious about this task as I was and more fussy. He had small eyes, shallow, and red at the corners, and high cheekbones in a flat face: he appeared at the moment of departure, dressed in a magenta cotton futah, a vest, and a red turban, which, on formal occasions, he used to replace by a white knitted cap of the kind used for winter sports. The only military thing about him was his cartridge belt, which hung well filled, and loose about his hips. He settled himself and his rifle on the step of the car which already contained me and 'Ali Hakīm, and two other friends who were to come as far as the road would carry. This was ten miles or so to the village of Thilē, at the back of the mountain of Makalla, round whose wind-eaten curves we jolted, north and then east among the desolate valleys where the citizens go in summer to sit in patches of rock-bound palms. We passed below the Sultan's garden, away on the left, and the two earth-coloured forts that hold the road, and Harshiyāt, a green thread in a hollow – and other forts, square towers "left over," said 'Ali Hakīm, "from the days of Fear," but still used by the 'Askar. The landscape was all stone, with samr trees in its clefts. If one looks closely, green shoots of leaf appear behind the mist of thorns by which their branches try, vainly, to protect themselves against the enveloping lips of the camel; but at a distance the grey skeleton trees scarce show; one can see them on the hills only if one looks at the skyline, where their rigid forms stand ready to rush into greenness after rain.

We passed a track on the left which leads to Do'an and a string of camels loaded with reeds from that country; then we rounded the block of the mountain, came out into the low wavelike landscape of Shihr, left the Shihr road and the marks of wheels, and reached a low ridge whence the mud houses of Thilē overlook their lake of palms.

The three good houses of Thilē stand together above the rest of the village in a strategic position, and belong to the Mansab and his family. They are not whitewashed like the wealthy houses of Makalla, but are solidly built of mud, five stories high. On the roof of the nearest, a woman stood and watched our coming; her arms and face were black as her gown, and she had a Byzantine dignity in the straight lines that draped her. I noticed how much was added to the grace of that figure by the darkness of face and arms, as if it were some statue carved completely out of a single piece of ebony, a thing one and indivisible in its beauty, instead of appearing, as most of us do, in bits here and there through our coverings. What is less harmonious than half a leg showing in contrasting colour beneath a modern skirt? – or an arm, which our dressmakers cut off at the shoulder, and leave to hang as an independent object outside the general design of their creations? This woman had no such incongruities: she was all one, and stood against the sky like the Madonna of Torcello against the gold mosaic of her dome: until she saw us and screamed, fluttering those dark arms in an abandoned way, unbecoming to Byzantine mosaics.

The Mansab of Thilē, Sheikh Muhammad ibn Ahmad ba 'Omar, is one of the most venerated people in the Hadhramaut, and his word will carry over the tribes of his district and beyond. He is the descendant of the saint, Sa'id bin 'Isa 'Amudi, who is buried at Ghaidun, between Sif and Hajarain, and whose pilgrimage and four days' feast in the month Rajab is one of the chief events of the country. This feast nearly caused the death of Von Wrede, the first European traveller in Hadhramaut; he reached Ghaidun at the dangerous moment, was suspected in spite of his disguise, and would have been killed by the excited beduin if some of the chief people there had not interposed and sent him, penniless but safe, to the coast.

The descendant of this famous saint, the present Mansab or religious chief of the clan, was in the palm grove below when we sent word of our arrival. He climbed up to greet us, an old man whose long and sensitive face experience and authority had sweetened and dignified, He had a large kind mouth which all the family have inherited. His two sons joined him, and then a curly-bearded son-in-law, dressed in a loincloth and cornelian pendant, in contrast to the long robes of the Sayyids. We all turned into the house, by steps of mud made shiny and smooth with use, and sat in a matted room, while the business of handing me over was undertaken by 'Ah Hakīm over the slow gurgles of two roughly made hookahs. The business did not take very long, for the afternoon was wearing into evening, and my friends had to return. Down below, in the lee of the house wall, my beduin had arrived and were settling for the the night. 'Ah Hakīm said good-bye, his white-rimmed eyes full of solicitude, his rough voice a cascade of recommendation, reassurance and apology. He had done everything that kindness could suggest: and now he packed his figure, which somehow seemed to be an object separate from himself and a little bulky for his own management, into the car: the other two fitted in beside him: the Afghan chauffeur shook hands as a friend and took the wheel: they vanished into the rocky landscape, and I turned to my hosts, who were accepting my unexpected presence with the reserved courtesy natural to the well-bred Arab.

This was my first entry into one of those Hadhramaut houses which appear to have come down, diminished in splendour but fundamentally unchanged, from the days of the Sabæans. Small models of these houses have been dug up, and they are little altered. The poet 'Alqama describes them in the early days of Islam when their ruined magnificence on the hill tops of Yemen still filled the imaginations of men.

"The proud Ghumdan and its dwellers. And this comfort for
     those who come after.
It climbs the height of heaven, in twenty stories;
The clouds its turban; girdle and cloak are marble;
Its stones are fastened with dropping lead; jewels and marble lie
     between its towers.
At every corner the head of a flying eagle; or of a bronze lion,
     roaring.
A water clock on its summit; it drips to count the parts of day.
The birds halt upon it; and the waters flow in its channels
. . . and a look-out place is above
Of smooth marble, where the lords may stand: entrance is easy
     to them."

Entrance, whatever it may have been to the ancient lords, is impossible to the modern traveller unguided; for the bottom story of the house is unprovided with windows from motives of defence. It is usually filled with goats or donkeys, and branches into turns and stairs as puzzling as a labyrinth, until in the upper parts one comes by winding passages and sudden corners to the various apartments, each provided with sanitary arrangements of its own that drain by a wide shaft to whatever street or open space happens to lie below. All these apartments are kept locked with wooden keys, stuck into the housewives' girdles and worked by pegs through which a corresponding series of loose little shafts of wood are pressed into sockets inside the elaborately carved lock; even the expert as a rule requires time to wrestle with his own front door; and to pass through the various apartments of wives, widows, daughters and mothers-in-law enclosed in the walls of a Hadhramaut house is not a task to be undertaken lightly.

As for the bronze lions and heads of flying eagles which the poet mentions at the corners of the ancient palaces, they still exist in the shape of ibex horns, stuck in pairs below the topmost balustrade, and I saw them for the first time at Thilē.

The house here was a shabby old place, used to much entertaining of the beduin who come to their spiritual leader for help or counsel; everything was well-worn and in constant use. An upper room was given me, with rush mats on the floor and many carved windows; and here the Mansab and his two sons, and a small grandson, all with the same charming expression of gentleness on their faces, sat and talked over clay bowls of coffee mixed with ginger.

The son-in-law came strolling in presently, swinging his hips, elaborately dressed. Red and yellow was wrapped round his loins, and red and black like a toga carelessly cast over one naked arm and shoulder. His curly beard and hair shone with oil. He might, indeed, have been an ancient Roman, bull-necked and sensual. He sat down beside the others, cross-legged, one hand playing with the silver dagger that shone in his red and yellow folds; he was accustomed to sit and be admired, and it was amusing to watch him beside the un-selfconscious refinement of his relatives, whose shabby old gowns took nothing from the quiet influence of their faces, marked by many generations of authority and learning.

Mr. and Mrs. Ingrams, who had explored the Wadhi Hadramaut to its outlet at Saihut a few months before, passed by Thilē but did not stop; though the news of them had accustomed men's minds to the fact that European women can travel about here, I was the first one actually to be seen by the Mansab's family. I tried to explain my presence by an interest in history, and found – as I was to do frequently during the next six weeks – that curiosity about the ancient Sabæans was taken as a form of European frivolity, a restlessness of mind to which no particular sympathy is accorded; but all entered enthusiastically into my feelings for the mediæval traditions of Islam, and realized them as an intelligible reason for a journey.

They presently left me, and the ladies of the house came rustling in behind the Mansab's daughter. She too had the gentle large mouth of her family, in a charming long face, rather sallow: her eyes were beautiful, soft and mischievous. The ice was quickly broken, since Providence has kindly granted me a real delight in clothes – a stand-by in many of the trials of life, but a special boon in travel, for it provides one with a subject of conversation whose universal interest never comes to an end. The room was soon strewn with flowered silks, all, alas, artificial silks from Aden: and I was learning the difference between the short-waisted Indian 'gowan' and the Arab kurti when the Mansab himself, bearing a light to see my supper put before me, was surprised to find us so strewn about with vanities, and apologized, smiling.

The ladies explained their different hair-dress to me. The parting down the middle, with no plaits, is the Indian fashion, chiefly used on the coast or by East Indian women whom the Hadhramis marry abroad. A straight fringe across the forehead is worn in Makalla, while a fringe coming down between the eyebrows in a point belongs to the interior. The making of the innumerable little plaits takes a whole day from morning to afternoon, and they last only ten days when they are made.

A woman presently came in and sat beside us, her face hideously streaked with the brown dye they call hudar. It was laid on in three broad stripes, one over the eyes, one across nose and cheeks and one under the mouth and jaw, and she told me that this was done daily for forty days after childbirth, and washed off every evening. She was a slave woman. Her son, a boy about ten years old, sat on the outer edge of the party. He suddenly shocked everyone by murmuring the word "Bakhshish."

I said nothing, but looked pained and shocked: the rest of the gathering were horrified beyond words.

"Where did you learn to say such things to a guest?" said the Mansab's daughter at last. "You must be mad!"

The little boy was already overcome by the weight of collective disapproval.

"Nasara," he mumbled. "They all give bakhshish. The Nasara who came before gave bakhshish to everyone."

This habit of scattering money is, I think, one of the most unfortunate things that European travellers are apt to do: by it they offend the best Arabs and spoil the rest.

"Perhaps they gave bakhshish on their road, to the poor," I suggested. "They would not do so as guests in a house."

"Let me never hear such words again," said the Mansab's daughter, while the simultaneous silence of ten or more women showed the enormity of his crime. He vanished into the outer dark. Our circle, restored to harmony, continued to chat of this and that until my soldier, with a lantern, came up and set my camp bed in a corner of the room.

He took his responsibilities seriously and thought or sleeping at the foot of the bed to guard me. But I was firm and the ladies were on my side. They trooped out after him, and left me with only the Mansab's little grandson and an orphan beduin girl, who lingered fascinated in the hope of seeing me get into bed. The little girl was smiling and gay till the boy told me she was an orphan.

"*Meskina*, poor thing. She has nothing," he said in a voice in which pity and contempt, nicely balanced, expressed exactly the attitude towards poverty of the East. The child's face had fallen into an expression of sadness.

"Is she a slave?" I asked.

"No, only an orphan," said Ahmad. He seemed to think it worse, as no doubt it is. "Slaves," he remarked, "can be bought in Shibam, and a young one costs five hundred thalers" (£37.)

I suggested that I would now like to sleep, and they went, and left me alone in the room with a mouse. I stepped out on to a terrace and looked over the houses of Thilè below and the palm-tree tops white under a misty moon. Only the Mansab's own houses are allowed on the ridge "so that no one," his son told me, "may shoot in at our windows." But there was no shooting now: only the cloudy peace of the night, and the murmur of voices over their pipes on a lower terrace. The temperature was pleasant, 79° Fahrenheit. Round the corner of the wall a dim glow showed where the beduin's fire had sunk. The oasis below was shut in the wadi bed like a picture in a frame; beyond it – a larger frame – lay silence. How few of us in Europe know silence in the night: even if we sleep alone in Alpine pastures we are comforted by the sound of running streams. But here, between one village and the next, there is nothing except the wind when it blows: and on a still night, that waterless silence is so still that you may fancy you hear in its arid quiet the growth of the desert scrub beneath its breastwork of thorns.

7

The Way to the Jōl

"Er gewohnte sich gleich nach der Manier der Landeseinwohner zu leben, und dieses ist notwendig wenn man mit Nützen und Vergnügung in Arabien reisen vell."

(NIEBUHR 'Reisebeschreibung.')

I was awakened next morning by a strong and beautiful voice calling the first prayer below my window. In course of time the soldier came to pack up the bed, and the Mansab himself appeared to say good-bye. No one else was yet about, so I left in his hands a small mirror as a present to his daughter, and he accepted it with surprise and a half unwilling pleasure on her account, having obviously expected nothing of the kind. He looked at the red silk case and its tassel with indulgent curiosity, as one who still had kindly feelings for other people's vanities; he was, indeed, one of the most charming and human of ascetics. But his mind was not of that worldly kind which dwells on the matter of breakfast, and I was glad to tear off a chunk of the Makalla bread as we descended into the light air of the morning.

It was six o'clock. The beduin were only just beginning to saddle: and we left them and walked down the short cliff path to where the gardens of Thilē and their prosperity begin in a spring of warm water which irrigates the whole wadi. The son-in-law was here already, washing his flamboyant torso, which might well have belonged to some pagan god. The sight of it somehow made one sympathize with the devoted wife who, having been through the Vatican Museum, said: "They talk a lot of Hercules and Bacchus, but give me Jones." Perhaps it was because he himself was so pleased with his appearance, and it is part of our unkindness, or possibly an innate sense of economy, that we do not like to waste admiration on those already provided with that commodity by their own efforts.

Here I took leave of the charming old saint and followed the soldier between damp ribs of cultivation, straight across the wadi and up the opposite cliff to open lands, almost imperceptibly tilted northward, along which our journey lay. They are really wadis, so broad and low as to be almost imperceptible, and dull in outline as they drift into the coastal plain. But the early morning light was on them with a certain pale charm, and the grey samr trees stood gracefully about them: and after an hour's walk our trotting caravan appeared behind us, and we sat to wait for it by the small white dome of a siqaya or water reservoir endowed and filled every day for thirsty travellers by the piety of some dead benefactor.

So far I had met only three of my beduin, Sa'id and Salim his nephew, and Salim's ten-year-old brother Muhammad, a skinny little boy with hair like rat tails and a smile always ready in his frog-like little face. They were all Murshidi beduin whose homes and grazing grounds are round the Kor Saiban, the highest summit of the Hadhramaut.

Sa'id was a gay and friendly little bearded man, with full lips and a straight nose and low forehead, horizontally wrinkled, from which his woolly curls were tied back in a girlish way with a broad, ragged band round his head. He was active and solid, like the figure of some lesser Roman god not of the best period, but inclining to the baroque. He had an ingratiating way of talking with his head on one side, and large spaniel eyes, very friendly and brown in the indigo of his face. When explaining anything he would spread both hands, turning them out as far as they would go, palms, fingers, thumbs and all. His nephew Salim had heavy lids, like a cat when it pretends to be sleepy, and a pouting, full upper lip; he was quite young and I had thought he looked difficult to deal with, but, as a matter of fact, he developed the most chivalrous devotion and never left my donkey out of his sight, stopping it twenty times an hour if I wanted to take snapshots, and rushing hither and thither to pick whatever desert flower my eye happened to light on, even before I spoke to ask for it. These three had been up with the Sultan last autumn. They were well known in Makalla and were to have been all the party, but two more – a silent lad called Ahmad Ba Gort and a second Sa'id, a cousin, had added themselves to it. The latter now appeared with a cartridge belt and French rifle, to the butt of which was added a rounded piece of wood covered with gazelle skin, as is the Hadhramaut fashion for all their guns. He was a sulky young man to look at, with long lean face and black tuft under the chin like a figurine from an Egyptian tomb: an indigo rag was wound among his corkscrew curls. The curls, and a silver armlet beaten out in a snaky pattern, and two silver rings on his little finger, gave him a dashing air, and he had, indeed, something of a Byronic temper, and would wander alone over the boulders a little off the beaten way of the caravan, or would suddenly pull out a reed pipe from his loin-cloth and walk ahead of us playing monotonous wind-like beduin melodies. His sulkiness, as far as I was concerned, disappeared by the end of the day, when I had shared the beduin coffee; it was nothing more, I discovered later, than annoyance at having to protect "Nasara who are so proud that they will not even eat with us," for he had been with Europeans before and the fact of their eating alone had evidently rankled.

These four now overtook us with six trotting donkeys, invisible, almost, under hills of luggage, which in their turn were hidden by a double covering of sackcloth and flies. The flies stuck like a black dust to every part that was not too steep, and we only lost them on the second day of our journey, when the air of the plateau grew colder.

For we were now rising gradually towards the watershed, that stony waste of the Jōl which lies many days' journey between the actual desert and the sea. In its extended monotony it is only the fringe of a greater monotony, the Arabian table-land, tilted downwards from Petra to 'Oman. This outer Jōl is cleft and scored like the dried mud bottom of a pond in summer, and these clefts are valleys, sometimes the ancient homes of cities, or sometimes, in their wildness and narrowness, the homes only of trees and birds beside the running summer streams. The Jōl has ever been the playground of the wind and sun and the free-moving beduin, little known and little liked by the inland townsmen, who cross it because they must, imprisoned as they are by it, a six or seven days' journey from the sea. Now in the distance we began to see flat waves and table-lands of limestone in the sun, the first steps, but not – said Sa'id – the proper Jōl, for that we could not reach until the evening of the following day, at the head of Wadi Himem which we were going to follow.

We trotted along gaily, the wadi gradually drawing its shallow far sides together into a recognizable wadi shape. There is a cheerful quality in the neat brisk sound of trotting donkey feet on hard ground. And it is pleasant too, to sit on a donkey pack, when you know how to do it, without rigidity, meeting the jolts and caprices of your companion with an elastic temper and a capacity for balance, riding, in fact, as one rides through life, with a calm eye for accidents and a taste for enjoyment in the meantime. My own donkey was called Suwaidi and was a stalwart little animal with hairy cars and a thick neck and grey like a dappled sky. When I asked his name, they told me he had none, he was just donkey – "himar." "That is impossible," said I. "He must have a name, or how can you tell him from the other himars?" Whereupon the small Muhammad, loping along with a stick beside me, gave me one of his smiles and told me the name, which his elders had evidently considered beneath my notice.

We followed a more or less even way to Lasb, two hours from Thilē. Here there are a few mud houses and a whitewashed one, and the path descends by a siqaya into the wadi bed, where pools and palms against the cliff wall look as if they had been arranged by a landscape gardener for effect. There were moist patches of vegetables, chiefly a low-growing convolvulus-flowered plant they call batata – and small fish and frogs in the pools, with red dragonflies above them. And here we really began to follow the white boulder bed of the wadi, coming upon scattered pools where the samr grew tall and nathb trees made handsome clumps of green with long leaves, and 'ashr trees grew in open places – pale leaves, large and oval, covered with whitish down and carrying, high up, little purple flowers, inhabited, the Muslim say, by Jinn.

The vegetation grew in clumps near the water, and changed as we became enclosed in the cliff walls, though some of the plants of the open still remained, like the poisonous harmal, with its white flower, no good to man or beast, scattered everywhere about two feet high. A bigger, oleander-like shrub with small velvety-white flowers also grew here, and yellow galaigula, of the acacia tribe but low-growing, which – said Salim – drives you out of your wits if you boil and drink it. The green groups hung romantically over pools in the white gorge. A cliff side now shut us in on either hand, so high that I could scarce distinguish the wild doves that fluttered in its upper sunlight. Thick pillars and rock faces, half formed by the winds and left, looked there like the work of gigantic hands. These cliffs are limestone, on sandstone bases. Against their rocky skyline, skeleton bushes show; one can imagine their surface faintly green in the season of rains. Up there the morning breeze and sunlight wander: but we walked in still air, heating slowly: the donkeys, flapping their ears with lowered heads, found places for their hooves among the round white sides of the stones: Sa'id II pulled out his madruf, his reed flute, and danced from boulder to boulder on bare feet, playing. Suddenly, by a common impulse, the other three pulled out their knives. I thought it was to prick the donkeys' grey hindquarters, just showing under the luggage, but they merely wished to dance behind the flautist, with short light steps, the curved point of the knives turned up from under their hands, a little above the level of their eyes. They looked as happy, and as unlike members of what Aden had described to me as a "regular and orderly government" as one can well imagine.

At nine o'clock we reached an overhang of rock, a sort of open cave, with a drip of water which must have made it a halting place for centuries before us. We settled here for the hot hours of the day.

Our soldier made me a bed with everything soft he could lay his hands on, while the beduin scattered to their work, collected firewood, and heated coffee before the serious business of lunch should begin.

This came later and was cooked by Sa'id in my new pot. It consisted of a mess of rice and red pepper powdered (bisbas). When nearly cooked, Sa'id crumbled into it some of the rotted shark which makes every caravan in the Hadhramaut smell as if something had died, not very recently, in its midst: he added oil out of a little oozing goatskin: stirred it with a piece of stick off the ground: and filled up my plate, which the soldier brought to me on a secluded ledge of rock, while he and the four beduin crouched over the pot with their fingers.

We rested here till two o'clock. The shade was pleasant and of the kind that does not keep one moving round after it: where it ended, along the way we had come, a smooth stone floor shone in the sun between high rocks, like an avenue to a temple, and Salim there was bringing back the donkeys from the pool. Sa'id II, the flautist, lay on a rock on his back, holding and gazing ecstatically at his dagger, the pride of his life. A stray beduin, a tall bearded man, who had stumbled in upon us dizzily complaining of a headache, lay on another rock with cotton wool and eau de cologne over his eyes: and the black slave, in a corner, was coaxing our four unfortunate live fowls with a few grains of corn. The routine of our journey had begun, unexpected in its small incidents, immutable in its unchanging lines: this interplay of accident and law, the surprises of every day worked into a constant pattern by physical necessities, compelling people along the same paths for one century after the other – this surely is the charm of travel in the open: and when our human methods of transport are so perfect that physical laws no longer regulate our journeys by land or sea or air, why, then we shall have outgrown our planet: and that delightful feeling of oneness with its animals and plants and stones, oneness in the grip of the same compulsion, will have gone from our wanderings for ever.

We started again at two, and Sa'id and Salim saddled the donkeys to a particular little tune which they kept for this occasion. "*Habbali, Habbali, Habbalit, Habbali*"; there was a certain monotony about it, as it went on and on in varying tones till the business was done; but the donkey seemed to like it and listened with his ears back, and when it stopped he knew that the load was tied, and moved away of his own accord. Sometimes they varied it, and sang "*Hot taht īdak,*" also over and over again: "Place it beneath your hand," a rather unsuitable remark, I thought, when the load is being tied on to an animal's back. As a matter of fact it was Sa'id who made up the verses and sang whatever came into his head. He used to sit and sing to himself as he cooked the rice, in a low, preoccupied, rapid voice like that of a Roman Catholic priest getting through his mass very quickly.

After leaving our camp, we came at two-thirty to Lubaib, a poor but open place where valleys meet. Two wadis come in on the left, Benahsa and Rayak, which leads to Qarn Rayak; south-east of Lubaib is Jebel 'An'ana, in sight, and beyond it, after skirting the mouth of Wadi Huti and Ras Barq, we entered the desolate defile of Wadi Himem, which was to lead us up to the Jōl.

Both M. Van den Meulen and the Ingrams' party followed and mapped this road, so that I did not intend to collect any geographical material until I came to new country west of Shibam, and I merely repeat here what the beduin told me, for what it may be worth; I did not go into the laborious process of verifying and comparing statements. For one thing, I still found my beduin difficult to understand; though they speak excellent Arabic, they do it with sudden amusing changes of voice, and a peculiar thick explosiveness at the end of the word, as if there were a volume of energy behind it: and this is much more difficult when one first comes to it than particular idiosyncracies such as the use of y for j, which are very quickly recognized.

As we stepped from the open into the walled stillness of Wadi Himem, we were brought face to face with ruins and convulsions, the ravaged history of the earth. The upper cliff is sheer and undercut, swept by the wind into striated hollows, like theatre boxes from which one can fancy prehuman presences watching the elemental drama, the action of daylight, wind, water, sun and frost, on the imprisoned powers that heave beneath the crust of earth. The steep sides are clothed with trees, ready for life when the rain comes, and rich in many varieties: and partridges, small crows, and wagtails were moving there. In summer, when water flows among the white boulders and when their slopes are green, these rock-imprisoned valleys must look like paradise; but now the sight of their naked power was overwhelming; mankind too insignificant, threading its barefoot way in single file between the silent walls, with the donkey feet slipping and clattering beside it: and the relief felt for any small oasis of palms or patch of maize field, made one suddenly realize the vast inhuman scale of all this land.

No such oasis showed itself that day. We followed the solitary uncultivated valley, until we came at three-twenty to a place called Hallaf, where in a sort of amphitheatre with smooth-shorn walls the wadi turns and the track rises to greater openness and climbs in a district called Rahba along the western bank over ancient debris worn from the cliff side: for these valleys, wild and majestic, are but rubbish heaps and outlets to the Jōl. Up there, centuries and the summer storms are carving new mountain ranges, whose waste material is tumbled down these passages, and eats their limestone sides and strews their sandstone bases: and caravans that travel in the zone of these terrific labours, are liable to be swept away by sudden spates which fill the canyons from side to side and sweep them clean.

Here, in the side valleys, incense still grows, and is brought down and sold in Makalla, but there is none to be found on a highway such as we were travelling. Many other things grew around us: samr, and humè, a dwarf tree with small dark leaves; 'asharik, like laburnum; abb, with red stem, a tree seen in Aden; and sarakh, like an olive, eaten by camels: thaulat adh-dhabi or *Adenum obesum*; dhubid, with a yellow flower, eaten by camels; khalsfa; qatara; and qaradh, an acacia rather like samr, of which we saw more and more as we climbed to the Jōl. There was a scentless plant like lavender called kohaile, and a shrub they call dhudà, with leaves sticky and bright, as if varnished, no animal would eat. Here, too, I first saw blocks of strange sandstone, with bits of iron-like rusty rock embedded in it and resisting with hard edges where the softer stone yielded around it. I found more and more of it up to the Jōl.

In all this time we only met one caravan descending. Little Muhammad, limping along and tired, refused the offer of my donkey: I got off to make him ride, and he smiled at the attention, but was down again in ten minutes or so, assuring me that he was rested. The valley, now tumbled and open, with its waterless stream, lay well below on our right: its cliffs, scooped and smoothed as if with giant planes, showed the cloudy evening sky and a triangle of hills behind us: and at four-forty-five, at a desolate steep corner scattered with boulders like houses, we took the packs from our animals and camped.

It was a place called Rash, and evidently much used, for the ashes of old fires lay about. The soldier put up my bed in the lee of a rock, and when supper was ready I distressed his conventional mind by joining the party round the fire. They covered the best stone with a sack, and welcomed me, calling me by the name of Frīya, which they adopted for the rest of the journey. It was then that they told me of the "pride" of the Nasara, which had evidently long rankled in their minds.

"We had a fire," said Sa'id, "but it was not good enough for them: they wanted a separate one of their own to cook on, and we were told to sit quite far away from them. And they are so proud that they insist on riding ahead, and we who belong to the country have to come after them."

I did what I could to soften these wounds, and felt, as I have often felt before, that to sit over the fire with one's fellows in the evening, when the work is over and the talking begins, is the only sure way of keeping harmony and friendship. I never had any difficulties with my beduin and found nothing but friendliness and an anxiety to serve in every way, and I attribute this chiefly to the fact that we had our meals together and that, except for the outraged soldier whose feelings throughout the trip were in a minority of one, I had no other servant of my own.

When darkness had already fallen, we heard the tinkling of another caravan against the stones. We kept quiet, hoping they might pass us by, naturally suspicious of people who come at night. But they turned the corner of our rock, and greeted us with "Ya hayya!" and borrowed a brand from our fire to cook their pot. They were grander than we, for they travelled with a sahn, or dish, for their rice, a tin affair on a stand, instead of scooping it out of the saucepan as we did: but they were peasant people from the settled lands, and therefore inferior to us for all their luggage. A strong, big-featured lad of them came up presently to join our circle and converse: he had a white woollen scarf for turban, with branches of harmal bound in it against the sun: he was a wag, with bold and careless features, and kept us all laughing. From my bed, into which I crept presently, I could see the party squatting at ease over the embers, their faces lit fitfully from below. The dim patient shapes of the donkeys seemed half shadow behind them: the rocks towered black, or streaked with firelight above their heads: and I fell asleep thinking of the entrance to Ali Baba's cave, in an illustrated edition of my childhood.

8

The Beduin of Kor Saiban

"Wer sich bequemen kann so zu reisen, und zufrieden ist wenn er in einem Wirtshause bisweilen nichts mehr findet als schlechtes Brod, der wird auch auf Reisen in Yemen eben so viel Vergnügen antreffen als ich deselbst gefunden habe."

(NIEBUHR 'Reisebeschreibung.')

The whole of the next day we followed the Wadi Himem, climbing steadily.

I woke at 4 a.m., and took the temperature, which was 74° – a pleasant cloudy morning.

At six we started and, keeping along the left-hand side of the valley, came upon camels, asleep among the rocks. Camels travel more slowly than donkeys and cost a little less to hire: they take eight days to the donkey's six, and the donkey is preferable from the photographer's point of view, because one can slip quickly on and off him. These camels were sprawling over the path; their owners, their hair tied up in nets, but otherwise almost naked, strolled up amused when I asked if they would bite; one young boy bent over to hold their gurgling necks as I passed with a gesture as free and balanced as the sculptured movement on a Grecian frieze.

After this we came to the first village, Zamin el-Kebir, fifteen
houses or so across the valley at the opening of a gorge, with bananas,
palms and millet round them. All these Wadi Himem villages are
poor little places, and belong to independent "Sultans" of the Ba
Hebri. They are separated by long waste stretches. We passed the
few mud hovels of Zamin as-Saghir, and then climbed up an untidy
slope of boulders, the 'Aqaba of Bathā, to Mahzama. Here the
valley lifted to a highland basin, with water-worn bare tops of hills
around it, on which lay clouds and sunlight. A battlemented mud
village, called Ghayada, rose on our left. Palms, limes and wide-
spreading 'ilb or nebk trees (*Zizyphus Spina Christi*) stood before it.
After the palm, the 'ilb is the most useful tree in Hadhramaut. It
needs no irrigation and grows in drier places, and provides food in
its powdery apple-coloured berries for the beduin, and fodder for
their goats, and timber for all the carved doors and columns of the
towns.

I walked here, glad of the openness of the flat-bottomed valley
and the normal slope of hills around me after those perpendicular
passages below.

All sorts of new plants and bushes began to appear. Madhab,
with red tongue-like flowers on bushes about four feet high; 'ebub
with purple, and dhora with red, small seed-like blossoms; ghulila;
da'aya, a yellow composite; hudam, a fat plant, and aloes called
quruf, sold for their juice. There were thorny cushions producing
delicate unexpected orange blossoms; and the ragged yellow daisy-
like duweila, which grows everywhere in the unwatered earth.

As we walked briskly over the alluvial land the beduin lifted their
voices together and sang words with no meaning:

"Wa ai daina, daina . . . "

They called it simply a maghāni and said it was meant for dancing;
and they ended on a sinking note, low and humming, which died
slowly on the waves of the air, as if it were heavier than they.

They were pleased that I should like to be sung to, and presently
started a Zeima, a man's song, Sa'id explained, "because it teaches
us not to fear death." It goes more quickly, three trochees, then two

trochees and a dactyl, and they ran in time to it with short steps, our one gun levelled, while the donkeys, evidently accustomed to the game, pricked their ears and began to trot quickly of their own accord, with a clattering of luggage and a faint desperate effort at a crow from one of the four cockerels destined for dinner. They travelled tied by the legs to the top of a pack beside the cooking-pot and kettle, and the sight of their misery, as they watched the world jogging past and closed and opened their small eyes, made me long to see them cooked and done with before sheer melancholy wore them to death.

And now, at ten o'clock, we saw the valley close in again before us, and Himem jutting on a hill above the opening, a feudal pinnacle of a village, with scant tillage at its base and many samr trees as one approaches from the south-west.

I am surprised that travellers have not found more to say about the samr tree. It is like an embodiment of the wilderness, so delicately austere – but graceful, and with almost the lightness of motion in its wave-like stem and horizontal branches against the immobile horizontal limestone in which it grows. It is a feathery acacia (*acacia vera*) with dark seed pods and thorns longer than its leaves, through whose spiky entanglement their green is soft and pale, and the scented yellow balls of blossom as unexpected as the flowers on Tannhäuser's staff; and whether it is the twist of the stem that lifts its wind-flattened canopy, or whether it is the contrast of its fragile grace, decorative and simple as a Japanese design against the weight of the rocky background, I do not know, but the samr tree looks, in the barren defiles, like a dancing figure, suddenly, just as one turned the corner, enchanted into stillness.

There were numbers of them as we rode by Himem, past a white siqaya, under the hill and the blank lower walls of the village to the wadi bed beyond, where we camped by pools of jade-coloured water in shallow windscraped caves that gave rather inadequate shelter. The limestone inside them was wrinkled like a bad imitation of tree-roots, and there was nothing to look out on but the glare of waterworn boulders, until a few villagers noticed us and came down to make a circle. From this our soldier managed to exclude me by bringing my rice and peppers to a separate cave.

He was showing a Victorian disapproval of females who do not keep themselves to themselves, a thing I find dull and difficult to do. He was, moreover, stupid, and when he got an idea into his head, clung to it with the tenacity of people to whom ideas are not an everyday occurrence. One of his ideas was that the management of our expedition was in his hands. The four beduin and I were not affected by such illusions, and our tacit understanding became amusingly clear during the afternoon. We were following a track which climbed roughly with sudden jolts up and down the valley side, and Sa'id, who was walking and gossiping beside me and my donkey, would put out his hand when he saw a bad place coming and hold me firmly on to my pack-saddle till it was past: I myself was not very anxious for this assistance, which left five indigo fingerprints on my shirt every time, but we were just then deep in the annals of the last Murshidi war, and Sa'id's kindness was of that absent-minded sort one would accord to a case of porcelain or anything else that might be damaged if it fell off a donkey on to stones. The soldier came up suddenly and pushed his hand away, saying that the lady was not to be held. Sa'id looked at him blankly, but he strode on, swinging his lank hips in a girlish way under the magenta petticoat. Sa'id looked at me: I smiled: he smiled: without a word we consigned our protector to the limbo of the imbeciles where he belonged, and returned to talk of reasonable things like tribal wars.

The Murshidi tribe, Sa'id told me, are descended from Murba' 'Abdalla Benhaim and Muhammad ba Salim Begdīm, whose origin was in the high cliffs of Kor Saiban, which their descendants own to this day. The Ba Surra of Do'an have the same descent and these are the only tribes from whom the Makalla government take no hostages, as their loyalty and fidelity are well known. They are related to the Humūmi, N.E. of Makalla, with whom they were at war eight years ago, when five hundred Humūmi attacked three hundred Murshidi and left seventy dead on Kor Saiban (the figures in these battles are apt to vary according to which side tells the story). Peace had now been made between them by 'Aiderus in Shihr, for the Humūmi, and by our host the Mansab of Thilē for the Murshidis, who, however, is not the proper Mansab, or religious head of the Murshidis: the real one lives in Wadi al-Aissar to the north, where a war with a neighbouring tribe was going on at this time.

Sa'id II, our flautist, had just been fighting them. He was scrambling up and down the rocks beside the path as his habit was, and joined our talk now and then, and I asked him if peace had been made.

"No," he said. "Fear lies between us. But it makes no difference; we carry on trade with safe conducts."

He pulled out his flute, and lifted his voice to sing "ai daina," and they all lifted their voices after him with the bell-like wind-like note which seemed to belong to the rocks and streams.

But my Sa'id was the real poet and knew the proper things to sing for various occasions, and qasidas, which he would rattle off to his nephew in a low tone, so earnest and argumentative that I first thought it must refer to money matters or to family quarrels; for, having sometimes sat on a bench in European towns and listened to the stream of talk as it went by, I have hardly ever heard that same earnest note deal with anything but money. So that when I asked Sa'id what it was all about and he told me it was poetry, I was pleased, and surprised and sorry that I could not follow the verses when he began again for my benefit; nor was it any good to ask the meaning of any word, for he would just say "it is poetry" and plunge again into midstream with one hand on my donkey's mane and the other outspread in the air, his brown spaniel eyes filled with delight, and his woolly curls, demurely rolled into a bun on the nape of his neck, making the most entertaining housewifely contrast with his sturdy little naked torso.

We had left Himem at one-fifteen and all that afternoon we followed the wadi of the same name, passing only one hovel on the left at the foot of a landslide called Ankedun, a dreary place. But as soon as we had climbed the 'aqaba, or steep, above it, the upper

Himem became beautiful and wild, with more and more trees in its narrow bed and greater boulders.

The path kept high and open, until gradually the valley clefts narrowed again upon us, and shut us in walls whose luxuriant green made a romantic landscape of the kind usually only invented in pictures. There are no houses here; a few shy men live in caves, which are everywhere in the cliffs, and it says much for the strength of government that travellers are not robbed where assault would be so easy and detection so difficult. Our valley turned left, and the trees grew taller, the green bushes thicker, the wind-ribbed weather-bitten walls fiercer with tilted strata as they pressed on us more closely. We met only one party of travellers, people from Khuraiba in Do'an on their way to India, and two slim little beduin girls round a corner, who ran up to our flautist and greeted him, and turned out to be his sisters.

We were climbing all the time, and into cloudy weather, which they say often happens before one gets to the clear atmosphere of the Jōl. We were very near it now; the wadi sides grew shallower; one kind of plant after another began to disappear as we emerged into harder air, until at last we came out upon open shoulders where the stone-scattered land rolls down towards the sea. It was near five o'clock and dark with cloud and brown like a moor, and on our right, but hidden in mist, was Kor Saiban itself.

"Al-Kor, al-Kor," they called to me, for the feeling for their mountain, the home of their ancestor, is pagan and mythological, such as a Greek may have felt for the spirits of his rocks and hills.

We were now really in the heart of the Murshidi country, and turned left and a little downhill to Hisi, where they had fields and a few huts in the shallow open wadi head, and where we were going to sleep.

Salim and Sa'id II ran on to get ropes of hay. We followed in the sail bed – now dry – and open like a stone-paved avenue bordered with trees; chiefly the qaradh, which is like the samr, but stouter, with a wrinkled bark, and grows in more exposed and higher places. The fields were enclosed with boulders or thorns, to gather the flood when it comes from the Jōl and before it rushes into the funnels of the wadis; it does not come every year, but when it does so, the Murshidi of Hisi hasten to sow and get their harvest.

They have a few square huts on tins open place, and we put down our packs at the door belonging to Miriam, Salim's sister, a one-year bride dressed in black, herself dark brown as ebony, with necklace and bracelet sand girdle of silver. She was pretty because of her youth and slenderness, and with her brother's soft and sleepy eyes. She stood smiling in the frame of the door and held a thin, sad baby astride her hip, while other women gathered from the huts nearby.

A roof of leaves had been built in the lee of one of the huts, and a circle of stones about three feet across laid on the ground for a hearth: it was called the mag'ad or sitting place – one finds such gathering places here and there in the open with a raised centre of earth. We settled round it, and my bed was put close by. We made coffee – pale stuff boiled with the husks of the berries and with ginger – disagreeable until you taste it in the cool night of the Jōl, where its warmth is comforting to people dressed chiefly in indigo. Here at Hisi the high air was cold and dank enough to make it welcome. The tribesmen, nephews and cousins, gathered round to help us and to share. One of our miserable cockerels was immolated and buried in the rice pot. We were anxious to cat them quickly, for they might die at any moment and make themselves unlawful by not having their throats cut in the name of Allah; they had already ceased to take any interest in the affairs of this world and looked with glassy eyes into space while our soldier spread tit-bits of millet before them. Round the fire, where Sa'id was pouring red peppers irrepressibly into our supper, a circle of dark men gathered.

They were friendly people, related to each other, and much alike. The same big mouths with pouting lips, wing-like eyebrows and long faces. They squatted and discussed the traffic of their highroad, which is in their hands between Makalla and Do'an. They talked of Sa'id II's French rifle and the matter of prices in general. He had paid £3 15s. for it, and cartridges were $4\frac{1}{2}$d. each, or four to the thaler. The daggers and their sheaths were considered as separate objects, fifteen thalers (£1 2s.) for the former and thirty-five (£2 12s.) for the latter was a good price. Salim's sheath was a handsome silver one and worth thirty thalers, but his knife had a poor edge, and was valued at only five by the company; whereas Sa'id II had an unassuming sheath with a fierce knife inside it worth thirty shillings, which he drew out and turned lovingly in the firelight, trying it gently on his own welt-padded rib. I left them, murmuring and smoking, and settled in my bed to write and sleep.

Next morning we started at seven-fifteen. The sunrise was fine, the temperature 56°. Miriam's neighbour knelt outside her hut grinding corn for bread, pounding it with a stone pestle in a slightly hollowed stone. Miriam stood watching her, her thin baby on her hip; it looked at us with eyes as sad and wise as those of an animal and suddenly turned away and banged its fists on its mother's bosom as if renouncing this unhappy world and its peculiar phenomena.

"Ya ibni," said Miriam, ashamed and proud, feeling among the folds of her gown. The baby sucked, its poise restored by one element of certainty at any rate in an uncertain universe; it gave us a sidelong glance, sad but blasé, for it had got what it wanted and could imagine nothing beyond – and if that does not make one blasé, what does?

I gave Miriam some of the small things I had for presents with me; money was not expected; she watched us go, smiling in the sunlight.

"She is pretty and sweet," I observed to Salim, who walked by my donkey.

He lifted his chin in a brotherly way.

"When are you going to marry, too?" 1 asked, judging him to be about eighteen and old enough for a wife.

"I have married, twice," he said. "I have no luck with wives."

"Why, what happens?" I asked.

"The first one left me. There was too much pepper in the rice; she just got up and left." He smiled shyly, as if it were a joke, for he knew my feelings about the pepper.

"And what about the second one?"

"Ah," said Selim, "she was disobedient. I lost a lot," he added with a sigh.

Whether the loss was to his heart or his pocket I could not tell, but I looked at him with respect, and thought he must be a little older than eighteen, after all, to have got rid of two wives already.

9

The Jōl

*"Mallefougasse vit d'une vie qui n'est pas végétale; les arbres qui sont là
ont appris à se taire . . . sous le léger rideau de chair . . . palpite
l'intérieur du monde."*

(Le Serpent d'Etoiles.)

The Jōl has usually been dismissed by travellers as a piece of
dull dreariness, a plateau where heat and cold are alike unbearable, where food is quite, and water almost, non-existent, a hard,
inhospitable, flat expanse.

To me this was not so. The Jōl has the fascination and the terror of
vastness not only in space, but in time. As one rises to its sunbathed
level, the human world is lost; Nature alone is at work, carving
geography in her millennial periods, her temporal abysses made
visible in stone. On that upland we tread the ancient floors of seas.
It has been lifted, sunken and re-lifted perhaps, how often? Its shells
are those which, before the beginning of man, lay in unnavigated
oceans. They have been raised 7,000 feet and more into the sunlight.
The sea-bottom has hardened to limestone; it rolls away now to
south and north in shining stony spaces. On its uplifted substance
the Sculptor is at work. Thousands of years already have cut the

perpendicular buttresses of Kor Saiban, as regular, one behind the other, as the wings of a Vauban fortress astride the watershed. Below and around them, farther than the eye can see, the plan is sketched for future mountain ranges, the first chisel touches given to what will be slopes and valleys, mounds now whose flat and similar tops still show the ancient level of the sea, and defiles yet unwidened that drop black as oubliettes out of the plateau floor.

Here the shallow catchment area gathers torrential rains, whose waters, swirling round to find the weakest loophole, eat out with increasing volume the ruinous gorges below; here they are but small steep whirlpool hollows, funnel tops down which the water rushes. Like a shallow amphitheatre, the ground converges on to these valley heads in tiers so strangely regular that they look like the foundations of walls set with loose stones. But they are not loose; though scored and wind-bitten to a semblance of separate boulders, you find them immovably set there with edges rectangular in spite of time, a part of the mountain core; only the caravan route, going over that rough surface into the far recesses of the past, has smoothed a slippery ribbon of rock, on whose polished smoothness forgotten Arabs have scratched their names.

In this clear altitude, where the basic forces of the earth are building, it seems absurd to reckon time in human years. The scrubby plants are scarce more momentary than men who pass in transitory generations, leaving no more trace than does a fly on the steady hand of a craftsman at his labour. Our origins and histories become almost invisible against the slow lifting of the Jōl. Only the beduin, who have little to lose or fear, walk over it with an unburdened spirit, naked and careless, "butterflies under the arch of Titus," and know its scanty pastures, and love its inhuman freedom.

Towards this majestic and sterile plateau we climbed steadily from Hisi, and looked back over the shallow saucer to the dip towards Himem and the invisible rift that hemmed our yesterday's journey. As we rose we had before us on our right, ever nearer, the great cliff buttresses of Kor Saiban, 2,150 m. high. Six of them showed, reddish, bulging from the perpendicular, with level tops;

nearer, like a separate outwork, stood the similar mass of Jebel Matar or Amtar, divided by a cleft from the main structure. Our track wound between the two, and skirted small funnel holes that mark the heads of Wadis Thwinne and Haram, by twisted samr trees, few and bent, until we came to where, like the gates of an Egyptian temple, the two cliff faces stand.

Here we entered, with primitive feelings of awe, into the highest defile of the land, and found in its shelter, amid chaotic boulders, trees again and green walls. And here the beduin, responding to the natural religion of the place, have built the shrine and grave of their ancestor, Shaikh Amtar, a poor, whitewashed enclosure and dome in the depth of the valley. On the 13th and 14th of the month Rajab, the Murshidi and their kinsmen gather together and roast their sheep and sleep all over the valley floor. The ashes of their fires were still visible. Dr. Helfritz passed by at the time of the feast a year or two ago, but he was preoccupied and says that the beduin toyed with the idea of killing him. For my part, as people hardly ever wish to kill me, I regretted that we could not stop over a camp-fire of our own to join in honouring the tribal ancestor, and told Sa'id that I would provide the sacrificial sheep if ever we came by again on the right date.

In the pleasant coolness of the defile, I got off my donkey pack and walked, and presently heard our gun go off behind me and saw our flautist loping across the boulders like a retriever as fast as he could go. The beduin have a rather knock-kneed way of running, swift but not beautiful as their other movements, and nothing like as free and straight as that of an English youth. I think it is the natural shrinking of bare feet from stones which makes them go gingerly and gives a light and catlike slope to their run. Sa'id II was covering the ground very fast, while Sa'id himself, beaming and with the gun in his hand, told me he had shot a wabar: if the flautist could reach it before it died and slit its throat in the name of Allah, we should be able to eat it for lunch.

Our soldier looked disgusted and shocked. "One doesn't eat a wabar," he said.

"Is it lawful?" I asked.

"Bi'l marra lawful," said Sa'id. "Other people don't eat it, but we bedu do. It feeds on nothing but grass."

The little beast appeared now, dangling from Sa'id II's hand and with its throat twice slit, once by the bullet and once in the name of religion; it seemed to my ignorance to be a sort of marmot with a ratlike coat, softer and greyer than those I have seen whistling on rocks in the hills of Piedmont and which the mountain people eat. I have since discovered that it was a coney of the rocks. I felt that, in any case, it would be nicer for lunch than the disgusting shark, and Sa'id promised to dry its head and keep it for me as a specimen. He was justly proud at having got so small a beast with his gun at one hundred yards or more. I suggested that he might make a poem about it, but he was not good enough, he said, at original verse; so we talked instead, and reviewed the Death of Wabar in all its bearings, until we emerged from the defile and turned westward over the sun-drenched roof of the Jōl, wind-hardened and so high that the sky seems to be around it, as well as above, with encircling arms.

Across the inhospitable expanse square one-roomed huts have been built at intervals with underground unwalled reservoirs dug close by, into which the slope of the land leads the rain-water. The huts are called Murabba'as from their cube-like shape, and mark the stages of the Jōl. At eleven-fifteen we reached the Murabba of Bain-al-Jeblain (Between the Two Hills) and settled there in the sun, for no trees grew so high. But the air was fresh and thin though the heat pierced it; and we were on the watershed. All on our north, to our right as we now moved westward, would drain into Wadi Huwayre; while to the south, Haram and Thwinne ran below us, south-east by Jebel An'ana along the route of our ascent; and the other left-hand wadis as we came to them, would drain S.W. into Wadi Hajar – the route of Shabwa and Cana from the sea. We could see Jebel 'Aqaibar in the south, dividing us from Makalla and the coast; and Naqsh Muhammad over Hajar, S.W. far away. Light, "that queen of colours," lay on it all, and pencil lines of shadow where valleys dropped out of sight in a wide silence, with no voice of bird or beast; the earth and sun embraced, and far motionless cumuli of cloud like pillars above the invisible sea, alone could overlook them.

The wabar, boiled in rice, turned out to be so tough that it was impossible to say whether it tasted of anything at all. We rested digesting it till two-thirty-five, and then set out along the watershed.

For near three hours we rode along the level backbone of the Jōl. New plants grew here together with the bright varnished green dhorar and the ubiquitous duweilah from below; sabr, or aloe, which they export; kaidah; qurith; shighle; rà, whose leaf is boiled for medicine; and round bushes called deni, which look as if they had meant to be cactus and then decided on being thorn, whose stems hold milky juice they use to stick the soles of their sandals. This bush grew everywhere; in the lower levels it had small leaves that spread out like a star at the end of each twig; but on the high ground it only showed as yet a tangled growth of wood, light grey and dark grey at the core, so like coral in its fossil beauty that one felt visibly reminded of the ocean floor on which in fact we trod. A few twisted qadah trees still grew here, but there was not enough shelter for them, for we were out on the open, with nothing between the pebble-strewn level before us and India. We rode in delight of freedom.

"Here the spirit turneth into a lion; liberty it means to have and lordship in its own wilderness."

"Why is there need of the lion in the spirit? Why sufficeth not the beast of burden, which renounceth and is reverent?"

"To create itself freedom for new creating; that can the might of the lion do. To assume the right to new evaluations; that is the most formidable assumption for a load-bearing and reverent spirit."

So spake Zarathustra and perhaps found in his words the secret of the wilderness. For it allows us to look for a while on our universe from a detachment of loneliness; to weigh our values at leisure; to judge them anew in the presence of things almost eternal. Some we reject, and some we make our own: whatever the result of our weighing, ignoble it cannot be, thus born under the majestic visible eye of Time; we come back with a firmer step into the general world of men.

To right and left of us the sudden whirlpools of the wadi heads dropped and drained to invisible valleys. The hard pebbles of the Jōl tinkled under our donkeys' feet. They, too, trotted of their own accord: perhaps something of the lion was entering into their souls also, for they jingled their luggage and sniffed each other's heels, and tossed their ears. As for a reverent spirit, no donkey has that even to begin with; but they keep their meditations to themselves, and if one does that one can think what one likes, independently of the rest of the world; so that, I reflected, looking at Suweidi's strong little neck and shoulders bobbing underneath me and my pack, perhaps he may be one of the lions after all, and no one know anything about it.

The beduin and the soldier behind me were joining in a war song. They trotted lightly with grasped weapons, two of them sang half a line and the other two completed it with a fierce short guttural ending; they repeated this over and over again, answering each other, running all the while; I began to count, after a time, and there were 130 repetitions between them before they stopped with a yell. But the peasant who had joined us last night at Rash and now overtook us, did not sing; he was an Arab, he said, and not a beduin.

So the time passed, and presently we had other distractions in meetings on the road. Prosperous-looking burgesses on quilted packs and swathed in shawls and turbans, with a black slave soldier or two before them, on the first stages of the long journey from inner Hadhramaut to Singapore or Batavia. My soldier and the other slaves kissed each other when they met, holding their rifles behind them. We learnt from these people that the Samuh tribe, on whose part of the Jōl we were soon to enter, had that morning robbed a traveller of his donkey and his gun. There was friendship for the time being between the Murshidi and the Samuh, so our donkeys were in no danger, but the other man belonged to an enemy tribe, and, said Sa'id: "The Samuh had every right to take all they could. The man should have paid for a saiara (escort) from the tribe, and he would have been safe."

Our soldier contested this point; he was a believer in regular government and gave us a lecture which might have come straight from Geneva; as such, it was listened to with polite nonchalance by the beduin who, I noticed, were now keeping a better look-out than before. But we saw no one on the wide expanse except a woman gathering thorns. We turned northwards under a cold clear sunset sky with pink shreds of cloud, and saw beyond a radiant dip the Murabba'as of Mathana, where we would spend the night. Beyond them a hill called Jebel Mūlah rose in a delicate triangle; a few qaradh trees in the foreground, flat-topped, made it look like Fujiyama in the vivid air where every detail showed.

At five-twenty we reached the camp; two huts, a third one in ruins, and a stunted qadah tree between them, made it a home; when our fire was lit a smiling boy appeared from nowhere and squatted to share the feast. No one greeted him: his presence seemed to be taken for granted.

"Where does he come from?" I asked.

"Probably from a cave. Men live in the ravines."

He ate and sat with us and vanished in the darkness as he had come.

There were ten of us round the fire that night, including the two fellow-travellers from Rash. It was cold, the wind came rushing over the stones and fanned us with smoke in circular gusts; it did not make the leaves quiver in the tree above us, so small and well-knit and close to their stems they lay, inured to this air from their birth; but the beduin shivered in nakedness, and wrapped about them their poor cotton shawls in which small bulges tied with string showed the hiding-place of tobacco, tea or sugar.

I sat in the sheepskin cloak kindly lent me by Colonel Lake in Aden and blessed his name and looked with an uneasy conscience at little Muhammad, who coughed desperately and looked ill even through his indigo paint, while he poked sticks under the cauldron where our supper bubbled. I tried to make him wear a cape of mine; but he put it aside after a few minutes. "A spark might burn it," he said; and added that the indigo kept him warm.

On the first day of our acquaintance I had insulted this small Spartan by offering him a toy whistle. At Hisi, when I gave fireworks to the beduin children, Muhammad watched with a smile, tolerant but superior, while the sparkling things snatched from the hands of the young were twirled about in the darkness by the grown men of the tribe: Muhammad at ten years was past – or perhaps he had not reached – the age of toys. He always did his share of work and spread the donkeys' oats on sackcloth on the ground, where, also accustomed to the art of travel, they ate carefully, so as not to blow the supper away with a breath of their nostrils. They moved neatly in and out of our scattered things, watching us at our meal.

All our doings were part of a ritual which many centuries have gone to elaborate, and which alone makes it possible for the beduin to travel in harmony through the hardships of their lives. They treat each other with a tacit formal courtesy, made second nature by custom; and I never saw any of them shirk a piece of work when it came, or wait for another to get up and do it after the heavy day. When one thinks how difficult it is for two friends to live together in tolerable comfort; how travel books are strewn with such remarks as "Here so and so and I parted," leaving much to the imagination – this good-humoured courtesy of the beduin, always on the extreme edge of discomfort or hunger, deserves to be remarked. Travellers who go among them with servants of their own are apt to find them quarrelsome, rapacious and difficult; but nearly all those who have been alone with them have a different tale to tell. One is then accepted into a rough but cordial brotherhood; its duties are made light and its comforts are enlarged for the weaker stranger: one sits in the best place available after a comparatively easy day, through which you have ridden and they have walked, and watches them in their cheerful labour; and realizes how the society of the wilderness has its social disciplines and restraints, its rules of decent living, just like any other society of men.

Our luggage had been arranged in a semicircle away from the wind round the fire, and we sat leaning against it, watching the rice cook while Sa'id made a dough of maize and water to bake under the embers; the two young men were greasing their thighs with our table oil out of the goatskin, a very restful thing to do, they said, after a heavy day. At this moment Sa'id murmured that someone was moving in the shadows. Sa'id II's gun was behind him on a saddle bag, with a sack over it against the damp; he swung round in no time, his oiled legs one on each side of my bag and the gun cocked and resting on it as on a parapet. Our soldier, our official guardian, had left his gun in the shed, and was told not to move, while Sa'id asked me to go on talking as before. Nothing happened; no further sound or movement; but later, as we were going to sleep, a halter was found to be missing. We returned to our supper.

Sa'id II presently put down his gun and played to us on his pipe; the maize pancakes cooked in the embers; the little twigs leaped glowing as they burned, lifted themselves in one last spasm and twisted into red rods before they fell to ashes, or the wind carried them off in sparks; in the dusky hght only the men's curved daggers with their cornelian bosses shone, and Sa'id II's white nails on his indigo fingers as he touched the five stops of his flute: it was a reed from the sea shore, brown at one end and dwindling to green; it was shiny with use; and it seemed to gather in its notes the voice of the perpetual empty wind. When I left them and climbed into my bed, a voice spoke to me from among the saddle bags through which I was groping my way in darkness; it was the dha'if, the peasant from Do'an, on guard over his belongings and anxious to make sure that I was not a robber.

I had had to be firm with the soldier before I persuaded him that I meant to sleep out and not inside the hut. I told him to put my bed close to the door, and then he and the rest could sleep inside; but this he would not do, and laid himself close to the foot with his flat black face shining in the moonlight. This was later, for I left them all talking by the fire; and I had fallen asleep before the discovery of the stolen halter caused shouts and argument and renewed alarms. No one, except I, slept properly that night: and whenever I happened to wake and look over our little camp under the moon, I saw one or more shawled figures shivering and wakeful by the fire.

10

Nights on the Jōl

*"La terre, la grande, la nôtre, celle qui, apres le déluge, est restée là;
elle s'est sechée, et voilà tout."*

(Le Serpent d'Etoiles.)

I woke at 3 a.m. and looked for a long time into the dome of the
sky, limpid as a well of light. Some bird, perhaps an owl, whistled
from the shadows: a great hard brilliance shone on our world of
stones. The wind still rushed through the motionless tree whose
leaves were too small and hard to bend before it: it showed its swift
feet in white clouds from the north that billowed up glittering to
be swallowed and melted in moonlight. The frozen air shimmered,
the moon rode high, but the opposite western sky was soft under
an avenue of stars. Orion and Gemini there led a friendly train, far
from the white abyss which steeps the moon in loneliness; like a
procession, unutterably lovely, they moved over the uninhabited
lands, beautiful to themselves alone in their nightly wandering. No
wonder the ancient peoples of Arabia worshipped these heavenly
beings: they seemed almost to touch the barren surface of the Jōl in
their passing: here, so near the Equator, they seemed to step more
swiftly over the enormous girth of the world. Presently a great bank

of cloud came and overwhelmed them; and drizzled upon us till the dawn.

Then troubles began, for everyone was tired and wet after the agitations of the night; and my sugar had come to an end, having had to sweeten tea for many more people than had been intended in Makalla. Salim could not bear to leave me sugarless, and soon appeared with a little ball tied up in his shawl. Unfortunately it was not his own: it belonged to Ahmed Ba Gort, the Silent One, who protested, but was snubbed by all; no one, they said, would grudge a little sugar to a lady who was, as it were, a guest. It was they – as a matter of fact – and not I, who liked handfuls of it thrown into the kettle. Possibly this is what Ba Gort felt. He walked by himself for the rest of the morning, too inarticulate to defend the rights of property. He had only one remark, as far as I ever heard, and that was an amiable one; for he used to murmur: "The beduin are pleased with you," whenever I came within earshot, with the air of a head master handing a certificate. I was sorry about his sugar, but I felt that he had had quite a good deal of mine; the tea made us all feel friendlier. The temperature had risen by 6 a.m. to 53°. At seven-thirty we started a little north of west towards Jebel Mūlah.

The Jōl looked brown like Dartmoor this morning and we continued to watch the valleys drop away: on the left, Wadis Sidūn, Trumwe and Beli from Qumra, Hasa and Sarab respectively, all draining as before into Wadi Hajar: on the right, Wadi Shiri from Jebel Mūlah draining to Huwayre, and Wadis Kenun, Bughlīt from Hasa, Ghar Dhabi from Sarab, draining into Wadi al-Aissar. It will be seen how the Jōl watershed, from Kor Saiban to Do'an, drains into four big systems; Himem with Haram and Thwinne flow east of Makalla to the sea: the rest of the southern slope of the watershed drains to Hajar: the northern watershed drains first into Wadi Huwayre until we reach Jebel Mūlah; after that everything flows into al-Aissar, which falls in its turn into the northern part of Do'an, and thence into the Wadi Hadhramaut inland.

As we passed the heads of these defiles, and deviated like ants that come in summer to cracks in the ground and wind about to circumvent them, we could watch the processes in the excavation of a wadi, its growth in concentration, as it were. Like our own affairs, it is first determined by some almost imperceptible accident, an invisible dip in the ground: the rain-water gathers by the chances of gravity, and pushes and labours downwards; the eating of the hard earth begins; the turn is taken to left or right; the force of water imprisoned in walls becomes irresistible and cuts its way victorious; and a purpose is born, a direction fixed, for ever (or at least for a very long time). We also saw here how the great pillars are made which buttress the lower defiles: sketched out by streamlets which trickle down the sides of the main cut, they eat inwards and leave the rock jutting between them. The landscape is hewn out like a statue from a piece of marble, a drama spread over æons of time. As I rode, I pictured what strange sea tides must first have washed these materials together, remote and incongruous as my own thoughts, which were lifted from such far places into this comparatively unthinking emptiness; scattered fragments inherited from Greece or Babylon or the Gothic forests, and goodness knows what yet shadowy worlds besides. They were here as actively at home as if the Jōl were the Athenæum, or some such place where people think; invisible phantoms around me as I rode – and with them possibly some echoes of those Sabæan musings which must have travelled up and down this track in ancient days. The world being so vast, it is very remarkable, and constantly surprises me, that the human brain should be vast enough to comprehend it: and perhaps our most important occupation is that of thinking. The beduin, living as unconsciously almost as the stones, belong to inarticulate Nature, but we, in our uncomfortable awareness, have the future on our hands.

We passed the Murabba'a of Qumra, where the land of the Beni Samuh – stealers of the donkey – begins; and then came to that of Hasa, and suddenly stood on the edge of the upper Jōl and

looked over its flatness, that shelves in imperceptible furrows far
northward out of sight. Small lizards ran about here, with strong
American jaws and tails straight up in the air; Salim called them
Zumi.

I was now taking photographs without descending from my donkey. Salim helped by holding its head and nostrils buried in his
tummy, to prevent it from shaking me by breathing. Suweidi, the
donkey, obviously took no pleasure in photography. During one of
these halts I asked Salim why he and Sa'id would not come on with
me into the Wadi Hadhramaut beyond Do'an.

"We would gladly," said Salim. "There would be no difficulty in
going, because you would be with us, and the slave who represents
the Government. But we would have to come back alone, and the
other tribes would rob us."

"You might come on to Shabwa, and then back with me."

"No," said he. "That would be fearful for us. We do not belong
to that country."

"And would you ever take me down to the south-west to Hajar
and Maifa'a?"

"No," he said, "we do not like to go to Maifa'a."

"Is there war between you?"

"Oh, no, but we don't like them. Our market is Makalla, and we
travel between Makalla and Do'an."

This strict trades-unionism of the tribes, which does not allow a
beduin to undertake any transport in any district except his own, is
a great nuisance to the traveller; he loses his guide just when he has
become useful.

At eleven-ten we reached the Murabba'a of Sarab and camped
for lunch. The temperature was 70° in the shade, the aneroid 24.1.
The murabba'a, about 20 × 16 feet, was built up to 3 feet in a band
of largish stones and mud, and above that with small flat stones
embedded in mud which hardens like cement in the sun. These
refuges are all on the same plan. They are not more than 6 or 7 feet
high, so that the edge of the flat roof is useful as a table to keep guns,
shawls and oddments out of the way when one camps. From the

waterhole beside them, lines of stones are often laid out to guide and collect the rain-water.

This was a pleasant place, and in a hollow below us a closed abandoned tower built of mud showed that there had once been a spring, and that we were nearing the end of the Jōl.

As we sat, a string of camels loomed up and passed. The beduin lingered a moment to exchange news, then kissed each other's hands and ran after their beasts. I noticed what ugly mouths most of them have, perhaps from constantly screwing them up against the sun, for they never wear the sheltering head-gear of the northern Arabs. When they had gone, I saw Salim preparing for departure and made my usual protest against this unnecessary hurry in the heat of the day. "Haste is of the Devil," I repeated every afternoon when this happened.

"And delay is of the Merciful," they all replied in chorus, but went on saddling nevertheless.

"If we do not start now it will mean an extra night on the Jōl and we shall have to buy hay," Salim explained.

I suggested a compromise. I would buy the hay, which came to ninepence for every beast, and we would spend an extra night, and not hurry after meals. So everyone was pleased, and Salim, coming up after a while to the small patch of shade in which I rested, asked if I was content. "It is good to be patient with the traveller," he added, with a virtuous glow.

I agreed that is always good to be patient, avoiding any concrete inference. Even so, I was made to start at 2.30 p.m.

We now left the high Jōl and descended very gradually into Wadi Dahme, which drains to al-Aissar and holds in its soft and shallow landscape the first village, Dahme, north of the watershed. It is only four acres or so of flat fields in the open upper wadi bed, with a few 'ilb trees, and a square tower to protect the houses beside it; but it looked civilized after the Jōl and Sa'id called it a town.

We left it on our right and continued over a low 'aqaba to Bureyira, while Salim went on to buy hay in a Murshidi village farther on, since both Dahme and Bureyira belong to the Samuh;

this was, I think, the reason for their reluctance to sleep here; for the Italian proverb: "To trust is well, but not to trust is better," is one which the beduin thoroughly appreciate. The hay they buy here is twisted in a thick rope, and a donkey eats half or three-quarters of one in a day besides $4\frac{1}{2}$d. worth of corn; a camel only requires the refuse of the oil presses, which is fed to him in cakes, so that he costs nothing, and the donkey is considered the more aristocratic animal.

Bureyira is a bleak little collection of cubic huts in an almost treeless dip with a few fields beside it. We reached it at five in the afternoon and pushed our donkeys through a door into a court just big enough to hold them, and settled our luggage in one of the two living-rooms beyond. These are poor windowless places, black with smoke from an open hearth. A few plaited food trays on greasy walls, a rush mat or two and a hookah on the ground was all that our reception-room contained: the stone roller and grindstone, which cost one and three thalers, were the housewife's most valuable property; hard poverty here was like an echo of the hard surrounding land. Even the children looked subdued, dressed in black. The little girls had their hair shaved in an ugly band across forehead and temples, leaving an isolated strip called hillāqa about half an inch wide over their brows, with the usual pig-tails, done once a fortnight, behind. They followed me, hiding, as I went round the few houses and gradually crept out at a safe distance when I stopped by the shrine of their wali, which stands above the fields. It was a plain sort of tomb, about 4 × 3 ft., whitewashed and rough, but decorated at the four corners and in the middle of one side in the ancient Sabæan way with the horns of beasts, ibex (*wa'il*), gazelle (*dhabi*) and goat, which the people called *saidi* – a colloquial term, I was afterwards told, for the wild doe.

When I came back I told our soldier that we would feast on a sheep that night. Our fowls had come to their end, one having died of fatigue and the other three cooked in rice, and I had no wish to see any more victims tied alive to our saddle-bow. The thought of a good dinner sent a wave of cheerfulness through us all.

A large sheep was brought in and paraded before me, but the price was thirteen thalers: the beduin sat looking at it with non-committal gravity until I observed at a venture that this was too dear. They then got up one after the other, felt the sheep all over, and bargained seven dialers off it. This was still too dear, for I had only five dialers with me, and I said that the sheep seemed unnecessarily large. Everyone instantly agreed, another frightened little beast was brought in, black with a white-tipped tail, and felt all over. I bought it for 4s. 6d. (3 thalers), and in two minutes the name of Allah was pronounced over its death in the courtyard; a woman sat down to skin it in the doorway, while the cooking water heated in the pot. Our fellow-traveller from Rash turned out to be a butcher, and the rest of the business was entrusted to him. He cut it up on a straw mat with a dagger and then divided it as it might be Africa among the powers, if people had their way. He used the insides to tie like string round odds and ends of anatomy, and then handed all over to the women to take to their room and boil in rice. The heart and liver, special delicacies, were brought to me fried in the coffee-pan as an hors d'oeuvre.

It was pathetic to see how popular this meal made me and with what silent exaltation its appearance was greeted, heaped up on the tin dish borrowed from our fellow-travellers. Round the edge of the dish the butcher now set out nine portions under our hungry eyes (one for the master of the house). They put one on my plate, no doubt the best, and then each chose in turn and, this anxious business over, settled down to enjoyment at an incredible speed; only Salim interrupted himself to tell me that he had kept a little of the uncooked meat for me next day, for he had every genuine instinct of chivalry in him.

After we had finished our coffee, I retired to the edge of my bed and attended to what little toilet I could while the beduin squatted in the smoke of the fire. Sa'id II sprawled in a corner, playing with his cartridge belt, loose over his hips. It had a purse in front with nothing inside it but matches and an address; in its first cartridge compartment it held, instead of a cartridge, a little pot of kohl to

decorate his eyes. Presently he pulled out his dagger and began to
breathe on it, turning to the company with a delighted smile when
the steam disappeared off its shiny surface. He caught sight of me
as I spread face cream over my face. He handed the dagger to little
Muhammad and told him to ask me for a little of that duhn to grease
it with. Rather regretfully – for it was very precious – I put a lump
on the blade, and wondered what Miss Lethbridge in Bond Street
would think if she could see. Muhammad carried it gingerly into
the firelight, where it was greeted with exclamations of joy.

"Yasmīn," said Sa'id II, smelling it. All the daggers were handed
up to him for a share; a little was left over, and this he spread over
his legs, remarking that it was "better than oil."

After this we slept, less happily than on the open waste, and rose
in a shell-pink dawn and left Bureyira at seven-thirty to climb again
from the wadi and cross our last stretch of Jōl. The temperature
at six-thirty was 58°. Before going, as our hosts did not belong to
our Murshidi tribe, I gave a thaler to the woman of the house, a
friendly battered creature whose only female vanity remaining from
her youth were brass anklets six inches high. She told me that two
men of the Samuh were hostages in the prison of Makalla.

An unfortunate thing happened in the little courtyard where
our donkeys were saddling. One of the sacks was seized upon and
claimed simultaneously by both Salim and the butcher of Do'an.
Salim, usually so amiable, would now and then lose his temper with
an unexpectedness which possibly explained his two divorces: he
was rushing at the butcher, when Sa'id and our soldier interposed:
a quarrel was a serious matter, as one could see by the anxiety of
everyone to stop it. The combatants were separated. The soldier
gave us one of his orations in the name of Government. He himself,
he said, would judge between the two claimants when we reached
our journey's end.

No one paid much attention: the carelessness with which the
beduin took his pomposity must have been a constant pain to him.
But his vanity was not personal; it was bound up in that of the
royal household to which his father and grandfather had belonged

before him, since first they were bought and brought over from Africa: to this his devotion was absolute: he regarded himself as its mouthpiece, humble, but inspired – a dangerous belief and cause of most of the world's persecutions. But he had no gift of authority; he was rather like a fussy nurse, and the beduin paid as much attention to the long and monotonous tale of his responsibilities as we used to do to those of an incompetent governess. Now, however, he was happy; he murmured about the excellence of government and the matter of the sack alternately for the rest of the day, and told me that when we came to Do'an he would make both parties swear to their ownership and would give it to the right one.

"But," said I, "supposing they *both* swear that it belongs to them?"

Either my Arabic was inadequate or this was beyond the modest reach of the African brain. I got no satisfactory reply. He and Sa'id continued to discuss the abstract merit of justice to the poor in the uninterested tone used for uncovered virtues; the sack, meanwhile, had been collared by Salim and remained with him, his party being four to one; one could only hope that justice and government happened, on this occasion, to be on the side of numbers.

We passed a second village called Bureyira on our left, with a fort and qaradh trees before it, and reached the level of the Jōl, lower but otherwise exactly similar to what we had travelled on before, except that far behind us the ridge of Kor Saiban lay in the sky, undulating and coloured pink and mauve, like smoke.

Wadi Kharit on our right drained with a number of tributaries into al-Aissar: on our left, Wadi Menwe ran to Do'an. It was hot here, and the sun shone white in a white sky: everywhere it shone on the hard edges of small stones. Sometimes, they say, a little grass makes the Jōl green, but now it lay bare as a gridiron under the rays of light. We passed the murabba'as of Hadje and Ba Khamis, and rested there at eleven-ten and talked with two women travelling to see their children at Makalla. Makalla, they said, is an immodest place, for the women wear no trousers under their short skirts as they do in Wadi Do'an, an uncharitableness probably quite untrue – but that is women's talk. We left, and rode till the sunset lit the western sides of the pebbles that strew the flat expanse: our shadows flickered over them like a curtain travelling before us. The lava stones lying here and there are the same variegated dusky colour as the beduin's skins.

I felt rather ill with a headache and was glad to see the men scatter to fill their shawls with firewood, for it meant that a camp was near. These poor cotton shawls are used for everything; even when they sew up a sack the beduin pull a thread out of their shawl to do so. At five-forty-five we came to the murabba'a of Jōl 'Obaid. Here there is no wood lying about, for the women come to gather it from Do'an. On our right we could see the cliffs of al-Aissar, a faint crack just showing in the distance. The temperature was 61°.

We were a smaller party, for Sa'id II and Ahmed ba Gort, the Silent One, had pushed on to their homes, and the butcher of Do'an had been keeping himself to himself after the affair of the sack. He came up, however, by the time we had settled round the fire, as friendly as before, and started to cook a mixture of flour, water and sugar for the general benefit; when it had thickened to a dough he sprinkled more sugar on it, made a hole to pour oil into the middle, and invited us to share – and very good it was. We had run out of sugar ourselves, but the butcher happened to be carrying a load for a merchant in Do'an, so we "borrowed" a little, to be replaced from a shop in the wadi. This was done after a good deal of hesitation, for the beduin are scrupulous about the loads entrusted to them: their credit depends on it, and their livelihood, and Sa'id told me that they do the journey between Makalla and Do'an or vice versa about three times a month.

"A vain life," he said. "Always on the road"; yet he would not gladly change the health of the Jōl for comfort in the wadi.

They were friendly with the thought of our journey's end so near, and thanked me again for having shared their food on the way. "It has been pleasant travelling," said Sa'id.

Salim was pouring coffee into the two grey bowls which are all the beduin have in the way of crockery.

"Here we are now," he said, "all together. And tomorrow?" – he opened his hand out wide – "all scattered, where?"

After this question, so sad, ancient and universal, we looked in silence to the darkness and the stars. We were suddenly astonished to see a small light flickering about there. I thought it was a lantern bobbing up and down with a donkey.

"It might be," Sa'id said dubiously. "But people do not travel by night. It might just as well be the Gedriya."

The light disappeared. "It must be the Gedriya," they said.

The Gedriya, they told me, is a great light which sometimes appears in the sky during the twenty-fifth night of Ramadhan, and it will grant every wish which is made while it is visible. At this moment the light reappeared, nearer, and a sound of feet stumbling over the stones. It was evidently human. A voice presently hailed out of the darkness, and three peasants or dha'īfs from the wadi, well draped and hooded against the nightly cold, appeared in our circle of firelight. They were friends and they had heard of our coming from Sa'id II and Ba Gort, and seeing our delay (due to my preference for slow travelling) they had come to protect us through the night.

This kindness was very well received, and the social circle widened round the fire. I left them and went to my bed in the moonlight, rejoicing in my last sleep out of walls – the last for many months as it happened.

Next morning we left at our leisure, for we had only a short way to go. The donkeys trotted gaily, knowing themselves near home; and soon in the flatness of the Jōl, and with another unending flatness of Jōl beyond it, we saw ahead of us the growing slit and the opposite cliff top of Wadi Dō'an, with an R.A.F. landing-ground on our right and two little watch-towers built of mud square on the edge of the cliff before us.

11

Life in Do'an

منزلنا رحب لمن زاره   نحن سواء فيه والطارق

"*Our abode is wide open to those that visit it; he that shelters there at night is the same in it as we.*"

(Mustatraf.)

If I were asked the most agreeable thing in life, I should say it is the pleasure of contrast. One cannot imagine anyone but an angel sitting with a harp in Paradise for ever. The ordinary human being needs a change. This is the secret charm of the oasis, usually an indifferent patch of greenery made precious solely by surrounding sands. The celebrated fountains of the world – Helicon, Bandusium, or that water of Salsabil which Solomon gave to the Queen of Sheba – all spring in arid places. The beauty of an Alpine dawn lies half in the sleeping world below. A warm chair by the fire after a day with hounds, a shuttered room when the wind is tossing, belong to this category of pleasures. The Greek shepherd knew the joy of the safe pinewood when storms tear the open sea; and a woman I know told me she had married her husband because what he said was always unexpected – a good adventurous reason for matrimony, I thought.

This subtle unexpected pleasure, this very salt of life, is the reward of those who, after crossing the Jōl, stand on the lip of the cliff and look down into Wadi Do'an.

The wadi is about a thousand yards wide and drops a thousand feet or so with sheer walls. On the rubble sides which hold the cliffs, little towns are clustered, built of earth like swallows' nests, so that only the sunlight shows them against the earth behind. Five or six are visible on the slopes as one looks down. Between them and their squared ploughed fields on either side of a white stream bed, the wadi bottom is filled with palms. Their tops glitter there darkly, like a snake or a river, with scales or ripples shining in the sun. The eye, sated with open spaces, rests on their enclosed greenness, and follows it to where it winds from shadow into sunlight between the buttresses that hold it in and turn it round a corner in the distance. The River of Palms, shut in the adamantine walls, held, as it were, in a crack of the Jōl, looks as valiant and prolific, as optimistic, as full of quiet resting-places and of shadows, as life itself in the arms of eternity.

The difficulty of the Hadhramaut lies in the steep descents into these wadis, the "'aqabas" whose causeways are built into the precipice. They are probably very old, paved with cobbly boulders like the paths which struggle between walls in Liguria; only much harder and sharper. A Queen of Yemen in the fourteenth century left endowments for "drinking fountains in the valley roads" and repairs to the steep hill-side paths and "staked ways." (She was a very remarkable woman and her husband, the Raisulid Malik Eshraf, was so devoted to her that he mourned her death for a month before he married again.) Down our particular 'aqaba, scooped in the cliff and sometimes overhanging, we made our way and took fifty minutes to reach the rubble slopes where the limestone precipices are bedded on sandstone.

The open Jōl of the beduin was behind us and above, and we were in heavier air, among peasants; they stopped to look with their mattocks half in the ground, but gave no greetings of their own accord. Sa'id led our little caravan under the palm trees along raised banks in high cathedral-shade, the donkeys trotting in the dry watercourse below. And soon, walking north down the wadi, we came to the Governor's castle of Masna'a, built high and square of mud on the wadi side, and with roofs and terraces crowded to see us. A welcoming shot was fired. We passed through a carved gate studded with iron bosses; up a winding enclosed path inside the fort and two more doors at different angles: someone to shake hands at each entry; and so by a narrow passage into a pillared and white-washed room, where the Governor and his brother, Muhammad and Ahmad Ba Surra, stood to welcome me.

They were surrounded by their tribal retinue, indigo beduin like my Murshidi, all owners of rifles which now hung or leaned like a frieze against the walls, while the men stood crowded together to watch me. At the upper side of the divan, on mats or carpets, a few members of the household were gathered; the head of the small garrison of soldiers; and a neighbour or two from the towns nearby, all looking very much dressed in coloured futahs, white jackets and turbans. Here, after depositing my shoes, I sat down on the ground; and took coffee in the usual earthen bowls, while the servants attended to the shisha, or hookah, and brought it round at intervals so that each of the more honoured guests could have a whiff of it.

I was to spend twelve days with the Ba Surra, and got to know them well, and it would be hard to find a more charming family anywhere. The two brothers live together in harmony in the fortress, sharing the weight of government between them. Their beduin love them and say: "Ba Surra is our father," as a Highland clansman might say of the head of his clan. And the wadi people, too, unite in praising them, and the fairness and firmness of their government, which they run practically independently of the Sultans of Makalla. They were both youngish men, much alike, the same gentle brown eyes, the same large mouth, rather full-lipped, used to smiling; the same long oval face, neither aquiline nor round, and long capable hands; the only difference was that Muhammad had a slight curly fringe of black whisker, while Ahmad only wore a tuft under his chin. Their father had held authority firmly in the valley before them and died as a very old man only two years ago, having married ten wives in the course of a well-spent life: Muhammad had already married six and Ahmad four: these details I learned later, and on this first interview merely stayed to exchange the necessary courtesies before being taken up through another winding pathway of the fortress to my apartment.

This had belonged to the old Governor, and his widow Ghaniya was mistress of it, and led me up its narrow mud stair to a decorated door whose wooden key she carried in her girdle. It was a big room with six carved windows through whose fretwork arches the valley showed below. One had to stoop to see out, for the windows are all made level with the floor, conveniently for sitters on the ground.

The good houses of Do'an are all more or less alike, their rooms supported on wooden pillars elaborately carved. The inner wall also is faced with carved wood, arched over the door and opening into niches where the store of quilts and pillows is kept by day. The carving is fine, and the old 'ilb wood is rich and dark: iron bosses, tinned over like dull silver, ornament it. The ceilings are built with strips of palm wood in a herring-bone pattern between small rafters; and supported on carved pillars with cornices flattened in the old Persian style; the windows are in four compartments, each carved in tracery over a small arched opening, for there is no glass at all: stout shutters, three inches thick to keep out bullets, close each compartment, and each window has a small round opening below it, with a gutter-pipe outside, useful to pour things on assailants below, and holes behind them for the barrel of a gun. For the valley has become quiet only in recent times, and many people remembered its little towns warring with one another, when the old Ba Surra was besieged in his own house, now so peaceful; and if a shot rang out, its echo beating from wall to wall of the wadi as if the sound could never escape that prison, the ladies of the harim would rush to their carved windows and look out over all the little towns spread in their sight along the valley sides, and wonder if it were beduin or soldiers, and then turn away rather disappointed when nothing further happened, telling me how wonderfully quiet the valley had become.

They took great pride in their rooms, and showed their riches by the number of brass trays which hung upon the walls, so thickly sometimes that they lapped one over the other: they can always be converted into cash because of the value of the metal, so that the ladies look upon them as a sort of savings bank, ready to their hand: the slave girls used to come and dust them with great care, though nothing else received the same attention, and they were always shining. Birmingham mirrors, odd plates, covered the rest of the wall-space, and rows of tin coffee-pots, one above the other and almost touching, ran up the corners of the room to the ceiling. Otherwise there was no furniture, except now and then one of the beautiful carved chests, brass-studded, from Zanzibar, such as you also find in Kuwait and Basra. The floor of the room was covered with rugs, and underneath them the mud was hardened into smooth ridges like ribbed sand, a decorative wavy pattern also used on stairways. On the walls of stain a frieze of mud was sometimes smoothed and whitened and worked over till it shone like distemper, with a zigzag edge to it: the cleverest workers of Do'an and Hadhramaut can use mud as delicately as stucco, and indeed nothing can be more dignified and decorative than the old fashion of their houses, which, unfortunately, they begin to despise in favour of bad showy things from Europe. When I next went down to the diwan, I found Ahmad looking lovingly at some panes of mustard-yellow glass, carried up at great expense by camel from Makalla: they were for the new house, which he was building close by: it would take six months to a year to finish and then he would move in and leave his rooms in the old fortress for his son.

He took me to see the building, where his masons sang to keep time together as they slapped the slabs of mud and straw into their mud foundation. Only the very lowest band of the house is laid in stone: the rest, even to seven stories high, is made of these slabs of mud and chopped straw, about eighteen inches square and three thick, dried for a week in the sun, and then set in a paste of liquid mud. Donkeys were trotting up with water in goatskins to mix with the earth. The walls began to show: they incline slightly inwards like the old Sabæan buildings, and give their massive fortress look to the Hadhramaut cities; even the heaviest rain will not penetrate more than an inch or so into their thickness, and they stand for hundreds of years. Whitewash patterns decorate the outside of the windows or run in bands alternate with the natural brown. When I said that I thought these houses more beautiful than the new cities of Europe, the two Ba Surras refused to believe me; but they admitted that perhaps their old carved doors were handsomer than the machine-moulded brown-varnished impostures just ordered from the West. The shades of civilization are closing rapidly over these feudal valleys: only the absence of transport keeps our hygienic vulgarity at bay.

The first thing I asked for in my apartment was a bath, and a quiet time to struggle with the dustiness of my luggage. The head of the wabar, which the beduin had peppered and salted for me, and which still smelt more than one would think possible of so small an object, had been put by the soldier into the tea-kettle when I was not looking: the governor's widow and I, in the disgust of this discovery, fraternized over the universal clumsiness of man; and she soon brought me hot water in a tin thing with a spout which would pour over me as I stood on the bathroom floor – for my room, like all these Hadhramaut apartments, had a bathroom of its own. An earthenware jar, four feet high, stood in the corner, filled with water every day: and the floor tilted down to a gutter which dropped the water over the face of the hill-side below our walls. The drainage, too, went down there in the same open manner, by a wide shaft on either side of which a small platform was built for standing on: and in the absence of toilet paper a niche was filled with clods of the hill-side earth, hardened in the sun. These bathrooms are clean and not unpleasant if they are well kept, and their disadvantages are felt only by the public in general if the area below happens to be a street. But nobody worries about that. When I was ill a few days later the ladies of Do'an assured me that my scented soap was the cause of the trouble; nor could I ever make them believe that their sewage might be more unhealthy than the perfumes of Houbigant, so anxious are people to think that what is good for one must also be unpleasant.

It took me some days to disentangle the inhabitants of the fortress of Masna'a, for it was a big place, like a warren, several stories high and with several houses built inside its encircling wall and gate, and the numbers of people who had been divorced and married other relatives made the line between one family and another almost impossible to follow. Ghaniya, my hostess, was simple enough. She had only a girl, and boy called Nasir, whom she would look at with adoring melancholy and say: "Unhappy one, he is an orphan," so frequently that I felt sure it was developing a complex in him, for he was a morose and taciturn little creature, quite unlike the gay and talkative swarm of cousins all around him.

His sister was gay, too; she used to come in with her little eyes dancing behind the two slits of her face-cloth and only looked serious if one talked about marriage, which was to be arranged for her in two years' time when she would be fifteen; fifteen is the age for orphans, though ordinary brides can be younger. Whatever the age, the whole thing is settled without the child's knowledge: dresses are made "for a cousin," and she only guesses what is happening when her hair is being washed for the event. Then her face is varnished yellow with zabidbud, a mixture of oil and wax and "hurd" *(turmeric)*; her hands and feet are covered with a brown pattern; and she sits all through the third day of the wedding feast under a red veil which her husband lifts from her face at night. In the morning he leaves ten thalers on the pillow; and after the second night, a tray with a handkerchief, ten thalers, a pile of cloves, scent and incense; and after that, no more. We had one bride in the community during my stay: she was a bovine, good-natured creature called Fatima, still dressed in all her finery: she would wear it, she told me, for forty days. Her black gown had a breastplate of solid silver plaited with cotton: her girdle jingled with silver tassels: her bare feet had anklets of gold. I covered her with confusion by asking her whether her husband kissed her, and if so where, for she seemed too highly decorated to be touched anywhere with any comfort. This indiscreet question caused her to be teased for days by her friends. Her mother, who stays with the bride for a fortnight after marriage, had just left.

The make-up of these ladies varied a good deal according to whether or not they had a husband to please at the moment. My poor Ghaniya divided her hair simply down the middle, "because," she said, "I am a widow." Her mother also, who was a gay and delightful old lady from the next village, had long given up these laborious vanities and looked on the world and the gossip of her grandchildren with wrinkled and smiling detachment. But when Muhammad's wife came in, the lady of the castle, it was like a ship under sail, so rustling with bangles and girdle, so decorated with necklaces, and with so smiling an air of prosperity and favour. She was still a beautiful woman, though Nur, her daughter, had been married already for some years. Nur was my chief friend and companion in the harim, and used to bring my food and sit and talk to me, with one eye on the window for the valley and its doings below. She had the soft eyes, large mouth and long fingers of her uncles, and the same charming nature, an easy kindness to anyone who came: her husband had left her three years ago to work abroad, as most of the men of Hadhramaut do, and he used to write to her with every third or fourth ship that touched the coast. As it was the first time she had been left alone, she was allowed to come back and stay with her own people: the second time she would remain in her new home, for such is the custom of Do'an. The men stay away sometimes fifteen or twenty years, and many other wives abroad, since their own women will hardly ever leave their valleys. They go chiefly to Somaliland, Abyssinia or Egypt from Do'an, while the upper Hadhramaut emigrates eastward to the Dutch Indies or Malay.

This habit of migration is quite recent and the Ba Surra told me that they remembered the time when any traveller would be known as Makkawi, or Massawi, etc., according to the place he had visited, so rare an event was it to leave the cliffs of Do'an. But some streak of enterprise must constantly have distinguished the men of these valleys, for even after the decline of their commercial empires, in the early days of Islam, one finds stray traces of them far afield. They settled in Syria and Egypt at the time of the Conquest and formed about one-tenth of the Arab population there, first known under the names of al Harith and al-Eshbā – derived from Shabwa.[1]

A standard-bearer of Sadaf, which is a Hadhramaut tribe, is mentioned in the army of the great conqueror of Egypt, Amr ibn al-As: and Shuraih ibn Maimūn, a Madadi from Mahra who went to Egypt, was in command of the Egyptian force in an expedition against Constantinople in A.H.98 (A.D. 716–7). Most of the Sadaf who left Arabia went to Egypt or North Africa, but they are also heard of at Kufa in Iraq, in close alliance with the tribe of Kinda, also largely a Hadhramaut tribe. It was a man of Hadhramaut who arrested one of the murderers of 'Ali, the Prophet's son-in-law, at Kufa; and they are said to have come to the assistance of Kinda when that tribe revolted from Islam; they certainly refused to arrest Hijr, a man of Kinda, on the plea of their kinship. In the war which overthrew the Persian Empire, Hadhramaut and Sadaf had 600 men in the armies of Sa'id ibn Waqqās. They must have been prosperous and learned at that time, for they paid one-tenth of the total Yemen taxes, and their Qadhis are particularly mentioned. The "8th treasure of Yemen" was at Hamra somewhere in Hadhramaut. When Islam finally triumphed, three governors were stationed in the south-west – two in San'a and Jened in Yemen and one in the Hadhramaut.

The ancient reputation of this country for learning is not upheld in Wadi Do'an, for there are no real schools – only a few philan- thropists who will teach anyone who is anxious to read the Quran. The Qadhi himself had got his learning from ten years spent in Mekka: anyone dissatisfied with him could appeal to another Qadhi up or down the valley, or, as a last resort, to Makalla. None of the

---

[1] Abd-el Haqam 47B fol. 2 and Hamdani 98.

women I met could read. How the women indeed managed to fill their days I never came to understand. They did no embroidery, though they would run up their dresses – a simple matter exactly like the sewing of a sack: but the elaborate breastplate, with its sequins and beads and tinsel, was sent out to be done professionally. They would cook sometimes, or superintend the cooking, and that might mean a good deal of work now and then in a household where any number of loyal tribesmen turn up to be fed at any time. But most of all the day was spent in calling on each other from one house to the other in the fortress and from the cluster of houses in 'Ora village below.

These calls had their formalities. The fact that we had only just seen each other in the house of Muhammad's wife did not absolve us from shaking hands all round when we met half an hour afterwards in the rooms of the mother of Ahmad. Every newcomer made the round of the assembly, lifting everyone's hand in turn and kissing her own as she did so, or sometimes – in sign of greater respect – kissing the top of an older woman's forehead. If you were talking, and happened not to attend to the new arrival, she would snap her fingers loudly till you turned to perform the necessary rite. "Hayya" or "Salaam," she would say. The visitors from outside came wrapped in their shuka, a square black shawl with two fringed sides which they wore draped over their heads and bodies, the two lower corners knotted together and the upper ones thrown over one arm: I never grew tired of watching the beautiful draping of this shawl, which made them look like Tanagra figures walking. They would put this garment on even to go from one house in the fort to another, and also the black face-cloth with a silver line stitched down the nose and two eye-slits, for a man might appear in the narrow alleys: but indoors they wore only an Indian silk kerchief tied under the chin and the black sleeveless gown askew over one shoulder.

No man could, without warning, come into these sanctums except Mahmud, the doorkeeper, who controlled the gate of the fortress by a chain from above. He was a privileged retainer, born and bred in the Ba Surra house, a cheerful, breezy little youth, curved altogether, with a round tuft of whisker on a round chin. He used to strut in like a bantam among so many hens, with two or three sorts of coloured cuff links arranged in buttons down the front of his white jacket. He chaffed the more modest visitors from outside who pulled their visors down. He would come up to me when I was ill, saying: "Taib, taib. Good, how goes it? All is well now, if God wills" – brushing aside any remarks of mine as if non-existent: for was he not a man? – and did not the sound of senseless female chatter lie below him, a mere noise and no more? Sometimes, when the babble of ladies talking seemed almost incredibly continuous, I was inclined to agree with him. What he wanted, he told me, was a European wife from Egypt. The one he had, he said, was dirty – so he never spoke to her.

"Why don't you tell her to be clean?" I asked, wondering at the same time what she could be like, for the general standard was not high. "Perhaps you prefer a silent wife? If you once let her talk, you might never stop her."

Mahmud looked at me as if this were an idea, and evidently determined to continue silent. He was troubled because his eyelashes curved inwards and hurt his eyes, and I had no medicine for such a disease: his small round face looked at me, puckered up with disappointment like a baby's.

"You must get a doctor for that," I told him.

"When you go to Egypt for your next wife," said Nur.

With this happy thought, his masculine swagger restored, he left to fetch me my water. It came from a spring in the cliff, which I preferred to the fortress well, and he used to go for it every day with a subtle nuance in his kindness. "If it were not for me," he seemed to say, "what would you poor creatures do, shut up and helpless?"

12

Khuraiba and Robāt

عجبت من منع امرئى جاهه   ما منع مَن يجتدى ولم يَغرم

يثلم وفر المال اعطائؤ لكن   وفر الجـاه لم يثلم

(ابن الرومى)

"I wondered that one so noble as he should withhold;
Why should he withhold who, by giving, loses nothing?
The money-hoard is diminished by its gifts:
But the store of honour is not diminished."

(IBN ER-RŪMI.)

The two governors used to come to eat in my room, fluttering the ladies in flight before them. They would come in without ceremony, Muhammad with a straw table-mat, and Ahmad with a plate or two in his hand, and settle down while Ghaniya did the rest, overcome in the face of so much condescension and as nearly speechless as was possible. She brought us rice, piled high, with fat and peppers; meat cooked in excellent gravy, and the local dish called harisa, of meat and flour pounded smoothly together like a gruel, with a cup of melted butter in the middle to dip each handful in as one took it.

Ahmad and Muhammad meanwhile talked pleasantly, and I liked them more and more. They brought with them the Sayyid Muhammad ibn Iasīn, a charming old merchant who dealt in cotton on the Red Sea coasts and wrote in Arabic to Liverpool. He too had the long face and large pleasant mouth typical of the settled people of these valleys; and their delightful good humour with each other had, in him, a special mellowness of experience and kindness. He might have been Ulysses settled down to a quiet old age:

> "Fussé-je comme Ulysse, qui fist un long voyage,
> Ou comme cestui-là qui conquist la toison,
> Et puis est revenu plein d'usage et raison
> Vivre entre ses parents le reste de son age"

Ibn Iasīn had come back to his wife and his native town of Robāt at the head of the wadi, leaving his son abroad to carry on the trade; and as he was a friend of A.B.'s, whose name is like gold in this country, he invited me to lunch next day.

I started early in the morning, and on foot, for I wished to look at the towns on the way. Robāt is the last of the wadi, where its palm trees end, and three uninhabited ravines lead up to the Jōl; and between it and Masna'a, Rashid and Khuraiba cling to the left side of the valley against the cliff. It is not more than an hour's walk to pass by all these little towns, and I set forth with the soldier and a beduin guide behind me, under the spiky shadows of the palms.

The palm trees are the great business of Do'an, and people will give as much as 500 thalers for a good one: 6 per cent goes to the Government on every sale, and there is a yearly tax of a quarter of a thaler ($4\frac{1}{2}$d.) per tree, equal to that on a measure of land, and more or less equal to a day's wage, which is about one-third of a thaler, or sixpence. As we walked under the crowned stems, dim in their green shadow, we saw men climbing up to fertilize the fruit with creamy spathes. "The smell does it," they told me. One would think that people who trouble so much about smells would be more particular over the kinds that hover in their streets.

I left Rashīd on my right and turned in to the black slits of streets that climb uphill between the piled-up houses of Khuraiba – so narrow that small wooden frames are suspended from opposite windows for fowls to roost on, out of reach of thieves and foxes. This is the chief town of the upper valley with market and mosques. The name means a ruin, and it may be the Do'an mentioned by Ptolemy and by Hamdani also, capital of Pliny's Toani: it is, at any rate, an old and self-satisfied town, and prides itself on a purity of religion which inclines it to violence: it was the Sheikh of Khuraiba who sent Von Wrede, robbed and penniless, to the coast in 1843; and fifty years later, the Bents avoided Khuraiba because of warnings from their guides. Later travellers, Van den Meulen and the Ingrams, have found it pleasant enough, and so should I, if it had not been for the ungraciousness of its chief people, the family of Sayyid Hamd al-Bar.

I had a letter to the Sayyid, and his house, they told me, was at the very top of the town, under the cliff. Before we had gone any distance, a charming stranger appeared from nowhere and welcomed us: he had been a clerk in Aden: the sight of a European delighted him: he came to show me all I wanted on my way. He led me to the chief mosque – a quiet place of columns – and lesser mosques built more like private chapels by pious householders, low and neglected, with open wells beside them – for the sewage goes down and the water is drawn up promiscuously in the crowded area of these little towns.

We came to the market, whose wonders I had heard of from my beduin on the Jōl: it was but a narrow alleyway, and on its high doorsteps the sellers sat, outlined against black rooms behind them, with baskets in their laps. They weighed their meat in red and yellow painted scales. It was the busy hour, and the children crowded round; but all were friendly. They asked questions and stood to be photographed – until, with a growing train, we came to the high palace, whose carved door and whitewashed battlements stand under the wall of the cliff.

Here the deplorable mistake occurred. The stranger went up to the door and gave my letter; there was a long pause and the answer came that no one was at home. I suspected, and everyone else knew, this to be untrue. The Sayyid himself was, as a matter of fact, away; if he had been at home, the disaster would not have been allowed to happen: but his sons and wife were there, and they are all known to dislike Christians, and to meet them unwillingly, as I was told later. Sheer inhospitality, however, I never knew before or since in the Hadhramaut, and its effect was catastrophic. The welcoming stranger came back silent, smitten with shame, and preoccupied; the crowd fell away a little, quiet and murmuring: the stranger began to lead me quickly downhill – for we had to go through the whole breadth of the town.

He refused to talk, and avoided open spaces; he hurried down ways so narrow that I had to go sideways between the houses: our descent began to take on the appearance of a flight. We were obliged to come out in the open near the lower end of the town, and here the crowd reappeared and, seeing our haste, began to look disagreeable, for there is nothing like flight to rouse the hunting animal in man, and they had been dodging round buildings to get at us. My stranger, I concluded, was losing his head and would soon bring about a catastrophe. I refused to be hurried any longer, and stopped to take a photograph of the gathering inhabitants.

This caused a check: the farther ones pressed on, but the nearer hesitated: I went up and talked to the foremost, and with the pretext of grouping them for my picture, began to ask if they had never seen a Ferangi before: no one answered, but the ones behind wished to hear what was being said: they were intrigued, for they could see that I was smiling. I returned to my guide, now biting his fingers in agonies of impatience, and we continued more slowly downhill, while the crowd, quieted for a minute or two by the interruption, gradually became troublesome again. But we were near the end of the town: and suddenly from his house an old man appeared whom I had met in the Governor's diwan, a merry-faced old man with a white chin-beard, who came forward beaming cordiality, but also fell away as soon as he heard what had happened, and instead of asking me into his house, hastily pressed me to follow on my path. I began to hate Khuraiba. As we reached its last houses, a pleasant thing happened, for my three beduin, Sa'id and Salim and little Muhammad, came rushing out of the hut in which they live when not travelling, and fell over me with handshaking and smiles: the crowd looked on, approved, and became more friendly: my protector, glad to get rid of me, had vanished. I took a farewell photograph to emphasize the fact that the town of Khuraiba and I were parting on terms of neutrality if not of friendship: and then walked off on my way, with my soldier and the beduin glum as could be behind me. The discourtesy of the Sayyid al Bar's family, the refusal of hospitality to a stranger, was too sad a subject for conversation: it was, I must repeat, the only occurrence of its kind in the whole country: and it showed how much the traveller owes as a general rule to the kindness of these feudal lords, who really have his life in their hands, since their attitude towards him will be imitated and exaggerated by all the lesser people.

With lacerated feelings we reached, in twenty minutes or so, the town of Robāt, which piles itself up between two ravines on a spur of the prison wall – so these cliff faces feel that shut one in without a gap on every side.

There were fewer palm trees here, and the wild nature of the country came tumbling down towards the town. But out in the street, the Sayyid Muhammad's son awaited our coming, and the Sayyid himself greeted us at the head of his stairs. All was welcome and friendliness. In a low room with carved doors and columns we sat on a carpet at one end, while the soldier and his gun settled among the household slaves at the other: the troubles of Khuraiba were forgotten.

Another guest was there, a gay old man who had worked for the British and had been made Khan Bahadur for keeping order among the Yafa'i tribesmen; until, unfortunately, they had been able to obtain some of his government rifles, after which he retired, and is now settled in private life: he told me part of this story, and spoke agreeably of the world and its echoes, heard even here. It is remarkable how closely political affairs are followed in these remote Arabian valleys. The Italians, who were then preparing their Abyssinian venture, were disliked in South Arabia at this time.

"When we walk along the streets of Massawa," said the old Khan Bahadur, "we are obliged to salute every Ferangi we meet and to give him the pavement; with you Ingliz at least we speak as man to man. And when the King of Italy came," he continued, "an order was sent round that all should prostrate themselves before him on his path: and we, as you know, only prostrate ourselves to God – and so we had to stay indoors that day, and only the slaves and the lowest of the people were able to go out to see the King."

"And," said a slave from the other side of the room, joining in the conversation, "they put their flags to the top of the mosques, as if it were their own house and not the house of God, may He be praised and exalted."

We left this delicate subject and talked of the tragedy of cotton, which had fallen from £40 to 10s., ruining, among others, the business of Sayyid Muhammad. And then we talked of the affairs of the wadi, and its poverty and little commerce, and the excellence of the Ba Surra government which keeps the peace amid so many difficulties, almost independently of Makalla. The strength of their rule lies in the tribal power they have over the eastern beduin – the only real basis of power possible in this country, I was to conclude later on. As it is, the security of Do'an is an island in a not very quiet sea: the tribes west of the wadi are kept in hand through thirty hostages or so imprisoned in Makalla: a war is going on round the top of Wadi al 'Aissar, where the villages alone are under the Ba Surra and at peace; and there is a strip of no man's land, now temporarily under a truce, in the north between Hajarain and Shibam. The difficulties of keeping the peace are added to by the fact that the beduin here consider it a disgrace to accept blood money, so that their feuds go on for ever.

Even the assistance afforded by Makalla is not an unmixed blessing, for the mercenary Yafi'is, of whom about 250 are settled in Wadi Do'an, were giving trouble at this time: they made themselves unpopular by feeding their goats on the people's plantations and, having been remonstrated with, had now entrenched themselves ready to shoot in one of the fortress houses of the valley: how the matter ended I never heard, and I have no doubt that the Ba Surra were well able to deal with it. As I went home that day I met the old chief of the Yafi'is and chaffed him gently on the behaviour of his troops.

"They never move them," he told me. "That is the cause of all the trouble. They have been here about twenty years, and they think they can do what they like."

He himself was an old Yafi'i, walking along under a big turban, with a long thin face, fierce but faded, and suddenly friendly and sparkling with fun like so many of his tribe: and he himself had been for thirty years in Do'an, having come as a young man "because his greatest friend was here."

After lunch, Sayyid Muhammad took me to see his bees on a little terrace. They live in a pipe like a drain-pipe made of mud, covered with blankets to keep it warm and closed at one end, with some small holes left for them to creep in and out. The other end is built into the warmth of the room, and closed with a circle of basket-work which is pulled out once or twice a year when the bees are smoked away and their honey is taken. The honey of the Hadhramaut is famous, and is mentioned by Pliny. It is exported, packed in round tins, and has a rich and heavy flavour, due no doubt to the 'ilb trees whose blossom is the bees' chief food.

After watching these creatures, I went upstairs to the harim and sat for some time among ten or twelve ladies, talking on that thrice-blessed subject of clothes, whose absence as a basis for conversation was evidently felt even in the Garden of Eden. What one would do without it in an Eastern harim is inconceivable. I was the first European woman to visit these ladies, for Mrs. Ingrams had not climbed up their stairs to see them, and they waited in groups to look at me, even when I lay down and slept, for I was now shivering with some incipient disease and longed for rest. They brought a mattress and quilts to cover me; an Abyssinian slave girl sat with my bared feet in her lap and pressed and released them in her two hands, drawing the fatigue from them more soothingly than any massage I have ever known. A beautiful creature came, one of the Sayyid family of al-'Attas, the nobility of Hadhramaut, descended from the Prophet: she was thin and long like a greyhound, with large eyes in a mâte complexion, un-painted, and with a shy and brilliant smile. Before I left, the Sayyid's wife brought me tinsel embroidery to decorate the hips of my black gown, for I had told her that I was having a Do'ani gown made to take to my home: and she gave me silver beads, such as all the women like to wear round their necks.

With these tokens of kindness I said good-bye to the charming people and departed, and the Sayyid's son took me some little way, with all the children of Robāt behind us. They were not objectionable in themselves, but their little feet made clouds of dust, and they advanced in a series of short rushes, to get as near a full face view as possible. They held on with me to the outskirts of Khuraiba, where reinforcements of a far more redoubtable kind came pouring down the hill, my enemies of the morning, who swelled the cortège, and retaliated with hooting songs when the soldier made clumsy efforts to whack them with his gun. They made me glad to see the friendly bastions of Masna'a above me in the sky, and to settle down to sickness in my own harim. In the evening at supper I told the Ba Surra about the children of Khuraiba. They were concerned.

"I will put some into prison," said Muhammad; "only to teach them."

And I hope he did.

13

Sickness in the Fortress of Masna'a

"And when she had lain a great while, she fell into a measle, and of no leech she could have no remedy."

(Morte d' Arthur, Bk. xvii.)

On the first day of my arrival in Do'an, the mother of Nur told me, as she sat with me over coffee, that the small scrap wailing in her lap was ill with measles. She turned its one green satin garment and many amulets upside down and showed me the spots, and I knew – never having had the disease before – what lay in store for me. Every three or four years, they told me, these epidemics sweep over the country, and I had unluckily fallen into the middle of one. Nearly every small child who came nestling up so confidently, had a spotty face when I examined it: they caught the illness not from each other, I was told, but from scented things like soap; Taveruier, in his travels, mentions that the "Abyssins and the Kingdom of Saba" use no soap, and perhaps this was the reason; even the ointment I used to give people who complained of rheumatism was often refused because of its scent. With so profound a difference in our medical theories, there was very little I could do to avert my impending fate: every object I touched had been touched by someone with measles before me: it was almost a relief when, feeling very ill, I took my temperature and found it to be 103, and decided that further preventative measures were unnecessary.

I now spent a delirious week. For three nights I was actually delirious, pursuing in broken and miserable dreams a search for some vague thing, undulating and alive, which had been given me and on whose recovery my happiness depended; it was, I thought, the secret of happiness, an object simple but elusive, as one might have expected, and I only wish I could remember exactly what: for I used to come upon it in the early dawn, when the fever dropped, and then slept peacefully, until Nur, with my breakfast in her hand, dressed in black and gold, rustling with bracelets, her lovely eyes brilliant with kohl under the oiled and plastered triangle of hair, appeared to my awakening sight as some strange continuation of the nightly dreams.

"Qumi," she used to say: "get up," regardless of my condition: and when I told her that I had a fever: "We all have that," she would answer cheerfully, and gave me her pulse to feel, which, as a matter of fact, was racing along. She, too, coughed, as did nearly everyone: the healthiness of patriarchal town-life I soon came to regard as a myth, for I never saw so many sick. But no one lay down unless actually incapable of rising. The ladies trooped in to me, surprised to find that I had crept to bed again after breakfast on the floor.

"Ma shī sharr," they would say; which means, in other words, that all is going as well as possible. But there is nothing so irritating as the optimism of other people at one's own expense, and I finally was driven to retaliate and to say that all diseases come from Allah, when they asked for impossible cures. And then I would be put to shame, for all they would answer was: "Praise be to God," in meek, unquestioning acceptance: and they would repeat this even when telling me of the deaths of their children, submissive to a destiny over which they have so little control. "A fearful lot of work is left for God to do,"I find written in my diary.

They told me that disease comes with the hot wind which blows from the sea. It beat the shutters to and fro and rushed in the organ

pipes of the valley, and I looked out, wondering to hear its noise
and to see only the motionless cliffs, their pure and sharp outline
and the shadow that falls and rises on their sides with the steps of
the sun, like a bucket in a well, measuring out the days. A sense of
prison overshadowed me between those perpendicular buttresses;
they seemed as unescapable as the delirium of the night.

In the daytime, however, there was plenty to occupy my
thoughts.

For one thing, there was the question of food. Milk, as the
Bents had found before me, and vegetables or fruit, were almost
unobtainable: everyone was anxious to give me all I could desire,
and they would send round for all the goats and wring from their
droughty udders a small and earthy tumbler-full, which I gladly
welcomed at breakfast. Raw carrots they sometimes ate, and Nur
cooked some of these: and they would bring meat which I was too ill
to bite; and would never believe that with a lacerated throat I really
liked my rice pepperless and fadess. I felt too ill even to touch the
flat bread cooked in oil and soaked in honey, and hved on eggs and
soup, on tablets of Horlick's milk which I had with me, and – one
day – on the luxury of a water-melon and apples sent as a present
to the Governor from the coast, and hospitably shared: the harim
would not have had a bite in the ordinary way; but my being there
procured a fat red slice for the child who sat beside me, her little
face framed in an orange satin hood stiff with grease and tinsel.

The babies were the playthings of the harim, and suffered, I
thought, from overwrought nerves due to the constant avalanche
of caresses to which they were subjected as they were handed from
one lady to the other among the coffee cups. The older children
ran in and out and brought the latest news from one house to the
other. They came freely into my room, and so did anybody else –
slaves and mistresses, beduin girls round-faced and healthier than
the towns-women, and old men and women in need of medicines.
A friendly democracy accepted all: the grubbiest could sit there on
the carpet, using it as a handkerchief, or lifting the edge now and
then to spit carefully underneath. It was the life of the medieval

castle in all its details; a life so much lived in common that privacy and cleanliness are almost unobtainable luxuries. Saintliness on the other hand, is made not only possible, but frequently essential.

All sorts of things happened around me as I lay in bed. Old peddling "dallalas" came to sell bracelets, their goods tied up in a kerchief full of coral, amber, silver girdles, and embroideries: they would go from town to town in the valley, and brought us gossip.

A pretty woman came, 'Atiya, from the village below: her husband, newly married, had just left her to go to Somaliland. She suffered from some pain so that she could hardly stand, and came for medicine: but I was asleep at the moment, and Mahmud the doorkeeper took her to an upper room, and there branded the soles of her feet with a hot iron: when I woke up, she came down to me, apparently perfectly restored and cheerful. She sang, shyly, a qasida, to wish her young husband a safe return: his aunt had made up the words, and his bride sang it in a light sweet voice, innocent and moving – five shorts, a long, and a short – three times, and five shorts and a long to close, when the voice lowered and dropped into a depth of longing.

"Return. Thy uncle's daughter is alone at the fall of night."

The girls laughed as they sat round. 'Atiya put out her little grubby hands, blushing with soft eyes.

"Is it not right?" she said. "Is he not my husband? Must I not wish for him to come?"

"And how long will he stay away?"

"Ah, who knows? Perhaps ten years. The Will of God."

They all sighed, for this is the sorrow of all in these valleys, and all, no doubt, were thinking of their husbands, married to others, far away. "The life of the world is hard for women," said Nur.

*   *   *

They were anxious to try a hot iron on me at the back of my neck, which they say is a good remedy for measles. I avoided this, but I was not so lucky with an old witch of a woman who came in one day from Hajarain, dressed in the black gown of that northern region, all decorated with little coloured patches, and with her elderly horsey face still painted yellow. She gave herself airs of holiness. Her husband had (very sensibly) divorced her, and her absence of youth, beauty, or human kindness were now devoted to God. When she saw me lying helpless, she pounced upon me: she uttered invocations, and whirled her indigo fingers and skinny arms like windmills about my head. With every invocation she tied and untied a knot in her shawl (a practice of sorcery already deplored in the Quran), and then she suddenly bent over me and spat. It was meant kindly.

We had dramas, too, within our walls. Ghaniya's son Nasir came weeping one day and told, between sobs, how a log had fallen on him and hit his arm as he stood in the alley: there had been some feud over a divorce with the house that overhangs the narrow way and for a day everyone, even the grandmother, were weeping at different windows of my room, though the ladies all continued to meet politely as before, and the log was explained to have fallen (as it probably did) quite accidentally. But the little boy sat for hours, sobbing quietly with rage. These feuds make history in oriental houses: shut in their walls, no later impressions would ever efface that childish memory: one could see plainly even here how, given opportunity and power, such harim bickering might ripen to bloodshed when the children of different mothers became men.

Such darker shadows flickered now and then amid the daily gossip. One day we heard that a kinsman had died in Abyssinia, a young trader from the neighbouring town, and one of the chief men there. Ghaniya told me the news, working her emotion up gradually and laboriously, to a pitch suitable for the visit of condolence, which would mean forty-eight hours of more or less solid weeping in public, in the house of bereavement. She bestirred herself to pull her satin dresses out of the chest in my room. At intervals she remembered to sigh deeply: but then she forgot, for she still liked her fine gowns and was pleased to show them. She ripped off a silver and blue front, and sewed a purple and gold one on instead, more suitable, she explained, for a house of mourning. And Nur and I watched her hooded in black, with nothing showing but her eyes through their slits, stepping down the castle path. In the village below, whose flat roofs we overlooked, an old minstrel beat a sort of tambourine and sang long qasidas at people's thresholds: he came from Yemen, Nur told me, and they called him Abu Alwān, the Father of Tunes. The valley, with its floor of palms, lay peaceful between the straight cliff walls.

"Have any of you ever been up these sides to look over the Jōl?" I asked Nur.

"Never," she said.

Beyond these ramparts all the world is the same, dim, vast, and unknown, to the ladies of Do'an; a place into whose recesses their husbands vanish, and whence, now and then, Indian pedlars come with machine-made silks and velvets, which the ladies sew up into the ancient fashion of their land.

When Ghaniya came back to us, she had a serious problem to attend to. Her black slave woman went on strike. She had been bought for 800 thalers ($£60$) "when the children were small" and something, no one quite knew what, had now annoyed her. She would neither obey nor answer: but she sent a message that she wanted to speak to her mistress upstairs, and everyone went amiably to hear.

Ghaniya came down annoyed and unsuccessful, and told me that Muhammad, as head of the family, would have to talk to the slave, and ask her if she wanted to be sold. In that case, said Ghaniya, a dallal from Hadhramaut would undertake the business. But she thought it would not come to that. The trouble was that the poor woman had had a little daughter. At five years old the child had been sold for 300 thalers ($£22$) to a family in Ghaidun (a day's journey away), and the mother hankered to see her child again.

Next morning, Muhammad talked to her and promised soon to send for the little girl for a few days. The slave woman reappeared in our family circle, her little eyes smiling as before above her bony cheeks.

"It is hard for a mother," I said to the brothers when next they came up.

"Yes indeed," they said. "So it is. It is the ordering of Allah."

In the West, spasmodically and with uncertain hands, we try now to eliminate the *causes* of sorrow: but it is only recently, and since the decline of formal religion. The East still holds religion in its established forms: and encourages philanthropy, which deals with effects and not with causes. For as soon as you investigate and try to alter the origins of things, you are no longer a philanthropist, but a revolutionary, and your disinterested movements are liable to make whole edifices crumble: and mankind is asked from successive pulpits to leave the fundamental things alone. So the East accepts slavery, mitigating its effects with kindness, and thinks no more of this bodily servitude than we do of the slavery of the mind, chained to the daily written words of more capricious masters.

I was better now, and the fever had fallen. I could walk about my room and insisted successfully on having hot water brought to wash in, a thing which my hosts had refused me out of kindness for a week. Forty days without washing is considered de rigueur for measles, and my relapse later was taken to be due to this premature use of soap and water. Meanwhile, I felt my strength returning: I recognized it by a renewal of fortitude in the matter of food. I could now, with an inward calm impossible in illness, watch Mahmud bringing us our supply of sugar in his well-worn skull-cap, or the slave girl wiping grease off the dagger she had taken from somebody's waistband to carve our lunch. In Terim I was told there was a doctor, and every European comfort: and meanwhile I had a cough which exhausted me and might, I feared, turn to pneumonia; this appeared, from a little book I had with me, to be a frequent consequence of measles, and I reflected that, if it developed in Do'an, I might as well call myself dead straight away. In Terim and the Wadi Hadhramaut cars were to be had, and they would come down to meet me as far as they could, at Hajarain: to reach that place was only a two days' journey. We wrote, and in a few days heard from the hospitable al-Kaf Sayyids that a car had been sent. Loaded with presents and kindness, I took leave of my friends in Do'an.

They had told me of ancient water cisterns about half an hour above Masna'a in a gap of the cliff, and I had seen through my glasses a little room and a window low and rectangular, opening from it, in the very middle of the cliff face, north of my lodging, in a place which is now and must always have been absolutely inaccessible by ordinary means. Doors into cliff tombs have been found by Rathjens and von Wissmann in similar situations in the Yemen, but this appeared to be built out, like a swallow's nest. As far as I know, none of the visitors to Do'an have noticed this little eyrie, or visited the reservoirs: I was too ill to do so, and recommend it to the R.A.F. on their next flight.

The Ba Surra spoke to me also of a chamber closed with an iron door just beyond Khuraiba in Wadi Khulle, also unvisited because of its inaccessible position: and they told me that in a cave in Wadi 'Aqrun, which flows into al-Aissar and the head of which I must have passed on the Jōl, a chest had been found full of black stuff which burnt with a flame like wax, and that a hand and some writing in red characters had been on the wall beside it. Van den Meulen and von Wissmann found ruins and Sabæan script at the junction of Wadis Thiqbe and Menwe, just off the Makalla route; and that is all that so far has been noted in the neighbourhood of Do'an. It was probably, as other evidence leads one to believe, a place off the main road in Sabæan times, and increased in importance with the growth of Makalla and the decline of the old route from Cana by the Wadi 'Amd: and that would explain the poverty of the remains hitherto discovered.

I was sorry not to be able to examine what there was, but I had little strength to spare.

I had been given new donkeys and beduin. My soldier, who had come to see me every day during my illness, reappeared in full panoply, with the addition of his white woollen ski-ing cap, peculiar in the tropical wadi. We set forth gently in the afternoon.

Soon the wadi turned north-west, and widened a little: its river of palms died away and was replaced by 'ilb trees, full of berries, in open stretches: the towns on its sides grew fewer and lesser, sometimes only a pyramid tower with small windows: the cliffs in unbroken ranks closed in on either hand.

Our stage was short; one and a half to two hours to Matruh, where a hospitable merchant had invited me to sleep: his new house rose in tiers of whitewashed lacework between the village and the cliff. It was a beautiful house, with painted rooms in the manner of Java, whence he came. The light gay colours made one feel as if one were inside a box of sweets: the front door, delicately carved, had cost him fifty pounds. All was clean, attended to by himself and his son: a satin quilt was spread for me on a red velvet mattress, a white tablecloth and tins of milk were spread for tea. He was a rich man, yet he told me he preferred his barren valley to the civilized delights of Java: but his son, who had been born out there, did not share this view: and this I found to be the usual attitude of the younger and older generations from abroad.

Next morning, with some misgiving – for my cough made me almost speechless – I left at six-fifty on the long stage to Sif and Hajarain.

14

The Ride to Hajarain

"A land of fenced citadels where blood is lightly shed,
Where a tribe must keep its borders and a man must keep his head,
Where the wayfarer benighted as he nears the village late
Sees the red glow from the matches of the guard about the gate."

(SIR ALFRED LYALL.)

We had left the narrowest part of do'an behind us, and its palms had long died out in park-like glades: but though the walls were now wider apart, their buttresses shining in sunlight, their outline faint in the whiteness of the morning sky, the walls yet felt like prison walls: truncated pillars stood gigantic against their wind-smoothed steepness, scored in horizontal grooves; their terrace tops were regular.

The Beni 'Ad, says Ibn Mujawir, before the prophet Hud brought destruction upon them, lived in these lands and built themselves terraces against the ants, and built fireplaces around to keep them from climbing up. Why the legend should have magnified so very small an insect to attack the giant forerunners of Islam, I cannot imagine: (the ants were big enough, according to Yaqut, to pull a rider off his horse): but as for the terraces, I feel that the early geographers may well have been impressed, as I was, by the extraordinary architecture of these wadis, and attributed them to the uniformity of man rather than to the accidents of nature: especially as I several times met people here who, never having read Ibn Mujawir, would yet point to some feature in those symmetric sides and say that surely the Beni 'Ad alone could be responsible for such colossal building. As for me, riding oppressed with illness in such a merciless landscape, I pictured this crack of earth as one of Dante's circles and imagined blue beduin dancing with flowing locks and shawls on the edge of their Jōl above, with pitchforks in their hands.

The wadi grew wider. Its shallow fields were terraced against flood, and 'ilb trees sat here and there, brooding on their shadows like a hen on eggs. Sunken paths ran where streams of water must rush in summer: we rode above on dry-walled dykes. If people met there, one or other had to give way and climb down the side, and we argued the point with a man whose donkey, half invisible under a copper cauldron, was difficult to dislodge: I would gladly have made way, but the black slave and the dignity of Government forbade.

Across the width of the valley, the towns on either side faded into the rocks; their lacework and inverted battlement designs, their small and variegated windows, merely made them look a trifle more crumbled than the works of nature round them. Slender shepherdesses were all about the landscape, in floating draperies, a small round basket for 'ilb berries beside them, and a chopper or a long pole in their hands with which to beat down fodder from the trees.

Alta sub rupe canet frondator ad auras.

It was amusing to see them so active, wound in draperies and with faces hidden by black veils. Sometimes the goats preferred to attend to their own food and climbed the trees themselves. They are sleek, black and white, short-haired, with ankles as pretty as a Frenchwoman's: and they pushed their blunt noses delicately to get the little oval leaves with three white lines running down them that nestle in the 'ilb tree's thorns.

The fields were still empty, waiting for the flood-water or "sail," which takes the place of rain. The earth lay in hard clods, bleached of all colour, and peasants just as dusty turned it over to a depth of about two feet with light and pointed hoes; they would sow millet there after the sail. But when we came below Beidha', a town about as big as Khuraiba that climbs with brown pyramid houses towards the western cliff, we suddenly found ourselves among palms again, delicious young plantations of small and tufted trees, fresh in the morning with grass and shadow, and quiet dusty paths soft underfoot. Here there were quantities of flowers – calamint, yellow daisy tufts, white convolvulus, yellow samr balls honey-scented – and birds sang a liquid song of six notes cool as water. Many dry channels were dug here, and came into the road by three or four sluices to distribute them among the palms when the time came: for every tree has a ditch dug round its roots to water it. And when we left the pleasantness of these plantations, and came out again into the open wadi, we saw fields of wheat – most of it miserable on dry and spindly stalks, but here and there a green patch and the shadow of an 'ilb tree thrown upon it; and I thought, as I rode by and saw that sight of home, that nothing in the world can be more lovely, restful and vivid than the softness of shadow on a cornfield, "somno mollior herba."

The only other sight of coolness in that sun-bleached rift in which we rode enclosed was now and then a flock of doves that wheeled towards their rocky nests; their grey plumage showed by contrast how arid, hot and red was all beside.

Our soldier, happy to be off at last, his gun on his shoulder, his hips swinging, his blue and purple loin-cloth newly-washed, striding beyond my donkey's head, added to the thirsty feeling of the landscape by stirring up more dust for us all to swallow than anyone would have thought it possible to do with only one pair of feet.

The whole of our route this day was through land under Ba Surra's control; but war was flickering in the right-hand wadis, and the governor, anxious to leave nothing undone for my comfort, had seized on a young Sayyid who happened to be passing through Masna'a and told him to keep by us for greater safety. The Sayyids are all descended from the first missionary of Islam, who settled in the Hadhramaut. They carry no arms, and can travel anywhere without danger, though a growing modern and secular movement, chiefly from the Hadhrami colonies oversea, is now undermining their influence. Our travelling companion, however, was considered to be a guarantee of peace. He was young, with a snub nose and a blue woollen turban – and he was very silent until we had eaten together, and discussed the pedigrees of various Imams, and then he became a pleasant companion, and gradually fell into a walk beside me, instead of striding ahead with flapping gown at an uncontaminated distance.

After we had crossed to the left side of the valley, where it turns east under the walls of Qam perched on a rock, we came by a barren stretch to where the Wadi al-Aissar enters in. Here is a wide and open space where floods must rush about, for the earth is congealed into fissures and ditches: the right-hand cliffs have retreated into distance and leave a sense of freedom, for al-Aissar is a great and prosperous wadi and drains half the northern Jōl from Makalla, as we had seen when travelling there along its sources. We left it behind us and turned north, and left the last of the villages, miserable mud-patches now, across the sail-bed on the west.

I asked the beduin who was trotting beside me about the war, and where the enemy positions were.

"There," he said, and pointed to one of the groups of houses called Koka. We were some way off, but we could see men bending at their work beside the walls. "That is one of their villages. But we do not fight here. We fight in the hills of al-Aissar."

We rode on in the increasing emptiness of the wadi: the heat of the middle morning beat upon us. At a turn we came upon a beautiful flowering tree they call 'adhab, and make a tisane of its bark. Its flowers were yellow and white, large and scented, and as delightful in their exotic way as the green cornfield had been before: I came to the conclusion that the secret of the loveliness of these two things in the dusty land was that neither of them had any dust upon them.

In three and a quarter hours from Matruh, we saw the mound of the houses of Sif pressed in a bay of the western cliff, below a mud tower whence the Yafi'i soldiers hold the town: a white minaret; and an amphitheatre of rocks wildly weathered, as if the cliff-side behind the town were crowded with giant statues half effaced. It is a poor place, with fortresslike houses. On the outer edge of it the Ba Surra's deputy is modesdy lodged, and welcomed us with friendly nervousness, due to the fact that he is bullied by the soldiers and suspected by the town; for Sif is an old-fashioned diehard sort of a place with little in common with our host and his wife, who had dealt in motor-cars in Jidda and knew both Mekka and Cairo. Ferangi-dressed photographs hung on the walls of their little sitting-room, above a fresco painting of a steamship done with that simple incompetence which modern artists call by grander names: all the facts were there, two funnels belching steam, the Captain's face like a full moon over the bulwark, and aeroplanes in the sky.

But there was none of the richness, the carved pillars and aristocratic massiveness, of Masna'a: and the deputy himself had no authority. He kept the neighbours anxiously at bay, seething in a tumult below and demanding to see me; while he told of the troubles they caused him. The head of the Yafi'is made his way in, blustered about, and snatched the medicine which I had just given to my host for his eyes – nor could he be made to go: he was a bully of a man, half naked, and treated the little governor with such contemptuous jocoseness as a Prætorian captain may have treated the feebler Emperors in Rome. And then there was a great to-do to find new donkeys, for my beduin here came to the end of their stage. The hours passed: the crowd shouted: women crept in to look at me; I longed for sleep and quiet. But at two-thirty the donkeys were ready: I descended into the crowd, which was quite out of hand, heaving with excitement, but friendly when I actually appeared. The Ingrams had stopped in Sif and broken down its record for unfriendliness to strangers; for it was here that von

Wrede was plundered and the Bents were nearly made to turn back, and the Dutch envoy spent a rather unhappy night four years ago. I, however, set forth with friendly w'Allahs on a donkey so small as to be almost invisible under the saddle-bags: three Yafi'i disentangled themselves from their fellows and came as escort: and we made north over the white sail-bed, dazzling in the sun.

There is a gradually lessening sense of security as one travels northward from Do'an: the chain of communication is kept open by the authority of government, but one feels in these lower lonely reaches of the wadi that it costs some effort to do so. There is very little cultivation between Sif and Hajarain, and I could never decide in my own mind whether these barren stretches were the cause or the effect of lawlessness: on the whole I think that it is the constant insecurity which first destroys the crops, and then leaves the land open to the ravages of nature. We certainly travelled through desolation in the afternoon light. Across the stony bed, some miles away in a western valley, Ghaidun showed pleasantly under trees: the shrine of Ahmad ibn 'Isa, the grandfather of the Mansab of Thilē is there, and I would have stopped to visit it if I had not felt so ill: it looked hospitable and open in the widening of the wadi. But we, turning eastward, rode in a shrivelled land, a rind of coagulated earth – limestone or sandstone – which time had crushed into gullies about ten feet high, most excellent for snipers. Few 'ilb or samr trees: no water: at intervals the small white dome of a siqaya, the pious human fellowship of some dead traveller. In the middle of this waste the sail-bed ran, a river of white boulders where the red crust was washed away. Here and there small observation posts were built square, one mud room over another, with a shot-hole in each wall. There were no houses, except far on either side in the bays of the cliffs, miserable human clusters almost invisible under the wide natural walls, and far apart at that. No human beings except a black-draped woman, who moved rapidly away.

The three Yafl'is scattered gaily over this land, walking carelessly, tall and thin. They were fine-looking, careless men, with a lawless swagger: "il devient malaisé d'après notre manière de voir, d'établir une démarcation entre le paladin et l'apache." They carried their guns on their shoulders and showed the dusky muscles of their backs and legs as they swung them. One of them was young, aquiline and handsome: the other two were oldish men, and it looked almost indecent to see them, clad only in loin-cloth and cartridge belt, with their lined and venerable faces, with a fillet round their hair and a ring on their little finger, skipping about the gullies after our straying donkeys. Every two years, they told me, they go home to their mountain villages in the hills north-cast of Aden.

"Is the time not long for you between one visit and the other?" I asked.

"Yes, said the old mercenary. He was walking behind my donkey and tried to keep its small invisible hindquarters in the right way with his gun. He smiled rather sadly. "All men." he said, "love their own home. Foreign lands are heavy to the heart." Presently, as the sun grew low behind us he spread his shawl out on the white stones and prayed his afternoon prayer, while his comrades walked on with our soldier, who had forgotten me altogether in the excitement of having real soldiers of the government to talk to.

I needed help, for my donkey was such a puny thing, it kept on stumbling: it came down with me four times, but was luckily so small that I could step over its ears before we actually touched ground. The Yafi'is were furious with the people of Sif for providing such miserable animals. There had evidently been trouble over the business, and no donkey driver appeared for a long time, and all of us were helpless except the Sayyid, who appeared surprisingly proficient in the art of talking to donkeys in acceptable language; until at last their real master overtook us, a beautiful curly-headed young beduin, furious evidently because he had been commandeered by the governor, and reluctant even to reply to my salaam. He took his animals in hand, however, and by a few well-considered noises drew them from the ridges to which their alpine tastes inclined them into the proper path. But he was sulky with us all, and as we stopped by a siqaya he stepped before us and passed his arm through the mud-wrought lattice work to find the dipper and drink, and would have put it back again without a thought for any of us if I had not asked him to hand me some water, and called him "my brother" as I did so. It had a soothing effect, and the rest of the day was spent in harmony; and this was as well, for we were all tired out before the end.

Our wadi turned northward, and as the sun set behind its walls we saw the rock of Hajarain before us, far away. It too, is flat-topped, but one step higher than the general cliff level, and is therefore a landmark from every side. Cultivation appeared here, fields of wheat and millet, and one or two more prosperous villages: and on our right a zigzag pathway up the cliff whence people go to Makalla in five days, my soldiers said. The way up to Hadhramaut from Makalla by Do'an is indeed the longest way, and only used because of its greater security: there is no geographical reason for it to be a main route into the interior.

The night was now coming upon us. A little crescent moon, very bright and pale, lit us along a dusty deep trench of path which never seemed to end. We walked enclosed, as it were, in a ditch. My donkey, tired as I was, dropped me at intervals into the deep soft dust: the young Sayyid trotted behind urging it on with noises, stopping now and then in the darkness to draw thorns out of his bare feet: there were quantities of them under every 'ilb tree where the young shepherdesses had pulled the branches down. I gradually became numb with fatigue, for we had been seven hours actually on the road and I was weak. In the dim night, four camels came towards us, looming under loads of reeds: we had to climb on to the high bank, where another path ran along the top, while they passed, like phantoms in the dust below, a seated black figure swaying on the load. They hailed us suspiciously: with our four guns we must have looked dangerous against the skyline in the night.

But now at last from our high pathway we began to look down on basins of moonlight with dim and rustling gardens. Hajarain, a shape of blackness, showed one light on a hill. We came beneath its walls, where a group of beehive roofs enclosed the city wells; flat ground dim with moonlight lay around. Worn cobbles zigzagged up under the walls, from which old rafters pushed out, and black streams of sewage. At the top we came to a studded gate and high threshold, and knocked, and heard a shouting within: we had been expected, but it was late now for our arrival. They opened and led us to where the representative of Makalla, a slave, stood by the mosque to welcome us, his black face disguised by a turban and the shadows of night. The mosque also had a well with beehive roof: its minaret, square and then circular and then square again at the top, is of the most ancient type found in the Hadhramaut: it shone dimly, lit by Cassiopeia above it: but the town was dark. Our little group led us to a door in a blank wall, the house of a Sayyid: we waited there while they looked for our host, for though there were people inside, they would not let us in till their master came: it is a mistake to arrive in Eastern cities after dark. But at last the carved door swung back: we were allowed into a sort of guardroom, with dingy walls, unfurnished, where the Yafi'i mercenaries, strolling in, hung up their rifles: I wondered disconsolately if this was where I was to spend the night, for the black slaves, unversed in the Arab aristocracy of manner, are incapable of dealing with the sudden advent of guests, and no one seemed to pay attention to the representative of Government.

After a while, however, the Sayyid came up and led me to the inner rooms of his harim. A sound of whispering, tidying and protesting, showed that I was to be given the ladies' own apartment for the night. A quilt was hastily spread amid the female litter: I admired the carved walls and doors and tried to concentrate on them to the exclusion of other things. The notables came to drink tea with me and told me they had been waiting here for the last two days to meet me; and when they had gone, I opened the shutters of my window and saw through its carved lattice, far down in the medieval valley, the stationary headlights of a car.

15

The Mansab of Meshed

"Car on voit de la flamme aux yeux des jeunes gens,
Mais dans l'oeil du vieillard on voit de la Lumière."

(V. Hugo.)

No one paid the slightest attention to the slave-governor of Hajarain; he hesitated in a corner and fraternized with our slave soldier, as neglected as a Lowland tax-collector in a gathering of clans, and a visible example of the uselessness of authority to uninfluential people in a tribal country. If I happened to mention him by the honourable title of Hakim of the Government, someone was sure to qualify the statement by saying: "He is only a slave, you know."

The Sayyids, on the other hand, sat round me, and presently rose with a flutter of respect to greet the entry of the Mansab of Meshed, the Patriarch, Ahmad al-'Attas. He rules the valley below Hajarain, where the jurisdiction of Makalla ends. He came in regally, voluminous in a velvet gown, green, with a yellow turban on his head; before him, in his hand, a silver-headed cane; he was portly, benevolent and active, his open face surrounded with curls of grey beard and hair; a ribbon of green and red velvet was thrown over one shoulder: he carried himself lightly, with the ease of sure authority and a manner paternally affectionate. He looked at me with quiet twinkling eyes while he sipped his tea, and a young man from Java, anxious to show off a knowledge of European ways, badgered me to show my non-existent diplomas.

"Diplomas," he said, "are what every Ferangi has who studies — and do you not study history? "

"They are not talismans," I remarked. "One does not have to carry them about. They are merely bits of paper to show that you have lived in a University."

"I have studied the English language," the young man said, "for six weeks; and the word university I have never heard." He obviously doubted its existence. But the Mansab of Meshed, now seeing me exhausted, rose and carried his company off with him to bed.

When I opened my door next morning, a girl with perfect features was standing there, dressed in the complete panoply of all that a young woman of Hajarain can wear, and her face done up to match. A thin scarlet line marked her plucked eyebrows, like lacquer on the yellow varnish of her face: her nostrils, too, were scarlet, and a green design like a 7 came over the left eyebrow down her nose: her lips, perfectly chiselled, had a blue tattoo line on the upper and a pattern of dots and dashes below,

人 and her dress, richer than that of Do'an, was short to the knees in front and trailed behind her, with bands of spangles from the shoulders and a spangly star just in the middle of the back, where a judiciously swaying walk could show off its prominence to best advantage. She had amulets in silver cases like a crown round her head and a cap of coral strings above them: and each ear under the many plaits was heavy with seven ear-rings. In her hand she carried a wooden platter, with eggs and some pancakes of bread soaked in oil for my breakfast. Two young and friendly eyes were smiling at me in that elaborate setting, and she explained that all this gorgeousness was put on in honour of the young man of the Diploma, who was carrying off a bride from Hajarain that day. He had come in a car, but his camels were on their way, and, when they arrived, he and his friends would carry off the bride to her new home, a long day's ride away.

The subject of clothes, so introduced, lasted us through breakfast, and other young girls came to show their finery. Some gowns were made of flowered cotton, from India, but the typical, and I rather think the older dress of Hajarain, is black and not coloured, embroidered with silver. They say that Abu Zaid, the legendary hero, warred on the men of Hadhramaut to avenge his brother: and only granted peace on condition that all the wells in the land should be covered over, the women should smear their faces with black, and wear black gowns short to the knees in front: and that having been first compelled to do so, they have now made it a fashion and continue to this day.

I asked to buy a gown to carry away with me, and by so doing roused feelings of cupidity in my host, a coarse-faced and commercially-minded old Sayyid: he took advantage of my position as a guest to charge enormous sums. He had entertained the R.A.F. before me, with the result that so often and depressingly follows British travellers – he now looked on us all from a financial angle. It is perhaps unfair to think of him unkindly: his wife, who had not been spoilt, wished to offer the gown as a gift. We insult and corrupt people by treating their goodness as if it could be paid for, and think the worse of them when they use us merely as creatures who pay. For there is nothing more subtly insulting than to refuse to be under an obligation. When M. Perrichon chose between his daughter's suitors, he gave his preference not to the one who had saved his life, but to him who had been tactful enough to allow M. Perrichon to save him: this fundamental fact of human nature we are apt to forget. I myself felt guilty of sending the price of ladies' dresses in Hajarain sky-high for future visitors, and disliked the old Sayyid who thought of nothing but money, and who, having got all he could, did not even come to see me off at my departure – a sad example of the influence of the West.

Not so the Mansab of Meshed, who reappeared next morning scattering around him an atmosphere of cheerful reverence. He seized my hand, and led me to the top of the house, where the view of the meeting wadis and their fields was spread below. From a pocket hidden in the folds of his patriarchal gown he pressed peppermints and cloves upon me, and gave me his horse to ride on through the amazed streets of the town – too full of donkeys with panniers for any exhibition of horsemanship, but a sign to all of the old patriarch's independent spirit, for he was a holy, venerated man, not obliged to be publicly charming to my inferior sex.

"They disapprove of it," he remarked in a breezy way. "But they are narrow minded, and I don't care." He left me to go on to Meshed and prepare a welcome, while I climbed to see the ruins on the hill behind the town.

They are discriminate heaps of rubble with a few cisterns: but they show that the hill must once have been covered with houses. Dammūn, which used to be the capital of the tribe of Kinda and still exists as a suburb of Hajarain, is mentioned in a line of Imru-I-Qais, the prince of Kinda:

كَأَنِّي لم الهو بدمّون مرّةً   ولم اشهد الغارات يوماً بعندلِ

"As if I had not once sported in Dammūn
And had not witnessed on a day the raids round 'Andal."

("Hamdani," p. 85.)

'Andal is a little town which I was later able to locate and visit in the Wadi 'Amd.

These were flourishing places in the early days of Islam, drawing probably uninterrupted prosperity from more ancient days. For I had now come into the part of Hadhramaut which is full of Sabæan vestiges, scattered on every side. There is a Sabæan cistern, they told me, on the very top of the rock of Hajarain. I climbed to the foot, a short way: the rock went up in a chimney delightful but impossible to my weakness: I had to leave it and turn back with a small and disappointed crowd, and sit in the sun and look at fossil shells I found there, while a man with a curly beard asked questions. He had been in Kenya, and was surprised to see me travelling without a servant.

"Peace is better than servants," I said, "and you cannot have both. They would quarrel with the beduin when I am away in the jōl."

"That is true," he agreed, "but no Ferangi goes without a servant. You should have one, and then you could sit in one room, and he sits in another, and whenever you feel like it you say 'Boy'."

This picture of European life and its pleasures amused us all, and we loitered, watching the town below, where every sort of excitement was going on. Down the zigzag path under the wall the bride was now descending with beating of drums, and black, veiled crowds of women; little girls, unveiled, with spangly dresses, flitted like butterflies about them. The bridal escort waited on the flat ground; the camels had arrived and with red festive rugs stood round the motor car. My car, which had gone to sleep somewhere else last night, now appeared and added to the general holiday sensation: it stopped by the beehive reservoirs, where water is turned in and kept in flood-time, and I saw the Sayyid's envoy from the Wadi Hadhramaut climbing towards me under the city walls.

He was, when he appeared, a stout, hearty and energetic young man from Mekka, European in clothes, socks and shorts, fountain-pen and wrist-watch, and with a lambskin cap on his head. He had been in Baghdad, and had fought in his time for King Husain, piloting aeroplanes for the Arab army at 'Akaba; his name was Hasan, and he knew all about the tastes and treatment of Europeans, having looked after both the Resident from Aden and the Ingrams on their recent visits.

He now hurried with unoriental energy to get me and my belongings to the car. Not half of them would go in, and we had to fall back upon beduin, who agreed for eight thalers to take most of my stuff and the poor little Sayyid, our fellow-traveller, with it. I thought that room could have been made for the Sayyid, but Hasan looked at him with super-civilized scorn, and he vanished: porters appeared from nowhere, and carried my boxes down hill: a little crowd, lured from the wedding, cheered us off: and I lay back under the canvas shade with a delightful feeling that we could now travel towards comfort and repose with no further effort of my own.

It was a dull tract too. We continued to wind among hardened red gullies such as had crusted the wadi bed the day before. This was the fourth car, counting the bridegroom's, to come south as far as Hajarain, and there was no proper track; but our chauffeur was an intelligent Berber with an instinct for what is possible in slopes; he wound in and out without speaking, and stopped of his own accord to let me see a mound of ruins, unrecognizable to the casual eye but for the rise of the ground and the scattered potsherds.

In the heat of the day we reached Meshed, and found the Mansab at ease in what might have been a nightdress, asleep with his faithful round him in a white and airy upper room between eight open windows. He came rolling down his stairs, which just contained him, cheerful and welcoming: called for coffee: turned everyone out to give me the room: called for water and Khoteqa – a local plant they use as soap, rather like fine, sweet-smelling sawdust – and fed me with an excellent meal.

The room was charming, upheld on four pillars beneath a raftered ceiling. It had pointed white alcoves over the carved windows, and whitewashed pillars at the door all worked to look like stucco: a hearth for tea and coffee in one corner: and on the walls a few guns, pikes and standard poles for processions, and shallow tambourines a yard across for days of pilgrimage, when there must be a continuous beat of tom-toms in the valley. For Meshed is one of the holy places in Hadhramaut, and pilgrims come even from San'a in Yemen for its feast day in Rabi' al-Awwal: the Mansab receives them all, and puts them into his guest house, behind the tomb of his grandfather, and reads the Quran to them in his whitewashed room, and now and then lets off one of the four small cannon, of which he is particularly proud.

He told me the history of the place, which bears in its openness, welcoming and bare, the character of its foundation. Once it had been a no-man's-land, a battlefield of tribes: agriculture and transit were alike impossible: the wide and shallow wadi lay uninhabited, except for the stones and potsherds of its ancient cities, long buried underground. Here the Mansab's grandfather settled, a holy man called Sayyid 'Ali Hasan al-'Attas; and by the unprotected sanctity of his life in the open lowland, and by his hospitable care, supplied neither from lands nor tillage, but from the spontaneous offerings of the devout, he brought peace into the wilderness, and came to be the paramount influence among the beduin of the surrounding Jōl. His bronze carved tomb lies with three others under three white domes, with two lesser whitewashed graves beside them, and a carved Himyaritic stone built into the threshold of the chamber.

This was a peaceful place to look out upon in its unguarded nakedness. The beehive domes, their white softened to pink with dust, rose behind an arched porch and carved doors, with a smaller dome before them. Outside the doors, three shallow platforms were built to sit on, shiny and soft-coloured with the passing of time. Here a woman or two loitered, and a few beduin with their guns. Across the open space a little mosque and minaret were built, sand-coloured as the desert; and two cisterns were there, made to hold about ten cubic yards of water, but empty now, their whitewash, too, made pink with the blowing dust. A large siqaya, a trough for animals to drink from, a few square box-like houses round about: no trees, and hardly any cultivation: but animals trooped through at intervals; a lost donkey was wandering about seeking water; and herds of goats returned to the village at sunset. Unlike the feudal towns of the valley, all here was unguarded and unwalled: the wadi itself, stretching widely from side to side, disguised in distance the prison of its ramparts, and took its colour from the evening or the dawn.

The Mansab lent me his horse (which also seemed to be tinged with the prevailing pinkness of the landscape); and a large company, with nearly all the Meshed children, took me to the ruins of Ghebun, near-by across the white boulders of the sail-bed, which in flood-time becomes so swift a torrent that donkeys cannot ford it, though horses and camels get across. The horse was a friendly animal, used to ecclesiastical pacings and only mildly worried by hands on all sides stretched towards him to prevent his running away – a levity of which he was quite incapable. One is always being warned in church about sins that one would otherwise not think of; perhaps the horse, brought up in a clerical atmosphere, was accustomed to preventive treatment: but he was obviously happy to get away with me by himself at last. From his added height and from the top of one of the little hillocks, I looked over the ruined city of the past.

M. Van den Meulen has described it carefully in his book. It stretches over a great area in uneven hillocks, with shards of pottery, dull red or black, slips of flint and obsidian, cornelian beads or carved chips of alabaster shed among its stones and Himyaritic fragments. The flakes and instruments of flint and obsidian are scattered there in incredible numbers, and their workmanship, according to Miss Caton Thompson, who kindly looked at them for me, suggests the stone age finds in Kenya. Some are smaller, but of similar workmanship to the Egyptian flints of *c.* 2200 B.C.: they point, at any rate, to something more ancient than the hitherto ascertained dates of South Arabian things. On the tops of several hillocks are ruined walls, their roughly-squared stones put together without mortar: and a well is there, lined with round mortarless stones to some depth, and then cut into the earth below. Nearer Meshed the ruined walls have smaller stones, rougher and put together with mortar; probably the old town continued to be inhabited over several periods, possibly into Arab times. I am inclined to agree with the Bents, that the sand has drifted round these ruins and buried them deeper, rather than with M. Van den Meulen, who suggests that all around has been washed away by floods: for higher ground would always have been chosen for important city buildings or tombs in ancient days, and the bits of wall now showing do not look as if they were near the foundations, nor are the hillocks undercut,

as they would be by action of water. The point is an important one
for any archaeologist, as it would determine how much one may
expect to find under the surface of the ground. Before I left Meshed
next morning, the Mahsab presented me with a small stand of
alabaster found in the ruins and with two Himyaritic seals, one with
the head of a goat and the other with the name Ha'asum engraved
upon it.

Meshed too, was celebrating a wedding. A thud of drums and
the sudden shrill notes of women came from the house where the
Mansab kept his wife. He left me there at the bottom of the stairs,
and I climbed up and found her, young and pretty as became the
wife of so gay a Patriarch, with all the Meshed ladies about her in a
small room, a vivid sight to see – for there was every sort of fashion
in paint, green chins, green spots on the cheek, hair plastered to the
forehead in a wave over one eye, tassels of many colours on head
or under chin to hold the veil or nuqba, and heavy silver collars.
The bride was in among them, sitting out her two days with a cloth
over her head. She seemed very limp, weighted down by bracelets
and huge anklets. Her yellow feet and hands were spread out to
dry the henna patterns painted upon them, and the noise of the
drums and the dancing of her friends were no doubt intended to
keep her cheerful through this exhausting ceremony with marriage
to a perfect stranger at the end of it. Several of the ladies in the
Hadhramaut have told me that they are happier on the whole after
their first or second divorce.

Their dancing here was like that of Makalla, but wilder, because
of the stranger patterns of their faces. They held their hands out,
stiff, heavy with rings, one before the other, below their breasts:
the pig-tails whirled in wheels about their heads; their mask-like
faces, seen slantwise, with eyes rigid from the strain of the stiff
movement, looked fixed as the faces of idols. A low drone rose and
fell with the monotonous thud of the drum, and now and then some
of the women would make their trilling noise, holding a hand up
modestly to hide their tongue, which beats from side to side in their
mouth like a clapper.

"You like it?" the Mansab's wife said to me at intervals, hospitable and delighted, and would have kept me there till the time when the bridegroom comes at midnight and the guests depart. But I was tired and left them, and find in my diary that I spent the evening writing in my pillared room by the light of what they call a "trik," or petrol lamp. I was "as comfortable as anyone can be with half-finished measles in a draught": for the fashion of having two windows in every wall allows of no corner free from ventilation, so that one is apt to surfer from cold quite as much as from heat in Arab houses.

In the morning, at seven-thirty, in a rosy light we departed. The Mansab pressed a last gift of cloves, peppermints and chewing-gum into my hand from his pocket and wished me well, more like a cheerful, busy and capable mother than the host of a night. No guest is ever turned away, and everyone who travels northward from Do'an stops for a meal or a night in that hospitable guest house: nor does his income allow of this without difficulty, for he is not enriched by commerce like many of those who have travelled overseas. If a banquet is spread by the eternal rivers, surely the Mansab of Meshed, when he, too, makes the universal journey, will find his place prepared.

16

Into the Wadi Hadhramaut

"Ah ! when shall all men's good
Be each man's rule, and universal Peace
Lie like a shaft of light across the land."

("The Golden Year," TENNYSON)

We had done now altogether with the narrow gorges, and were fast approaching the place where Wadis 'Amd and Do'an (now called Kasr), meeting together, flow more like a plain than a sail bed into the equally open spaces of Wadi Hadhramaut.

We travelled easily here, on hardened sand, with the delight of having no road to bisect the landscape before us: there is a feeling of independence in a car when once it gets away from roads. On either side of us the ruin mounds of the ancient city or its gardens swelled softly underground; its loose stones were laid on the top of every hillock as if by children at play: they were the only pattern in the landscape, except for a white siqaya with a well beside it, or some indistinguishable earth-coloured village on the right of the wadi, behind a dark pool of trees. Light and air were the beauty of the day. Wadi 'Amd was on our left, with a ribbing of sand-dunes in the middle – drift of the desert: and now we too came into ridges of sand, to the two fortified houses of Dhiar al-Buqri, alone in the middle of the landscape.

All who go up or down to Hadhramaut from 'Amd or Do'an must pass in sight of Dhiar al-Buqri, and figures hailed us from the roof. They are hospitable people, rich hotel-keepers from Java. In Batavia you may see them, fathers, sons and nephews, attending successfully to the intricacies of finance and running establishments with lifts and taps of running water: but here they carry on a hundred years' war with their neighbour, a town visible two miles or so away under the cliff.

Into this Montagu and Capulet feud outsiders have been drawn: the little town to the north, also under the cliff, was on the Buqri side, and harassed its southern neighbour. The Buqri family itself, explaining the geography of their war from their own roof, pointed to a white square tower on the edge of the precipice as an outpost of theirs, from which – as they declared – one could shoot straight down on the town. The odds seemed to be fairly even. The Buqri house, though completely isolated with a sand-dune approach on every side, was not easy to attack without artillery: it was composed of two tower-like buildings, one for the men and the other for the harim of the family, and a smooth mud wall with only one gate ran round them. Some years ago the whole valley had been a garden of palms, but the "town" had allied itself with the beduin of the Jōl, who came by night and poured paraffin over the roots of the trees and killed them (a confirmation of the theory that the desiccation of the Hadramaut is probably chiefly due to war). Now only a few patches of millet were sown in the hollows, and would be watered and grow green in the sail. I remarked that war was all very well, but one should not kill trees, and evidently voiced a grievance felt by all the assembled family: it had been considered an unsportsmanlike thing to do.

When the Sultan of Makalla came up to visit his lands of Shibam, a six months' truce had been arranged between the Buqris and the town, so that he might pass by in comfort. Two months of this truce had still to run – so there was peace for the time being, and when we came, the head of the family was standing outside his defences, surveying the drying of mud bricks in the sun, while the walls of his harim were being decorated in whitewash patterns by a man seated on a small platform suspended from the parapet. Even when the truce ended, they told me, the daytime would be more or less quiet, for raids are made by night and ordinary intercourse continues through the hours of daylight.

They received us with pleasant easy manners, as it might be in some rather remote country house in England. We had all the news to give of Hajarain and its doings, while they could tell us who had been up or down the wadi during the last few days. They led the way to the top of their house to show the view. The ground floor was windowless and an inner stair led up six stories, with easy steps and a wave-pattern frieze of the smooth Hadhramaut whitewash, polished like distemper. At each landing an invocation carved on the wall exalted and invoked the blessings of Allah: on the top a terrace with sloped shot-holes provided for more tangible defences. From here, they said, they could shoot at the town "with a mauser." We looked at its clear-cut houses like square boxes in the sun.

"Do they never besiege you?" I asked.

"Sometimes. But we keep four pairs of field-glasses and can see them coming." They seemed to think this ample protection. And indeed sieges never can have been very strict in South Arabia.

A siege is recorded in the Yemen which lasted seven years, in the eighteenth century, at Umm al-Lail. Defences were knocked down with shovels rather than with weapons, under the mud walls where the gutters of the town found an outlet. In the Yemen too, ordinary intercourse went on in spite of warfare. One of the attackers of Zabid is recorded as standing before the gate so that his friends inside could send him out his food – a thing evidently not considered unusual, though in this particular instance the dinner happened to be drugged. There too, a truce would frequently be made till after the date harvest was divided. These old wars were conducted on the excellent assumption that the enemy of to-day may be to-morrow's friend.

The Buqris, when they leave the tinkling of the trams in Batavia, return with equanimity to their mediæval code, though the head of the family told me that he found Singapore more restful. But he said so with none of that passionate yearning for the repose of civilization which M. Van den Meulen found generally in the Hadhramaut. Indeed, I hardly found this anywhere. I was also unable to discover, as M. Van den Meulen seems to have done, the preference for Dutch to British rule. I came to the conclusion that one is apt to find what one expects, or wishes, in the opinions of people who often think politeness more important than truth. "It is good to know the truth and speak it, but it is better to know the truth and speak of palm trees."

I wondered what a pacifist would make of the Buqri family, or of any of the merchants of Hadhramaut who, after a life of money-making, retire to an old age of guerilla warfare in their valley – as an eighteenth century burgher might have retired to end his days in an animated manner in the Highlands. If the human race really longs so intensely for peace, there must be some anomaly here.

For my part, I do not believe that peace is what most of us most ardently desire. I can imagine it pleasant to the young and active to live in a world where there should, indeed, be fewer wars, but more fighting; just as I can imagine that a young and active fox enjoys being hunted. One would enjoy it oneself if one knew the country and could run as well as a fox.

We are all hunted by one thing or another:

> "At my back I seem to hear
> Times wingèd chariot hurrying near:
> And yonder all before us lie
> Deserts of vast Eternity."

With muscles good, and a high courage, we *like* to pit ourselves against the powers of the universe. It is not warfare that breaks our spirit: to think that the horrors of modern engines will deter us, is to rate the heroism of the average human being far too low. What we suffer from now is that we are usually given ignoble motives to fight for. To struggle for blind supremacy no longer satisfies our spirit: we feel that we have come to a more consciously constructive point in the affairs of men: far less are we happy to give our lives for finance, however clothed in names of honour. But for a selfless cause, for some vision built out into the misty future of mankind, people will die as they have always died, whatever the penalty. They are led astray by will o' the wisps, charlatans, pressmen and dictators: *these* let the peace-lover denounce and watch against, and keep his instrument of war pure and sharp, to be used only in the real need of his soul.

But the people of the Hadhramaut, who have not yet busied themselves with such universal questions, fight unquestioning each for his town or tribe: and the general eagerness with which they do it, and the fact that they come back to it when they might quite prosperously stay away, shows, as I have said before, that fox-hunting is not so immoral, and that the human being enjoys a fight if he has something to fight for more soul-satisfying than petroleum.

With these thoughts we left the hospitable house of Buqri to look through its field-glasses at its enemies, while 'Ali the Berber raced us in and out of sand-dunes towards the Wadi Hadhramaut itself. He was skilful and took the ribbed yellow places quickly so as not to stick: it felt like Russian railways at a fair: and at the sharpest corners he always had to rearrange his yellow turban with one hand.

He was a silent man with protruding under-lip and small features, the white of his eyes large in his black face: he would listen expressionless as a block to all we said, and suddenly break in on Hasan's vagueness with some exact and useful information, or give me the sort of fact about the landscape that I most desired to know. He had been the first man in the Wadi Hadhramaut to put together motor cars, which all arrive in pieces by camel from the Jōl; there were now eighty in the wadi, and he was thinking of attempting the overland route into Yemen: the beduin who come thence with merchandise say that there is only one aqaba or cliff along this route and that it can be circumvented, and a way for cars opened not only to San'a but to Mekka. San'a at present is twelve stages away, and the opening of a motor route would greatly facilitate the pilgrimage which now has to go by sea round Aden. The great Ziadite Wazir, Husain ibn Salāma, built mosques and minarets, wells and milestones along the Hadhramaut-Mekka Road in the tenth century, one mosque at every stage. It is said to be a distance of twenty-four days.

At the eastern outlet of our wadi we passed the little town of Ajlania, mentioned by Hamdani in the tenth century. There are only fifteen to twenty houses left round a crooked crumbling tower, and 'ilb trees in the plain below. Children came running and offered us the berries, which they call dōm: they are floury, with very little between skin and stone, and the beduin grind them and take nothing else by way of provision when they raid into the north.

With Ajlania we left the strip of no-man's-land, and came into the district of Shibam, again under Makalla. Here the Yafi'i had first descended from the western hills and gradually conquered one place after another for the present Qe'eti dynasty, four centuries ago according to the rather vague local tradition. We passed El Furt, under the cliff, where they first entrenched themselves, a Dürer fortress against the débris of the hill.

We were in the great wadi now, the longest in Arabia except Wadi Rumma, seven miles at its widest and seemingly more so because of the opening of the Wadi Kasr, down which we had just driven, behind us. It was first entered by Hirsch in 1893. In the far west the cliff-rampart, along the Yemen road, had vanished in the dusty blue of midday haze: it gave the illusion of a clear horizon, an open freedom, like the loosening of a band round the heart. And on the other three sides, where the cliffs were in sight around us, their distance showed slight accidents, humps and hollows, and the embracing air had room to play and cast its gentleness upon them. There was even, I thought, a slight *tilt* in the line of the Jōl, but this may have been illusion; it made me realize how oppressive is that dead level with no wavelike motion in its making, no crest, no sense of anything but the gradual grinding away of Time at the enclosing walls: the sense of movement gives life to mountain ranges no less than to trees and water, and this infinite monotony of the Hadhramaut cliffs, buttress behind buttress exactly the same, has something of the immobility of death.

The width of the wadi varies enormously with incoming valleys and open bays. Its bottom is so smooth and flat that aeroplanes can land. It was brown now, with strips of tufted grass, yellow-green and coarse: but in the years when a sail comes, they sow corn and millet, and the great expanse must look flourishing and lovely. Its openness is hard to describe, too flat for a valley, too barricaded with cliffs for a plain, too enclosed for an island, since one is not master of the view beyond. Watercourses scarce a foot wide run across it, slightly raised and with tufts of grass, or onions planted along their edge. We kept by the southern side and saw, far off on our left, the roofs of Henin above the dunes that drift down from the west. As we advanced into the lands of Qe'eti security, the scene grew milder with human labour. Women walked about there with witchlike pointed straw hats above their veiled faces, and wore the cobalt blue cloak of Shibam, short to the knees in front and trailing behind, a good dress for them when they turned from us in flight; many wore white or blue trousers underneath, not wide but wrinkled in folds about their ankles.

We came to palms, and houses more apart than in the fortress valleys. On the flat land, wells creaked with camels or oxen, for the water here is near the surface of the ground (it is only four yards down at al-Qatn). Three camels abreast sometimes draw the rope along the inclined way made for their pancake feet: sometimes the work is done by the poorest of the peasants, veiled women and almost naked men. The triangles of poles, from which the pulleys are suspended that draw the leather buckets from the well, are as conspicuous in the level land as windmills in Holland.

Presently we came to thick and rustling green corn, with patches yellowing for harvest four and a half months after the sowing. And on the flat ground below the cliff, brown behind a mud wall round a whitewashed mosque and palace, we came to al-Qatn, the home of Sultan 'Ali ibn Salah al-Qe'eti, cousin of the Sultans of Makalla.

There was the feeling of a little independent sultanate about the place. Retainers lounged on the palace steps below a heavy door. They led us through the inner labyrinth by easy stairs, and at the top the Sultan waited to receive me, a youngish, tall and lanky man with straight black hair under a red tarbush, shy with a pleasant boyish expression. He led me into a carpeted room. It was decorated with paint and European shutters, and a small table and four chairs stood in it like an island. Over tea, pine-apples and biscuits, we talked of the history of the Hadhramaut and the route to Shabwa.

Here, as with the Ba Surra at Masna'a, one felt again the sure hand of authority. The Sultan of Qatn's manners were gentle; he had soft brown eyes and a deprecating smile, but his word was law in his own dominions, and no one has more influence over the difficult beduin of the west. Until two years ago he was governor of Shibam for his Makalla cousins; but he had left this post – most unfortunately for the prestige of government there – and now lived in the palace built by his father, where the Bents stayed in 1893. He knew little of Makalla and its sea, but lived and cared for his own people, and when he found me interested in the history of the land, began to talk less formally, and to tell me the Arab traditions of the old trade routes – for he has a library of Islamic writers, and knows more about these things than anyone I met.

Sabæan objects and inscriptions, he told me, are found at al-Qatn; he had given Colonel Boscawen – who stayed with him the year before – a bronze lion of great beauty, dug up under the cliff. "If I had known you were coming I would have kept it for you," he said, filling me with regret. The Bents, who spent some time at Qatn, went into the Wadi Bin 'Ali which leads up from the south, and there found Himyaritic stones and foundations (as well as incense in the gullies) and a way "much used and apparently ancient" up the cliff. The Bin 'Ali route from the coast to Shibam is shorter than the Do'an route, and is almost certain to have been one of the ancient roads. Another must have gone by the Wadi 'Adm to Shihr. The Wadi Hadhramaut itself, in its continuation, which is known as Wadi Masīla, is the beginning of the unidentified track between Hadhramaut and Dhufar: the Sultan thought that it probably followed the Wadi Hadhramaut to its estuary at Saihūt, whence caravans carrying dried shark still travel up from the sea. It is the route explored for the first time by Mr. and Mrs. Ingrams a few months before my journey, and they told me they found no traces of ruins in the lower wadi: an old dam, however, is known to exist below Qabr Hud and is marked on Squadron-Leader Rickards' air-map. The whole district is much silted up. The destruction of the dam is said to have ruined the land around, so that much may be covered and invisible, and the geographical arguments for this route appear to be so strong that it would still repay a further search. What little evidence I could collect on the obscure subject of the Hadhramaut trade routes is placed separately at the end of this book.

Having discussed the Dhufar Road at some length, the Sultan of Qatn then told me that he had been talking with one of the beduin who accompanied Mr. Philby across the Rub'al-Khāli. I asked him his opinion on the delicate subject of Wabar. Wabar is the deserted city, the abode which the Jinn took over when the people of 'Ad and Thamud were destroyed. "Most fertile of God's countries," it is unapproachable by men. "If any man nears it," says Ibn Faqih al Hamadani," they cast dust (probably sand-storms) in his face, and if he persists they make him mad." It is inhabited by the Nisnas, inferior creatures with only one leg, one arm and one eye, who have given rise to the proverb one quotes at certain sorts of parties: "The Nas (real people) have gone and the Nisnas remain." The famous Mahra camels are also said to be descended from those of the Jinn of Wabar.

The controversy as to the site of this legendary city has made it far too dangerous a subject for me to venture on, but the Sultan, who knew nothing of the difficulties which beset it, told me with the serenity of faith that everyone in Hadhramaut places it between Hadhramaut and 'Oman. The geographers, however, are not nearly so sure. Yaqut says: "In Yemen is the qaria of Wabar." El-Laith, quoted by Yaqut, puts it between the sands of Yabrin and Yemen. Ibn Ishaq, who mentions the Nisnas, places it between Sabub (unknown to Yaqut and Hamdani) and the Hadhramaut. Hamdani, a very reliable man, places it between Najran, Hadhramaut, Shihr and Mahra. Yaqut, presumably citing Hamdani, puts it between the boundaries of Shihr and San'a, and then, on the authority of Abu Mundhir, between the sands of B.Sa'd (near Yabrin) and Shihr and Mahra. Abu Mundhir puts it between Hadhramaut and Najran. With such evidence it seems quite possible for Mr. Thomas and Mr. Philby *each* to find Wabar in an opposite corner of Arabia.

As to reaching Shabwa, the city of my desire, the Sultan of Qatn assured me there would be no difficulty. The King of the Hijaz and the Imam of Yemen had now made peace, and the effect of it had been to open again all the eastern routes along their borders. For the first time in many years the way that leads by 'Abr to Najran was used by caravans: the incense route, by Shabwa and Marib into Yemen, and that which led through the desert once called Saihad, were now peacefully open to traffic.

"Behold the desert of Saihad is an empty desert, a wilderness where the winds blow in all directions, a country where the crows are king." I could well believe it of the winds, because it is what they seem to do everywhere east of Suez, but as for the empty desert, the Sultan told me that it was only a three days' journey to Shabwa and five days or so after that to Marib by Baihan. He himself promised to find me the right beduin, for the Shabwa inhabitants are not inclined to welcome strangers, and, when Colonel Boscawen tried to enter, had shot at him from their walls and hit one of his men, who later died: they had not liked his beduin, it appeared.

"Perhaps," said I, "they were shooting at the beduin and not at the colonel?"

"Oh no: it was the headman who shot, and he tried to get the colonel, and afterwards, when some British aeroplanes happened to fly across the desert there, they all rushed from their city and hid, fearing vengeance. But you have nothing to fear now."

Twice a week or so, caravans with rock-salt from Shabwa pass by al-Qatn for Shibam. The salt is prized all over the country and down at Makalla: it is mentioned in the old books; and a man from Baihan told me that they call the north wind there milhi – the Salty – because it blows from the region of Shabwa. If I would give the Sultan of Qatn a few days' notice; he would choose reliable men out of the passing beduin, would prepare all things for me, and await my return.

This was great kindness. Not Shabwa only, but new, unvisited places, the dead valleys of Hadhramaut, Tamna' the Katabanian and Gebanite capital, even the far north-western Jauf, where the giraffe is still improbably rumoured to exist, which contains, according to Halévy, "plus de vestiges de l'antiquité' que tout autre pays Arabe" – all these opened in my sight. I thanked the Sultan with gratitude in my heart, for the difficult part of my journey, impossible they had told me in Makalla, now lay smooth before me. All I had to do was to get a little stronger and then go.

Meanwhile I felt ill and tired, and asked leave to sleep. A mattress was laid on the ground, and I rested in coolness and solitude, and looked at the pleasant room, its columns and windows, and white green and blue paint, and niches for lamps in the walls. There were some mirrors, and the carpets were laid inside out, to preserve them. From the windows one looked into the square of the walled city, dilapidated and irregular. A hobbled camel limped in one corner of it; the houses stood separate like sugar cones with whitewash decoration round their brown sloping walls. The windows are no longer painted red as the Bents saw them, neither does the Sultan wear a canary coat with pale blue lining. The mosque opposite was an open court with three rows of columns at the back and one down each side: no columns in front: Glaser says it is a pattern of Sabæan temples and has probably come down with little alteration: its minaret shone white and gay amid the palm boughs, with trellis-work tip the same shape exactly as the high crowns of the women's hats.

Our tablecloth, too, looked gay when lunch was spread on the floor. It had a blue pattern of knives, forks, glasses, etc., stamped all over it on a white ground. Persian pilau, Indian pancakes, Arab soup and boiled mutton were piled upon it. The Sultan, my friend

Hasan and I, squatted at one end and at the other 'Ali the Berber, with the little Sayyid. I had seen him during the morning, a small speck walking in front of our baggage camel in the empty width of the wadi: and insisted on having him put into the car, though Hasan looked pained. Hasan disliked the unprogressive poor – but he had not been picked up four times off a falling donkey the day before, so had no particular cause for gratitude as I had.

Before I left, the Sultan of Qatn sent me up by the dingy inferior steps of the women's quarters to an airy room on the palace roof where the harim sat and watched the wadi spread like a map below. His wife was there, with eyebrows blackened to meet, and a dress of Indian brocade, and lion bracelets: five children, all with measles, sat around, their eyes like black saucers heavily surrounded with medicinal kohl. They pressed close to me, so that I was glad to tliink myself immune; and the Sultan's wife, shy at first, for she had never met a Ferangi, gradually thawed as I gave her disinfectants for her young son, who had run a piece of wood into his cheek. We talked on the sisterly topic of infantile diseases, till I was led back through other narrow passages, crowded in their shadows with blue-gowned servant maids to see me – out to where the car waited to take us to Shibam, now only twelve miles away.

17

Shibam

"Built by the hands of Giants
For Godlike kings of old."

("Lays of Ancient Rome.")

The city gate of qatn was opened to our passing. We drove into the hot afternoon and the emptiness of the valley, fringed now almost continuously on its southern side with palms. Here and there was a white siqaya; a camel or two, pitched along with spout-like neck and half-closed eyelids. The camel is an ugly animal, but, like some plain women, has lovely eyes, brown and soft with long lashes – often the only gentle things to look at in its sun-hardened world: but this one beauty is little noticed, for – though the adored is often compared to a gazelle – who has ever heard anyone say of her that she has eyes like a camel? We passed wells and solitary house-forts, with four corner towers if they were old or otherwise with plain and naked walls. The cliffs ran out into the sunlight, the open bays lay still in heat between them: an R.A.F. landing-ground we crossed was scarce distinguishable from the general smoothness of the valley floor.

And now it looked as if a lower cliff had wandered out into the middle valley: wrinkled and pitted, as we drew nearer, with beehive holes; split like the valley sides in vertical fissures; the top of it splashed with white as by a giant paint-brush: an old and wrinkled city, made of the earth that made the hills around it, built on a mound wherein no doubt lie buried its ancestor cities of the past. This was Shibam, that belonged to the children of 'Ad; the city where in the middle ages: "the horses of the King are kept"; built in "the middle of the lands of Hadhramaut," where five valleys like the veins of a sycamore leaf branch out and give an illusion of open sky to the town that lies between them.

As we drew nearer, it gradually differentiated itself from the cliffs around it. The pitted holes were windows, high up and small; the fissures, long shafts of drains that add to the high look of the houses, or alleys in perpetual shadow. The houses leaned away to their whitewashed tops and climbed to seven stories above a thin foreground of palms, and in their shadow minarets clustered delicate and white. The hill of Shibam is scarce a hill: it is an imperceptible rise in the ground where, like a phœnix, the city has no doubt renewed itself many times. Here, it is said, the people retreated from Shabwa under pressure of northern tribes, and established themselves anew. On the western side, from which we came, a graveyard fills a hollow, and its desolate acres, wider than the five hundred houses of the living, add to the sense of age and river-like immutability of time.

No motor road yet leads to Shibam. But our car thought nothing of a water channel on one side, the graveyard on the other, and a steep bank in between. We skirted the walls, which are not walls but merely the blank fortress floors of houses – windowless with here and there a postern – and came on the south to sandy ground where camels camp, and indigo dyers ply their craft, and women in blue gowns with trains carry goatskins of water from the well. The city gate stood above, on a cobbly rise, and camels laden with timber were lifting their feet over the threshold in their deliberate way. We had to wait while people came running, beduin, soldiers, citizens in turbans, and women with rubbish baskets on their head. (Municipal jobs like water-selling and the collection of refuse seem to be in the hands of the women all over the Hadhramaut.)

As we waited, I became aware that our soldier's plaintive voice had been droning on for a long time in argument with Hasan behind me. He had been eclipsed by Hasan, whose standards of civilization were beyond him, and who, moreover, had no sort of respect for the government of Makalla, since he belonged to the Kathiri powers, the eastern Sultans of the Hadhramaut, whose border runs just beyond Shibam. Between these two, though peace has been made six years ago, no love is lost.

Our soldier was explaining that I must be made to sleep in Shibam; the representative of Makalla must entertain me. I must not be allowed to go through without stopping one night. At the back of his mind was the thought of a public leave-taking, with an unsympathetic audience when he dunned me, as he meant to do, for those large sums which had filled his simple meditations as he strode before me day after day. That my own ideas as to where I meant to sleep should be taken into account, never entered his uninventive mind, nor did Hasan, as a matter of fact, think of this in particular. Hasan paid no attention beyond sticking his plump chin out in a pugnacious way. He had fetched me in a car; he would carry me off into Kathiri lands: he said so in monosyllables, conscious that the winning forces were on his side. A fountain-pen, sticking out of his breast pocket, showed him to belong to the progressive West: his lambskin cap and bullnecked head were not native to the long-faced, aristocratic Hadhramaut: he was an ex-Colonel from King Husain's air force in Mekka, trained there in the Turkish school, and had been wounded by the Turks in the air. Now – an exile from Ibn Sa'ud – he was full of modern plans for the wadi, and had already trained the boy scouts of Tarim. He was, indeed, very much more civilized than I was. My soldier felt inferior. His monologue became more urgent than ever as the last camel heaved itself out of the gateway and we, in our turn, bumped up the cobbled slope through the small court of the inner gateway of Shibam.

We were in a square crowded with leisurely hobbled camels; the tall houses looked down and made us feel as one does in a trough of the sea with high waves overhanging. A white minaret opposite, seen against them, seemed as lowly as we were ourselves. All I wanted in Shibam at this moment were my letters and some money from A.B's agent, for I meant to come back to stay later, when I felt better: we hurried into a gap of houses, with sky far above us and a gathering crowd behind, and were welcomed at his door by Ba 'Obaid the agent himself.

He was a little lively man, dressed in white cotton, and active as a grasshopper; he led us up narrow stairs on which he turned with smiles at every landing to ask after the friends of Aden. In his office his clerks sat crosslegged on rush mats: a corner was cleared and a rug spread beneath me: a packet of letters was brought whose familiar postmarks suddenly made the world around remote and strange. I roused myself from them to find that our soldier's monologue was still continuing, now addressed to Ba 'Obaid, who listened with a worried look, while the room filled around us with curious faces and the authorities of Shibam came trooping in to greet me.

These people afterwards became my friends, and helped me with unwearying kindness: even now, in our hurried passing, I noticed how cordial and welcoming they were: my future hosts, Husain al-A'jam and his brother, were smiling with flashes of gold teeth, while the old governor, one of the slave household of Makalla, portly in draperies, and with a silver-headed cane, his hennaed beard worn like a frill round his huge and fleshy face, settled his bulk on the floor in portions, as it were, and with one knee nearly on a level with his chin, studied the Sultan's letter from Makalla.

They had prepared a bungalow for me in the gardens outside the town and the fact that I had to drive straight through to the rival comforts of the Kathiri dominions farther on was painful to all of us except to Hasan, who treated this as a last interlude of the Dark Ages and was all for hastening its obsolete formalities: our soldier, on the other hand, now driven to his last defences, burst into open oratory to say that I must be kept.

"The Government *wishes* her to be kept," he said, revealing his real feelings as to freewill and the rights of women with a cynicism which shocked me. I ignored him and explained how ill I was, and the necessity of a chemist if a doctor could not be found: I would return in a few days' time and send word of my coming. In many eastern places this would have been taken as mere politeness, meaning nothing: but I noticed on several occasions that all over the Hadhramaut the English word is accepted at its face value – a tribute to all travellers there before me.

In haste, for the afternoon was waning, Ba 'Obaid came from the recesses of his diwan loaded with a cotton bag and counted out a hundred silver thalers in little heaps on the floor. The Governor and my future hosts escorted me through the alleys to the car, while our soldier – now completely disorganized – buzzed about bakhshish in our ears. I handed him six of my thalers – the equivalent of a month's pay – but he had been dreaming dreams of El Dorado – and what were six thalers? He knew that I had a bag with ninety-four more in my hand. I asked my new friends: they begged me to give no more: the scene was painful altogether, for their sense of hospitality was shocked – and I had some difficulty to reach our mercenary slave through their disapproving ranks to press two last thalers upon him: I felt sorry to leave him so – though I had no great affection for him, for he was a stupid man, with never more room in his head than for one idea, and that usually a poor one: but if one has only one idea, it must, of course, be doubly trying to discover it to be a wrong one.

When we had left this interlude behind us, and the tower-like houses of Shibam, we followed the northern, more desert, side of the wadi, where many ruined heaps on hills remind one that six years ago the Qe'eti and Kathiri Sultans were at war. The Kathiri are the older family in Hadhramaut: 10,000 of them came, according to Hirsch, from near San'a about A.D. 1494 and took first the inner lands east of Henin and then the coast lands from the Beni Ghassan. They owned all about us when first the Yafi'i tribesmen and the present Makalla dynasty descended from their hills. These pushed them gradually to their present border, just east of Shibam.

As a rule one may say that in the Wadi Hadhramaut, as in most places, the old towns were on the slope of the hills – which here must be the wadi side – and the new are built in the plain. Except Shibam, only one town mentioned by Hamdani – Teris – is, so far as I know, out in the wadi centre: the others all cling to the more defensive side or have, like Tarim, slipped down from the immediate neighbourhood of the higher fortress which once protected them.

As we ran from Shibam along the northern shore, through tufts of grass and new plantations of palms, we could see almost a garden suburb against the cliffs opposite – white houses hidden in palms like the outskirts of Cairo, sprung up with the security of the last years. The slanting sun shone on them and lit the cliffs and bays with tranquil light: one could understand why the rich Java merchants long for this oasis of their childhood, and ride to it across the desert as to a secret island of their own surrounded by high walls, where the noises of the world come like waves in a lagoon, scarcely troubled by storms of the outer ocean.

A negro slave-soldier, barefoot and noiseless on the sandy track, held up his hand for a lift: Hasan, anxious to do the right western thing, would precipitate himself at a nod in any direction: the nod was given in favour of Help to the Wayfarer, and the slave sat on the mudguard, fye crossed the sail-bed, crusted with salt; shallow patches of water lay where the ground must be too hard to let it through. The sail comes down once in a few years, and sometimes carries palm gardens before it as happened around Shibam six years ago: in the narrow wadis it will overtake and drown the caravans. But here all was open and shallow, and on the far shore, among wheat trees and palms, running back into the great bay of a side valley, was Sewun.

Its gardens were full of birds. We crossed the town and wound round sightless walls and asked the inhabitants, as we met them, for the keys of my lodging called 'Izz-ed-Din, the Glory of Religion: it is the Sultan's pavilion, where he goes in summer for coolness. The keys, when found, opened a court, arcaded and white. Steps led to the house above: a pool was built before it, with white balustrade and green and running water: a drawing-room and bedroom under a porch beyond. All was whitewashed, one-storied; the stiff branches of palms brushed against its walls and windows. The rooms inside were white and expensive, with velvet chairs and sofas in a circle, small tables, and in the bedroom a pink mosquito-net and pillows with pink frills.

Here was a haven. And I had barely time to change the more dusty of my clothes for a yellow satin dress with black spots which I discovered the Hadhramaut approved of, before the Sultan and his brother came to call, and the three Sayyids of the al-Kaf family whose kindness had brought me so far. They sat in a half circle, and talked with easy hospitality, which would never let one imagine that it may be tiresome to entertain all European strangers who appear. They had kind faces, used to dealing with the many and difficult affairs of their fellow-men, and they watched me quietly while they talked of this and that. I soon understood how they can make their fortunes among the Europeans of the East and run the politics of their native land as well.

When they left me to rest, Hasan showed me a small bathroom: one stepped into tepid running water to the neck, a Roman luxury. My supper was laid on a table under the porch, with a white tablecloth and all the tinned delicacies of California; milk, hitherto almost unattainable, came from a cow in a mud hut in the garden: and before I laid my head on the pink frills of my pillow, I looked out of the window and saw, arranged in little squares below, not only beds of zinnias to delight the eye, but carrots and other vegetables beside them.

18

Sewun

*"Je consens q'une femme ait des clartés de tout;
Mais je ne lui veux point la passion choquante
De se rendre savante afin d'être savante."*

("Les Femmes Savantes," MOLIÈRE.)

There was a chemist in Sewun. He was very slight, young, timid and soft-spoken, with a Malay cast of face common from the mixed marriages of the Hadhramis abroad. He had spent his boyhood at Port Darwin, in Australia, and now, Hasan explained when he brought him to my bedside in the morning: "He has been made to come back to the Hadhramaut so that his religion may not be spoiled."

Hasan, from his portly height – now no longer tailored in shorts, but swathed in checked cotton so that he appeared rather like a Roman Emperor in dust sheets – looked kindly down at the modest young man, a brand snatched from the burning. Australia seemed to have done him no harm: he handed me some medicines and ran an injection into my forearm: and, hesitating with a melancholy smile on the doorstep, remarked that I might get better if God willed. His theology, at any rate, was sound.

I visited him later in his dispensary – two rooms with carved windows and whitewashed decorations in an old house. The scales and microscope, and bottles ranged in rows, were all scrupulously clean in that unlikely place, and a treatise on medicine was on the table. But few ever came to him, he said: the people of Sewun, on the whole, prefer to run hot irons down the back of their necks. He was independent of them, for his salary is paid by the al-Kaf Sayyids, but perhaps the moral solitude had made him so modest: when I praised his arrangements, he looked round at them with gentle eyes and merely said: " There is a lot of dust; "and I came away feeling, as I often do, that there is something heroic and pathetic in this apostleship of modern culture so guilelessly believed in, the dusted room solitarily clean in the middle of the unhygienic town, which continues incorrigible and light-hearted on its accustomed way.

Sewun is, as a matter of fact, the most delightful of towns. I never got tired of driving leisurely through its scattered ways of houses white and brown. From their slanting walls and upper lattices they look on dusty streets unpaved and silent, and solitary save for a woman here and there trailing her long blue gown by some carved doorway, or beduin camels that brush the roughened mud-built corners with their loads. The houses are rich with every variety of delicate lace-work: from the warm shadows below, their parapets rise into sunlight, often with outcrops like the machicolations round old castles where hot oil was poured on assailants, but here made with the more peaceful object of letting the harim look down invisible on what goes on below. The harim often, too, has a humble little front door of its own, beside the big one. There are many quiet sunny lanes, with a white mosque, or an ornate siqaya, and a palm or two to shade it: and the drains in Sewun are all covered, and run into covered cisterns of mud made smooth and shiny outside, so that one can wander about with no thought of sanitation, in perfect peace. It is, indeed, a clean and pleasant town, with a mosque built in the old fashion with seven rows of columns, a market, the Sultan's castle, and the cemetery all in the centre, as in a feudal town it should be: and on market days the white mass of the palace rises between its four corner towers out of a sea of camels, a crowd of sellers of goats and sheep and donkeys, weavers of baskets, squatters over vegetables on the ground, weighers out of salt, dried fish, peppers, and odds and ends of nails and cords and sandals, and women in tall hats selling shawls.

When I was able to walk here, during the last days of my stay, two slaves with palm branches and an occasional rifle butt had to sweep the crowd before me, which had hardly seen a Ferangi woman, for the Ingrams passed through Sewun and did not stay. Then, too, I climbed the many stories of the Sultan's palace to visit his harim, and found them friendly and gay, dressed in the Hadhramaut fashion but with a touch of Indian splendour in their silks, colours of all sorts worked into the gown and the star at its back, and golden anklets on their feet. Some wore the Java fashion, a straight silk coat, nothing like as graceful as the trailing gown: and only their lips were painted. They were full of compassion for me and regarded with horror my freckled hands, which they attributed to measles. From their high upper terrace I looked over Sewun and its gardens, and saw how it lies in cornfields and palms, with walls that slope enclosing it from under the cliff. The gates are open and the walls are crumbling, and show the peacefulness of to-day; for the Sultan has a firm hand and his slaves obey him, and the beduin respect him; he is a tribal chief, a descendant, he told me, of Hamdan, and no amount of money or bought allegiance equals this hereditary claim to respect among the tribesmen.

I grew much attached to Sultan 'Ah ibn Mansur. He was middle-aged; his hair still curled, almost black, in small ringlets on a head completely round and usually swathed in a loose, voluminous turban. He was all loose and voluminous, and liked to wear the cloak or abba of the north, and sat like a bundle on one corner of the sofa, missing nothing with his small eyes, that twinkled amused behind their glasses in his round and unpretentious face. Before I left we persuaded him into his best uniform, a thick blue serge with golden epaulettes strewn lavishly about it — it made one think of the American girl's remark to the Scots Guardsman: "My, what a lot of cute little knick-knacks you've got hanging about you!" It was, indeed, a thing of beauty for a photograph, but extremely hot. He thought so, preferring his abba as any sensible man would: but made no protest against the standards of the West. Just so, I felt he had taken my visit – a phenomenon of the new age, tiresome but not to be resisted; for he and his brother beside him – a thin and silent man – sat saying very little the first evening, while the al-Kaf Sayyids talked of modern things, roads, motor cars, and aeroplanes, and such: and only when I confessed that I rather liked what was quiet and old, the Sultan smiled and began to see that we might have tastes in common: for he liked the old-fashioned ways himself, and even the most progressive may prefer praise of their own inferior things, however much their conscience tells them to venerate the new: I always think that the compliments we often pay the East are in rather doubtful taste, when we praise only what they have copied from ourselves!

Sultan 'Ali was a comfortable, sociable and pleasant man. His two wives, "down in the city" and "up at the villa" among the gardens, surely thought him so. He loved his garden, and to sit and drink tea with his friends under a palm tree, and watch the square beds of lucerne and maize, cabbages, carrots and onions, zinnias and marrows, and the convolvulus-flowered plant they call batata all growing casually among the young and bushy palms. There was no view, for a high mud wall enclosed us and showed only the cliff-tops behind: the harim moves in summer to the Glory of Religion, and it would not do to be able to look in from outside; but in its own quiet and untidy boundaries the garden had an atmosphere of peace: there was a well in one corner, dry-walled like the ancient well of Meshed, with a cream-coloured siqaya beside it, and holes in the wall to let the floods through when they come; a woman and her daughter laboured in blue gowns among the trees; and there were birds and crickets and lizards. I tried to collect them in the interests of zoology, but decided to leave them in peace when I discovered how unpleasant it is to put a living grasshopper in alcohol to die.

In the morning Sultan 'Ali used to come and, before settling in the shade, would call on me, and talk about Arab history, and read my copy of Hamdani, which enthralled everyone who saw it – for it is full of traditions known in the Hadhramaut now. For his part, as I had nothing with me to read and spent my days in bed, he lent me a history of the pagan Arabs: I wish I could find it again. It began with a chapter on women as the Arabs like them: they were to be, among other things, "grateful when well, and patient when badly treated"; and there was more advice of this kind which I have unfortunately forgotten.

After a few days in the peace of the garden, I began to feel better. I came out on to the porch for meals, and Hasan stood over me and fanned away flies, and talked about education.

It was à propos of a neighbour Sayyid who had given me three beetroots. "He is," Hasan told me, "the author of a book on Language, and they say that it is the best that has ever been written. Before his time no one was able to write more than six hundred chapters on the subject, but he has done a thousand."

"It is very modern to go in for records like that," I said to Hasan. "Everyone is doing it with motor cars: why not with grammars?"

Hasan looked pleased. "We *are* getting modern here," he admitted.

The noise that had kept me awake – a strange booming and humming – was, he told me, the telephone which they were trying to instal between the Sultan's palace and us: they had got the wire fixed at both ends, but could not pull it tight, so that it swayed and sang like an organ, filling the wadi with its twentieth-century voice.

"Everyone," said Hasan, "has telephones in Tarim from one house to the other. But one cannot have them between town and town, for the beduin cut the wires if they go beyond the walls." Hasan disliked the beduin because they were not modern. If he saw me talking to them, and saw their easy way of considering themselves anybody's equal, he would stick out his jaw and look straight in front of him, till I saw fit to disentangle myself from such familiarity and climb back into the decent aloofness of a car.

We drove out after a time, by the sail-bed full of stones and grey-leaved bushes, called ya 'būr, which are used in faggots to hold up the mud of roofs, and are the Sultan's monopoly and a good source of income: they had a red pea flower, like a small flame.

Beyond them was the new house and garden of Sayyid Abu Bekr al-Kaf, which we visited as soon as I was able. It was still being built. The garden, the first in Hadhramaut to be copied from Europe, was still an emptiness of round beds with stone borders, a tree in the middle of each: a hedge of dipped henna bushes beside them; a fountain in the middle. The house was the first in Sewun to be built with concrete, "so that the rooms need have no pillars": the old Hadhramaut woodwork, with its leaded nails, was discarded, and there were to be European moulded doors and windows, expensively ornate. Everything was expensive: even the bathroom – otherwise a delightful place with sunken floor filled with water – had a gilt centre to its ceiling; and the hall was to have a glass roof like hotels in Singapore. What more terrible punishment could one imagine for mid-Victorian decorators than to place them – their hearts now purified by the contemplation of heavenly Beauty – in such a position that merely by glancing down from the eternal parapets they must see their own inventions spreading like a cancer over the uncorrupted world?

And what is wrong with the human race, that, having bought at so high a price the fruit of the tree of knowledge, it cannot even use it to tell what it likes from what it doesn't? Not ignorance, but laziness and cowardice prevent us from knowing what we like. Left to themselves, the untaught make lovely things, but when we begin to think that we *ought* to admire or despise, then the devil gets loose in the minds of manufacturers in the Midlands, and we accept the things they give us wholesale, as the East accepts the West; we think the thoughts of other people, too indolent or too fearful to discover our own: and the dear old Sayyid, who loves his carved doors when he looks at them, and finds happiness in his ancient town – the only city I have ever seen whose dignity and beauty no jarring note distracts – considers himself bound to bring our Western ugliness to spoil it for ever.

I tried to say this: but what is the voice of a woman? Merely a noise, pleasant or otherwise according to time and place. When I explained my feelings, Sayyid Abu Bekr smiled, thinking mat I was being polite about the beauty of the Hadhramaut houses. Did we not ourselves live in and produce these things? And why should we do so if we did not like them? He took me to the tower structure where his family still lodged in the old-fashioned way.

Here at the top of many stairs in a red silk gown, his wife stood, with hennaed fingers and beautiful rings, and farther on, through many passages, a young daughter-in-law was being made beautiful on the fortieth day after having a baby. Her hands and feet were being painted with an elaborate lace-work of brown hudhar, which looks very pretty, and like mittens when it is finished. She was going in a few days to a wedding in Tarim to which I also was invited. These were charming ladies and I called on them again, and liked to be with them. They had not been in Sewun very long. Sayyid Abu Bekr had come when a revolt of the slaves in Tarim caused him a lot of trouble, and he sought for peace among the gardens and brought one of his families. The ladies were all looking forward to the new house, which is one-storied and in the middle of a closed plot where they can wander – and from the point of view of female comfort, has something to be said for it.

As we sat there, a message came from a learned widow of Sewun to ask me to call. A handmaid took me, trailing her green surplice through a sandy palm garden up other whitewashed stairs to where, in a pleasant room, columned and carpeted, about twenty ladies with amber bracelets and flowered cotton gowns sat in the formation of a square round their spiritual leader. It was very like the learned ladies of Molière. The widow was young, plumpish, and bright-eyed, with a gay little curl on either side of her face. When she saw me coming, she was hastily absorbed in a copy of Bokhari propped on a stand in front of her on the floor. She read from it with the expressionless drone of the expert, too much absorbed to notice my presence, while her flock moved restlessly, torn between their docile listening habits and the fact that they were dying with curiosity to see me.

I approached; skirted the sitting ladies; and bent and kissed my hand to the mistress of the house, who welcomed me with an affectionate oration into the sisterhood of learning. She did not rise to it gradually, but turned it on like a tap, holding me with one hand and the corner of her eye while she exacted the attention of her flock with the other. She punctuated her periods with pretty little hennaed fingers, quoting the Prophet, the Quran, and the poets – for she was a poetess herself, and had entered open competitions, and once won a complete tea-set as a prize. Every day, she said, the ladies gathered here and listened to one of the five books – the Quran, Bokhari, Muslim and two other traditionists I have forgotten. I happened to know a little Bokhari and got half-way to a sentence about him: it carried her, with not a second's hesitation, into the realms of philosophy and the excellences of religion. "Why do you not live here?" she said. "Every day we would meet and meditate."

I was meditating as it was, for I had no talking to do: but the flock, which had the privilege of listening to the Sayyida every day, but had very few chances of seeing a female European, now began to show signs of insubordination, and finally sent a message across the room by the green-gowned maid to ask if I would mind removing my hat: they would look if they could not listen. I took it off and smiled towards them: several opened their mouths, but none quite ventured to interrupt the second sentence, which with flowers of eloquence and fancy was winding on its way. Before it closed, I had to rise, for the afternoon was waning: I left the Sayyida with friendly feelings in my heart, for her pedantry bubbled out spontaneous and gay, as artless, in those arid theological pastures, as a mountain stream in rocks. There were other learned ladies in Sewun, she told me – for it and Tarim are cities of religion and learning – but they were "very bigoted." She was not so: her arms were open to the Christian listener, and she was full of genuine friendliness: when I came back through Sewun, she came to see me. Her husband was dead, she had lots of children, and she lived in a house of her own: she was, I imagine, one of the happiest women in the Hadhramaut, for she did what she liked doing, and was virtuous and important as well, and people told her that she was so all the time.

Next morning, February 16th, Hasan and I left the Glory of Religion on a three days' visit to Tarim.

19

Tarim

يا حضرموت هنيئاً ماحصمت به   من الحكومة بين العجم والعرب
في الجاهلية والاسلام يعرفه   أهل الرواية والتفتيش والنلب
(قال بزيد بن مقسم السدفي)

Greeting, Hadhramaut!
The followers of tradition, research and study know thee
distinguished by judgment amid Barbarian and Arab,
In days of Ignorance and Islam.

(YAZID IBN MAQSAM AS-SADAFI.)

The car that was to take us to Tarim already had a dusty blue beduin settled on the front seat nursing his gun when I descended to the courtyard next morning. He was our "saiara" from the 'Awāmir, whose lands lie between the two cities. I was just going to photograph him, hunched up in what looked like his mother's shawl, when Hasan murmured that I had better wait: the fact that an escort is still necessary gives pain, and one does not like to emphasize it, though it does not bother anyone very much: the al-Kaf Sayyids settle the problem by giving a permanent salary to a few of the beduin and putting them on any car that travels.

Our 'Awāmir was a friendly, quiet man, with that simple, direct and contented mind which makes the beduin pleasant. He treated me with respect, for I had just overheard Hasan explaining that I was "one of the Sultanas of England." He smiled when I let him look through my camera at the landscape. "It make things smaller," he remarked in a disappointed way.

I noticed that the butt of his gun was not covered with ibex or gazelle skin like those of the Kor Saiban beduin. "It is not our fashion," he said.

"Then what do you do when you kill an ibex?" I asked.

"We make its horns into war trumpets. Its head is carried on our head and we dance with it while our men shout: we call the dance a zàmil."

"Everyone has a dance," said Hasan. "The Sayyids call theirs a sherh: and the women's hair-dance is called zafin here and narsh in Makalla."

"But now you are all at peace," I said, going back to the ibex. "You will not need war trumpets for a long time."

"When they want money," Hasan observed, "they ambush this road: and then everyone has to go up and down the 'aqaba and over the Jōl to Tarim, by a road there on the north which the Sayyids made seven years ago when the tribes held up their dealings."

The 'Awamir smiled again, as if we were referring to the indiscretions of his youth, long past but not so very much regretted.

We had left the garden suburbs of Sewun and had come to a part of the wadi where the water, having made itself a slightly deeper channel in the north, causes the southern side to be dry and barren.

We passed through Mariama, a modern town on the west and an old one on the east of the jutting cliff base. They say there is a reservoir in the rocks above, and M. Van den Meulen mentions an old road to the south. The way to irrigate the Hadhramaut is obviously to dam these narrow side valleys, and this was probably done in many places in ancient days, just as it was in Yemen. That the country was *potentially* more fertile than now I very much doubt: the value of the trade made it worth while to attend to the general security; this in turn made it possible to maintain irrigation and agriculture; and everyone knows what incessant care is needed to preserve these vital things in scantily watered lands. In Mesopotamia, the destruction of canal banks in a very short number of years reduced the Babylonian fertility to a Turkish desert: the poverty of South Arabia is said by legend to derive from the destruction of the Marib dam. What actually happened was probably a gradual decline of trade and consequent carelessness in watching over irrigation and repairing dams and reservoirs, as in the Wadi Dam, mentioned by Bakri as: "once cultivated, but dried up and deserted a little before Islam." That the caravans from Hadhramaut to Yemen ever marched through continuously fertile lands, I do not believe. The Roman expedition under Aelius Gallus reached Marib and there had to turn back, threatened by starvation and thirst: and this was long before the destruction of the dam (which occurred in the sixth century A.D.), and at a time when, according to Arab fancy, "one could travel in continuous shade for two months through the lands of Marib!" If it had been truly even moderately fertile according to any but Arab standards, he would have been able to rest and refresh his army.

Between Marib and Hadhramaut, the earliest Islamic geographers mention the "dangerous desert to Shabwa, first town of Hadhramaut" (Bakri); or "the desert of Saihad, where only the crows are king." The Libyan slave route described lately by Capt. Bagnold, where caravans travelled, all through last century, 150 miles at a time without water, shows what distances, discomforts and dangers will be overcome for the sake of a profitable trade: the old Incense route probably went, as the Yemen caravans do now, from water to water, though the places that *were* fertile then, were probably far more so and more extensive than now.

That the population of south-eastern Yemen at any rate was more numerous under the South Arabian empires than it is now, may be inferred from some of the figures given on the great Himyaritic inscription of Sirwah: 26,000 killed and 65,000 prisoners show that the strip of country stretching roughly south of Najran to the sea must then have been more thickly populated than now. The enumeration of 200,000 head of cattle on the other hand, points to a good proportion of nomad shepherds, who probably lived there in uncultivated steppe-land, as they do to this day.

One cannot help pondering on these problems, as one drives down the wadi, for anywhere here one may come upon the Himyaritic[1] cities. There are ruins on a little island-rock, before Tarba: and at Qariat Sané or Sanahīye beyond it, a ruined city under the cliff; and where the Wadi'Adm breaks off, and the modern road to Shihr and the sea, there was probably an ancient road, since M. Van den Meulen found there the ruins of Sūne, and copied inscriptions and reliefs which I saw later in Sayyid Abu Bekr's garden in Tarim, and two of which he very kindly gave me.[2]

Apart from these things, we had plenty of other objects to amuse us as we drove along the southern wadi side.

We passed the place where a female saint – Shaikha Sultana – is buried, now visited not only by women but by men also: and farther on the grave of the Muslim apostle, Sayyid Ahmad ibn 'Isa al-Muhajir, ancestor of all the sayyids in the land. He came from Basra, and settled first in Hajarain, and then here, where he lies under a white dome tucked into the débris of the cliff. He proselytized the land of Hadhramaut, and the sayyids descended from him are now one of the four classes into which its inhabitants are divided – sayyids, qabīlis, or people who, though settled in towns, are descended from a tribe, meskīn or labourers, and dha'if, the lowest class of all. The sayyids bear no arms and have been held in immense respect until recent times, when a modernist movement, started abroad among the Hadhrami emigrants, has begun to undermine their authority.

After these holy places, we passed through Tarba in a side wadi, the capital of the 'Awāmir and a bad place according to Hasan,

---

[1] I use Himyaritic or Sabæan in a general sense; there is, I believe, no general name to embrace the various pre-Islamic empires of S. Arabia.

[2] These, together with a small statue bought in Shibam and said to come from W. Baihan, are now in the Ashmolean Museum.

though it would be hard to think of anything more innocent in looks among its gardens of young palms in the morning sun. The valley had narrowed a little, but some way beyond Tarba it opened on the south to low sandy distances of Wadi 'Adm, that lead to Shihr and the sea. A string of camels was moving there, as it must have done since the beginning of traffic; and there was our camel man, the one who brought my luggage up from Hajarain, smiling like a friend and jogging as he sat sideways on a beast with a red sore on its back.

Our main wadi, after the crossing of the 'Adm sail-bed in a moist luxuriance of plants and reeds, turned north, and narrowed and changed its name to Wadi Masīla. We crossed its sail-bed also, with ponds of water still unabsorbed in it, and ithl, or tamarisk trees overhanging. An old fort with round corner towers overlooked us on the left as we skirted that side of the wadi: the ithl trees were frequent here in sandy soil. Their shadow lay near a well on raised ground, at whose leather buckets three men and a woman were pulling; they walked up and then ran backwards with the rope in their hands down the smooth mud incline: they did this for four hours, they told me, at a time.

I strolled up to look at them. "No leave to photograph," they shouted when they saw me.

"Salaam to you. God give you strength in your labour," I said.

The leather bucket rose against the blue sky and splashed a sparkle of water as it crumpled over: a string is ingeniously arranged to pull at the bottom when it gets high enough, so that it folds on itself and the water pours out. The three men and the woman explained that they did not like to be seen in a photograph by all the world while doing this menial labour: "hewers of wood and drawers of water" – the humiliation is still felt in the east.

My beduin meanwhile had strolled up and with no fuss or explanation settled for a pull at their hookah in the shade of the tree. A mass of yellow climbing flowers ran up the poles above the well and made them gay against the sky. The wadi lay below in sandy hummocks dotted with ithl, solitary and peaceful, except where Hasan and the chauffeur struggled with the mechanical world, which had expressed itself in a puncture. When it was mended, they called us with a hot and virtuous air from our plot of shade and leisure, and we soon drove up to the old gate of Tarim, cream-coloured in the sun; a flock of black and white goats browsed before it with talismans round their necks, their udders carried neatly in calico bags.

Tarim is an ancient city, with a Sabæan slab with the letters A.L. M.'.D. let into the steps of the Shaikh 'Ali mosque: a grave, too, had been found and shown to Mr. and Mrs. Ingrams on the northern outskirts of the town. It was the home of the Kings of the Bani 'Amr ibn Mu'awiya, one of whom went to the court of Chosroes; and in the days of the apostasy, after the Prophet's death, Tarim alone is said to have maintained the faith of Islam in the Hadhramaut. Most of the apostates belonged to the tribe of Kinda, which still exists in the Wadi 'Amd, and they met and fought the Muslims at a place called Mahjar az-Zurqan. The Muslims were led by al-Muhajir ibn Abi Umaiya, who came from San'a, and by 'Ikrima ibn Abi Jahl, who, having defeated the apostates of 'Oman, had marched through Mahra to 'Abyan (just east of Aden) – presumably along the coast, since the inland parts were in the hands of the insurgents. Some of the men of Shihr are mentioned as following him. From Abyan at all events, he joined the Muslim host at Marib, and they then traversed Saihad, the "wilderness between Marib and Hadhramaut," and so by the Shabwa road. Mahjar az-Zurqan must be somewhere on this route. After being defeated there, the rebels shut themselves up and finally surrendered in the castle of Nujair, which – I have since heard from friends in the Hadhramaut – still exists at a place called Hujail near Mishta, between Tarim and 'Enāt.

Tarim prides herself on this ancient faithfulness, and is still the city of religion par excellence in a country which is all considered as a stronghold of religion in Islam. Tarim is said to have 360 mosques, one of them founded in the fourteenth century by Muzaffar, the conqueror from Yemen of Dhufar: sixty of them are said to be in use. This is as may be, for the European visitor gets little chance of converse with the religious circles of Tarim. The fact that the al-Kaf Sayyids are very broadminded and progressive, and that their

noble tradition of hospitality naturally attracts all Europeans to
them, rather obscures the very strong, narrow and uncompromising religious party they have to deal with in the town. It also
automatically identifies any European with the local progressive
modern party and makes it more difficult to get in touch with the
other. Strange sayyids passed me now and then with eyes averted,
their white gowns drawn carefully away from pollution if we happened to be in a narrow street where our garments might touch.
I was anxious to visit the school of Robāt which, they told me,
is as exalted and as religiously famous as the al-Azhar in Cairo: if
they let me see it for myself, I said, I would gladly contradict the
peculiar and improper calumnies written about it by Herr Helfritz
in a recent German book. But even this could not persuade them to
let my inferior sex overstep the threshold of learning: I remained
on the modern side of Tarim, and there, in the house of Sayyid
Abu Bekr, enjoyed the luxuries of civilization in a guest room richly
carved, enclosed in four doors and eight windows of coloured glass,
which made me think either of the Brighton pavilion or of a church,
according to the humour of the moment.

Here I was visited by Mahmud, the chemist of Tarim, who later
saved my life. He was an Aden citizen of Afghan descent, a most true
and honourable man. His father, he told me, had married an Aden
woman and settled in Abyssinia as a carpenter, the first foreigner to
live in Adis Abeba: had become a friend and adviser to the Emperor
Tafari; and, when Queen Victoria sent robes of honour from India
as a gift, it was he who had been asked to buy and take them. After
many years' service, Tafari had given him land and offered him any
reward he might choose.

"My father," said Mahmud, "chose to ask for a British Consul in
Adis Abeba; the Emperor said yes, and it came to be. And my father
received from Queen Victoria a letter of thanks and two china vases
with the royal arms." The letter has been lost. The father died, and
the mother took the family back to Aden. They still had land in
Abyssinia, but it had been seized by a sister-in-law and there was a
lawsuit. Mahmud told me later that his own greatest ambition was to

be the means of establishing a British Consulate in the Hadhramaut, for he felt himself to be, as he was indeed, a citizen of the Empire: and when, the other day, a young Englishman told me that we might well eliminate our troubles, get rid of our possessions, and retire as it were into private life as a small nation, I saw suddenly the round face and conscientious eyes of Mahmud, opening out his thoughts to me in that remote Arabian valley, and I wondered how the young man, who talked of shedding nations as if they were gloves, would manage to explain the matter to his satisfaction.

Meanwhile Mahmud banged my chest and said that the danger was over. I was only very weak.

"After measles . . . " he said, "bronchitis; then broncho-pneumonia, then . . . " but I interrupted this; we agreed that Allah had saved me for the time being, and after an interval of rest I went to call on the Sultan of Tarim.

The Sultan of Tarim and his brother live in a fortress-square palace on the edge of the town. The houses of Tarim, where they are not touched by the influence of Java, are different from those of Sewun: equally windowless, the lower floor is ribbed in a horizontal pattern like corrugated iron: the front door is cut into this massive blankness; an open shaft for sewage descends close beside it into a covered cistern and, with its long black shadow, gives the impression of a half portcullis. There is more brown, too, and less whitewash about these grim old houses than about the streets of Sewun, for most of the richer people in Tarim live in gardens outside, in new structures elaborately decorated in a casino style. The difference between the old and new takes away the sense of unity which is the charm of Sewun, and the wadi at Tarim is narrower, with less softness of cultivation round the outskirts of the town. The young men of leisure drive out to enjoy their sunsets in a hollow emptiness of stones in the lap of two uncompromising cliffs: but there are gardens hidden there in walls, and in these pleasant places they gather with carpets and cushions, and glasses of tea.

The Sultan's palace is in the old style, and the Sultan and his brother, two pleasantly-mannered indolent young men, received me there. One wore a loose pale blue turban and the other a tight white one, and as both their faces were rather alike, one could decide which headgear one liked best. They soon left me to look through their carved lattices at a wedding reception gathered below, while they themselves went off to feast with the notables in the house of the bride.

This was a huge palace a little way off across the open space, and thither all Tarim was flocking. Motor cars stood about with a multitude of women clustered around them in yellow, orange or green gowns of Tarim, or sometimes in blue of Shibam, their heads smothered in black veils. The cars which carried women were curtained, and decorated with bows and paper flowers, and most of the headlights tied up in pink or flowered calico. Little girls with sparkling trains, beads and girdles, played about from group to group, unimprisoned as yet in the rules of decorum. Across the way were groups of men, slaves or townsmen; they squatted, with shawls tight round their knees and the back of their shoulders, a device which enables them to sit comfortably for hours more or less in space. There were beduin with guns, but very few, for Tarim is not a beduin town, like Sewun.

Presently the bridal procession came along, or rather that of the bridegroom visiting. He wore a white turban and walked slowly, under a rather feminine parasol, while someone fanned him from the side. Three pipes and three shallow drums (Akhdam as-Saqqaf) preceded him, and all the notables of the town. They wore every sort of head-dress: neat white skullcaps with gold embroidered tops, from Java; shallower ones with coloured strips plaited in patterns and adorned with small turbans, from Mekka; sidaras from Iraq; tarbushes from Egypt or Syria; huge turbans made with any old shawl, or close white caps that look crocheted but are not: the heads, seen from my lattice above, showed into how many and how distant lands the Hadhrami has travelled. The philosophers go about

in white, and the people of the better class are spodessly clean; and
the fashion of the al-Kaf family, if they wear a European sort of coat
at all, is to wear it with golden buttons all the way down, usually
sovereigns.

While I was contemplating all this, and causing an addition to
the wedding excitement by showing my face at the window, a small
apparition was brought in behind me by her attendant slave. This was
Salma, the Sultan's daughter, ten years old, all in magenta biocade
with four rows of gold beads round her neck and a crescent moon
below. She stood gazing at me, shy and gorgeous, her little hands
done in lace patterns and wheels of indigo with henna tips; her hair
in seventy-five plaits at least, fluffed out on her shoulders in curls.
An amulet was attached to the top of her head by a safety-pin. She
turned herself slowly round to let me look at her, murmured her
name, and vanished, her little hand in that of the dark old servant.

I then descended to find Hasan at the door, and the Sultan too,
in a yellow car upholstered with panther-skin cloth from which, to
my distress, Hasan evicted him and drove me home.

Late in the evening I, too, called at the house of the bride. Mountains of rice, crowds of servants were hustling about downstairs;
upstairs Sayyid Abu Bekr's Tarim wife received me hospitably and
presently took me into a large room where the ladies of Tarim were
being entertained in one vociferous mass: but she let me stay only
a minute, for a straight-laced matron started in horror from my
outstretched hand: I was hustled back to where the kind old Sayyid
sat with his daughters, all gowned in red – the colour, they told me,
for evening.

I was too tired to stay, for the feasting and dancing had not begun,
and would go on till midnight, when the bridegroom is taken to
his bride. They are left till the beginning of dawn, then he and she,
with all their friends around them, go to the bridegroom's house.

I felt unable to sit this out, and walked home with Hasan along
the moonlit street: and there saw, in the pool of shadow beneath
the Sultan's palace, the procession with the bridegroom arriving
as before; but he was now lit up by lantern light, and dressed in

a rose-coloured coat, and had a fringed band hanging over his left ear from his turban. They were still fanning him, and he must have been very tired. We stood in the shadow to watch them: and long after, in the night, I heard the sound of drums and singing as groups of people passed, dancing the dance they call Shabwani, from days of Shabwa, long before Islam.

20

Departure from Friends

يا ضيفَنا لو زرْتِنا لوَجدْتِنا ⁣ نحن الضيوف وانت ربّ المنَّزل

"Oh guest, should you visit us, you would find us the guests and you the Master of the House."

(MUSTATRAF.)

I was awakened next morning by guns: they were going off to announce that the bride was taking breakfast in the house of the bridegroom.

After this, Hasan appeared in due course and guided me in a car through the streets of the town, by the crumbling ruins of the old fort, by suburbs rapidly growing, for the building trade flourishes now in Tarim, to the eastern gate of the town that opens on to cornfields. The wall is manned and guarded by the Sultan's slaves, and a little stronghold above is used as a prison. A man shouted questions down to find out all about me, and turned out to be the solitary prisoner sunning himself in comfort there. Crime is practically unknown in the Hadhramaut; such things as robbery and murder, being done according to established rules, come rather under the heading of legitimate warfare.

Even these were at a standstill just now: the al-Kaf Sayyids keep peace in the wadi, at a heavy cost of energy and gold. Hasan showed me a valley where two suburbs, facing each other across a narrow space, had been enjoying a small war of their own till Sayyid 'Abd ar-Rahman made peace between them a month before. The al-Kaf indeed may justly be called "children of God," if peace-making warrants that name. There are about forty branches of them now in Tarim, Hasan told me – all issued from one home, all prosperous and beneficent. They run the Sultans, the schools, the trade, the army – all, in fact, that there is to run. Their young men ride about the town on bicycles, brushing by the shocked and flowing gowns of the old-fashioned mullas. They have minted a small coinage which has a local value. They have every sort of difficulty except poverty to contend with, and riches in themselves do not carry enough weight with the beduin to give safe rule over the tribes around. The five hundred or so negro slaves in Tarim are also a turbulent lot. They had revolted a year before and the heads of al-Kaf had retired for a while to Sewun, leaving them to strut about, fractious and half-naked, like a Prætorian guard en déshabille: sometimes the beduin are set against them to keep the balance. Hasan told me that he had been trying to train boy scouts, and to make soldiers out of the peasantry.

"But what can we do without guns?" he said. "We are at the end of the world here, like mice in a mousetrap. At Shibam you can buy all things for nothing, and they get dear as they leave the gates there and come towards us."

This brought us to the burning question of the road to the sea, on which the hopes of Tarim, and incidentally its feelings towards the British in general, depend. Most of it has been made at the al-Kafs' expense, but the last lap to Shihr must await the reluctant permission of Makalla, afraid to lose the stranglehold it now has on the inland valley. Makalla, if it were sensible, would make a road of its own to Shibam and keep the trade of the future. Its merchants hoped to do so, and after the Sultan had visited the place last autumn he sent them four thousand thalers to build a minaret and to begin the

road (of which the whole cost is estimated at ten thousand thalers):
but in a month or two he asked for the gift again, and they were
obliged to send it to India, where the royal family spend most of the
Hadhramaut revenue. The people of Tarim, meanwhile, unused to
constitutional procedures, think that a word from us would settle
the question of their road. The part already made, a pathetic white
streak mounting to the Jōl, is being washed away by rains, while
camels still plod their eight days to Shihr, and the large overseas
business of Tarim is carried by swift barefoot beduin runners, four
days to the sea.

In the pleasant evening hours, when the cupolas of the cemetery
grow pink in a pastel sky, we would drive out among the stones and
patches of cornfields, where peasant girls, with trains and pointed
hats, shot clods of earth from slings to scare birds from the corn. We
would end beside the painted swimming pool in Sayyid 'Omar's
pavilion, or on a carpet in some garden, with pomegranates in
flower, to eat roasted maize cobs and sit in a circle and talk of
history or religion, the ancient borders of Hadhramaut or the policy
of the League of Nations, with the agreeable feeling that these
matters were all about equally distant from our repose.

I met many pleasant people here; and on the last day of my stay
was invited by the Shabāb club, of which Sayyid 'Omar is president,
to sit on a red velvet sofa in the middle of a horse-shoe of chairs
filled with listeners, while – conscious of the poverty of my Arabic –
I did my best to answer questions about the Education of Women.
A learned eager little man rose presently to make a speech. He did
it in beautiful language; it fell like honey from his mouth: out of
its richness, he chose suitable phrases to welcome me as the first
woman to travel by myself from Europe to the Hadhramaut, for the
love of its learning alone. The love of learning is, indeed, a pleasant
and universal bond, since it deals with what one *is* and not with what
one *has*: I was touched by the well-chosen kindness of the words,
but too appalled to think of anything except the fact that I myself
would have to speak next: the inevitable moment came; the little
man sat down. I rose and murdered the Arabic language as shortly

as I could. The end of a speech makes one realize that the Cessation of Pain is one form of Pleasure.

The club and I took each others' photographs on the terrace of Sayyid 'Omar's house: they were all as agreeable as could be; they took me back in one of their cars past the Sultan's palace, where the cannon – a thing like a telescope about four feet long – was being put away in readiness for the next wedding; and left me at the door of my home, whose coloured windows, like time and eternity, were staining the white radiance of the Arabian sky.

Everybody, and especially the little al-Kaf boys who came to visit me, each with his attendant slave – for each boy is given a slave of his own age, more or less when he is born, and they grow up devotedly together – each of them told me what a lot I had missed by not seeing the cannon go off. But this loss was made good that evening, for one of the al-Kaf families invited me to see their private cinema, and there the cannon was, in puffs of white smoke, going off on some former occasion and greeted with cheers by the audience.

We drove to the show after dinner, through the mediæval depths of Tarim over bumpy ground, in moonlight, until under electric lights, beneath corinthian pillars, we stepped into the modern world squatting about on cushions in a large and decorated room.

The cinema was there on a sheet at one end, showing us life in Tarim just as we had been seeing it. The two Sultans come strolling in: they have a rather blasé sultan-like manner of strolling, produced no doubt by the habit of innumerable processions; but everyone greeted them with shouts of laughter, for we had just seen them going through the same movements only more so, on a slow film. They laughed too; they are philosophic Sultans and leave to the al-Kaf family the toils of government: they sat down pleasantly beside us and joined in the running commentary on what we saw.

Hasan's brother, a clever fair lad like an English schoolboy, and wireless operator to King Ibn Sa'ud, was here on a visit from Mekka, and attended, with some young al-Kafs, to the machine. The young men from Java, the visitor from Mekka, the Abyssinian slaves, all mixed pleasantly and easily; I have never seen ill-humour in any gathering in the Hadhramaut. We watched the pictures of the valley and then turned to gardens and family homes in Singapore, with English-seeming lawns where the children ran in starched and frilly frocks from Europe. When the lights switched on again, little ten-year-old Salma, all green and gold with her five necklaces, was asleep in her father's arms. We drove back into the Arab world and called in the darkness outside our house: "Slave, O Slave," to have the carved gate opened. A barefoot bustling, a dusky figure with a lantern to lead up passages and stairs, past the divan with a jumble of slippers at its threshold, by the goatskins full of water hanging in the draught of a window to keep them cool, through the open high court in moonlight to my room.

I had a busy time next morning because I could not leave till my developed films were dry enough to pack. I was luckily able, what with swimming pools and thermos in which drinking water was kept cool, to develop nearly all I had with me, and by this time Hasan had become so expert that I could leave everything except die reading of the thermometer in his hands.

While the little rolls were hanging up to dry, I paid a hurried visit to the school – not the religious one of Robāt, but a modern one for little al-Kaf boys. New benches were being made for them and are now no doubt in use, but I still saw them sitting in rows on the floor while three wise men sat before them, examining. This happens once a week. The whole education, Hasan told me, when I asked him, "lasts all their life." Under the circumstances a certain want of concentration was excusable, since they had so many years before them in which to make it up: Tarim, I thought, was justifying her reputation as the City of Learning. The three wise men looked at me with disapproval; it gradually lessened as they discovered that I knew such things as the difference between the "Man Who Does," and the "Man to whom it is Done," equally vital in Life and in Grammar. But our time was short. A small victim was selected: he rose and was asked to tell us where words come from.

"From our father Adam," he said, "who told them to his children."

"Do you think it was really our father Adam?" I asked the nearest wise man. "In our country some say that most of the words come from our mother Eve."

A learned ghost of a smile hovered on his lips. I was sorry I had to go, for he would soon have become human. When we reached our courtyard, there were three can, ready and packed to overflowing, for Sayyid Abu Bekr was also moving to his favourite Sewun, and the cook and servants and all the kitchen things and a precious plant tied on at the back under an umbrella of its own, were joining in the exodus.

The cook was an Indian, engaged by the hospitable al-Kafs to make British travellers feel at home with their own familiar dishes: he had been brought to Tarim with the news of my coming, and I realized what a responsibility we undertook when, together with our Empire, we allowed things like anchovy sauce and tapioca puddings to run uncontrolled over the continents of the world. If Dupleix had triumphed and Clive had failed, one might be eating delicious omelettes in Africa and Asia to-day. And if missionaries allowed more goodness to overflow from prayers into cookery classes, it might, in the long run, be better for the salvation of the average man, who, as any wife can tell, is frequently inclined to sin by indigestion and very rarely rescued from it by piety.

These reflections were punctuated by the bumps of many raised water-channels as we retraced our journey to Sewun. Again the wadi shone in heat, and widened as we turned the bend beyond the track to Shihr. We passed one of the two taxis of Tarim broken down in the stream bed with the "Music of 'Urfa" inside it, four ladies and three drums, returning from the wedding. We did not stop to look at ancient sites, for I wanted to reserve my strength for Shabwa: but I got out among some beduin camped in the heat round a siqaya, their packs in the sun and camels grazing, caring little for anyone or anything: they were Kathiri, of Sultan 'All's tribe, and Hasan watched with pain while, my picture taken, I let them look through my finder at the landscape while they crowded about me.

At one o'clock we were back among the dusty walls and sweet-smelling cornfields: with a feeling of home-coming we mounted the white steps, sunny and quiet, of the Glory of Religion. I could understand Sayyid Abu Bekr's love for Sewun. It must be a relief for him here, to be away from the feeling of insecurity and wealth; to see the brown and white houses, whole streets of beautiful fancies, without any foreign intrusions.

The Sultan came presently, padding in his slippers, and sat and quoted Arab poets on the unnecessariness of riches. It was all very pleasant.

In the evening coolness, with half a bar of sunset cloud pushed like a sword from behind the rim of cliff, for the whole sunset is not visible from Sewun, I called on the Abu Bekr ladies: they were listening to the Music of 'Urfa, which we had left stranded in the river-bed: the four female musicians with their drums sat cross-legged in a row against the wall, one young and two middle-aged and one old: they had rough and hardened faces, for it is not a reputable profession and they are little thought of. One of the mediæval kings in Yemen is said to have poisoned himself when, his city having been taken by the enemy, he saw his concubines forced by the victors to dance and sing in public on the wall.

The music was wild, with a low falling cadence, like a waterfall: the women sàng in parts, taking on the story from one to the other, beating on the three little drums with an occasional bang on the biggest: I listened hypnotized, as one listens to the breaking of waves.

The incense burner was handed round to be held a moment to our breast to perfume gown and hair. Roasted coffee-berries too, on a straw mat, to be smelt at and handed on. And when we had sat there a little while, two beautiful gowns were brought, with silver girdle and silver crescent-jewel for the neck, a present to me from the Sayyid's wife, who knew I liked these things.

As we were admiring them, the Learned Sherīfa came also to say good-bye, with a quotation on her lips before she was over the doorstep. Her side curls were as engaging as ever when she emerged from her green gown and thick black veil: her little forefingers pointed as emphatically as before to let no crumb of wisdom wander. Under her strenuous influence our mere female gossip melted away and died. She began straightaway on the virtues of erudition, and went on to the letters of the alphabet, which are divided into fire, water and air: "Fire letters," she said, "will keep one warm if one happens to be suffering from cold. This," she remarked, "is Learning." I was not given time to agree, or to ask which are the letters possessing so useful a property, for she was already telling us that the three sorts of learning enjoined are religion, medicine, and the stars. "Languages too; there are two thousand seven hundred and sixty in the world." She could not stay, she said: her gathering of ladies was waiting: she had come merely out of sisterly kindness to wish me godspeed: she wrapped herself up again and left us, full of admiration but incapable of speech.

When I reached the Glory of Religion, three other ladies were waiting there from the Sultan's palace. Our talk here was on less intellectual levels, for they had all my things to look at and sips of cough mixture to try; and they stopped in horror before my soap dish, for no one in the Hadhramaut, among the old-fashioned people, will think of soap for the first forty-one days after measles.

"The smell says nothing to you?" they asked. "With us, if you smell any scent when you have measles, you die that very day: the scent rushes to your head, and because of the dryness of the air, it expands and bursts."

"Is that why a woman snatched her child away from me and cried: 'the Smell, the Smell,' when I went near?"

"Yes, indeed," they assured me, rather rudely I thought. "And we often plug the children's nostrils up, to save them from danger."

They left me, blue butterflies fluttering down the white steps.

Next morning, Sayyid Abu Bckr, the Sultan, his brother and his nephew came to see me off. I was sorry to leave them all. 'Ali the Berber sat ready in a two-seater car, with Hasan, rather too large for the dicky, behind, his appearance more gay than usual, due to the combination of dark glasses with a pointed, hat with tassels which I had just bought from the gardener's wife, and which he seized upon for shade. It was nine o'clock in the morning; we were going by the little towns of the southern side to our lodging in Shibam and thence next day by car to Wadi 'Amd – a three days' trial journey to see what strength I had before attempting Shabwa.

21

Into Wadi 'Amd

"weary bands
Of travellers in some shady haunt
Among Arabian sands."

(Wordsworth.)

I left Sewun on February 22nd. The spring was already beginning to make itself felt with warmer days: it was 88° in the shade at noon.

The patches of yellow had spread in the cornfields, and here and there men were squatting with a sickle to their harvest. The sickle looked a poor sort of tool, a crooked knife with a few inches of saw-edge in the middle of it, and the men worked in rows of three or four, sitting on their heels. They left a few inches of stubble to be pulled up when dry and mixed with mud for bricks. Women, too, were at work planting onions; they looked like rows of witches, the pointed crowns of their hats at all angles and their faces veiled in black with eye-slits below. A man in a field was ploughing with oxen, the only ones I saw – for this labour is mostly done by hand. The southern valley-side and its towns was fertile and at peace. Peasants and produce trotted on donkeys to and fro. Now and then one smelt the sweet scent of the corn. In the dusty green of the palm groves houses had been built recently, unprotected and open. For these little towns, still fortress-square beneath their cliffs, had now five years of peace behind them. Sayyid Abu Bekr and Sultan 'Ali of Sewun pacified them at a cost of seven or eight thousand thalers, and obtained this garden-suburb atmosphere of ease. Men could now build houses in safety among their palm trees in the plain.

The towns themselves, like Ghurfa, still showed the signs of wars – their houses blank to where shot-holes began at the second story, each a citadel to itself: from their midst a covered way ran, sunk into the ground and screened by a series of arches: it had allowed the inhabitants to reach their palm groves in the plain unharmed by enemy fire. The eastern enemy of Ghurfa ran a trench to within about two hundred yards of her houses, and built a small fort where ten soldiers were kept to harass the town. The soldiers were marooned by day, but revictualled or changed at night: and the war under these conditions had lasted ten years.

We did not stop at Ghurfa, but passed beneath it, and turned into Wadi Bin 'Ali, where the palaces of 'Uqda are white against cliffs, above the fountain-shaped tops of palms. I was reading the *Morte d' Arthur* at this time, and found it harmonized strangely with the life of the wadi; its sudden contrasts, the splendour of its castles, the general uncertainty of things round them, the delightful feeling that anything might happen anywhere and not be surprising. The average inhabitant of the Hadhramaut takes much the same view of life as did Malory's knights on the marches of Cornwall or Wales: a stranger under a tree has the same lively possibilities in him – a suitable object for either a fight or a feast: and the fifteenth century ideas of convalescence in England must have been very much the same as those in Arabia now, where you are expected to rise from your bed ready for anything, just as Sir Tristram, lying ill, was badgered to joust by his friends.

'Uqda, thanks to the five years' peace, is now a place of gardens: the palms grow unwalled, in young and bushy luxuriance. Our car nearly stuck in the soft sand, and we stopped under the white pinnacles of a palace which some rich hotel keeper from Java has built, alone and unprotected except by its own mud walls.

The inhabitants trooped out to greet us, inviting us to stay: but I was anxious to reach Shibam, now visible in the open space of wadis meeting. We were going on next day to see about the Shabwa beduin in the palace of al-Qatn, and I knew I was to have some difficulty over this with the Governor of Shibam.

No sooner, in fact, had we penetrated once more the cobbled threshold of that town and stopped to wait in the tower-like shadow of its houses for the Governor, when the difficulty began. A little beduin, agile as a rat, sprang up from where he lay amid some camel loads: he grasped and shook my hand.

"Three days," he said, "have I waited for you here in the dust. The Sultan of Qatn has sent me. It is we who will take you to Shabwa."

The Governor advanced at this moment, swathed in draperies like a ship under canvas, and bearing ahead of his portly presence his silver-headed cane. He shooed the little beduin away.

"Take no thought for anything," he said to me. "We shall send you with the best people there are. You need have no fear."

The market place in a crowd did not seem the most suitable spot to unravel this tangle: I retrieved the small beduin, who was looking at each member of our group in turn with quick and puzzled eyes, told him to greet the Sultan, and to tell him that I should be in al-Qatn next day to arrange matters. Hasan, visibly swelling with combativeness – for he disliked Shibam and all its inhabitants – was gently urged back into the car: and with our positions taken, but no actual hostilities engaged, we all made for a bungalow outside the town, where my lodging was to be.

It was a charming place, out in the openness of the wadi, though the cliff wall hung above it in the south. It stood alone, enclosed in two walled gardens, of pomegranates and palms, beside a pool of clear water built up with a colonnade: the dining-room opened there with green shutters against which palm branches rustled. We, however, climbed in procession upstairs to a large and airy room with seven windows, and terraces opening on either side for morning or evening shadow: the style was more or less European, painted in light colours, mitigated by whitewash and sunshine. It is the home where the R.A.F., when they land in Shibam, are hospitably entertained; and it was carefully furnished with green velvet chairs and numerous ash-trays.

Here, when the key had been found, together with Iuslim, the servant, who had disappeared with it in his sash, we all entered and sat down: my two hosts, Sa'id and Husain al-A'jam; the Governor, his red beard very like a halo which had accidentally slipped; little Ba 'Obaid, A.B's agent, friendly and anxious to please everyone: and two Sayyids from the Wadi 'Amd, 'Aluwi and 'Ali, who had been on their way to Sewun but, hearing of my intended visit to their district, had then and there, with the usual Hadhramaut hospitality, changed all their plans so as to go back with me and entertain me. When we were fairly settled and after a decent interval of non-committal politeness, we came to the delicate subject of Shabwa.

The Governor was afraid that if he let me go under the auspices of the Sultan of Qatn, he would be blamed in Makalla. He was one of the slave families of the royal household there and – in accordance with the south Arabian tradition, which numbers many famous wazirs among its slaves – he had been made Governor a year before, when the Sultan of Qatn resigned. Sultan 'Ali of Qatn is still the most powerful man in the upper Hadhramaut: he resigned, Hasan told me, because two of his soldiers were killed by the Jabir beduin at the gate of Shibam, and he was not allowed to bring troops and guns to punish them as he wished to do, but was made by his government to buy them off with money: the Jabir are lawless people, and killed a man and took two camels from a Shabwa caravan during my stay in the wadi. The Sultan of Qatn, respected in his own lands and beyond, was able to make the Qe'eti name respected in Shibam – a thing which few outsiders, however excellent, can ever succeed in doing among conservative tribesmen. As far as I was concerned, I was quite determined not to venture into the western borderland without the support of someone whose name carried authority beyond the borders of Shibam: and apart from this, I liked the Sultan and had already engaged myself with him. I explained the two latter points with necessary firmness.

"That is of no account," said Ba 'Obaid, anxious to conciliate. "We will send a messenger to the Sultan to explain, and when a caravan comes, the Governor will send you off from here."

"I am sorry," I said. "This could have been done before, but it is too late. I have given my word to the Sultan of Qatn. Not for the King of England himself would I change it. The word that is given is finished."

These sentiments left a pained silence. The little circle sat, looking at the ground, expressing nothing either way. The impossibility of dealing with female obstinacy by mere reason was apparent to all, and the Governor rose laboriously, with a sigh. He could not be responsible for me, he said: he would write and say so to the government in Makalla, and he would ask me to write also and tell them I was doing this on my own initiative and against his advice.

This seemed fair enough. The Governor left; the little circle departed too, rather subdued. When all had gone, the door opened and one of them reappeared with a most cordial expression on his face."

"You were right," he said. "The Sultan is the best man in this neighbourhood. He is a friend of ours. And as for the Governor, poor man – one does not listen to him: he knows no History."

So I felt justified, though in an unexpected manner.

At eight-fifteen next morning, Hasan and 'Ali the Berber and I, with the two Sayyids in the dicky behind, started for Huraidha in Wadi 'Amd.

The two Sayyids were the most charming companions one could desire. They made an amusing contrast as they sat in the dicky: 'Aluwi plump, good-natured, guileless, friendly and reliable at sight, while his friend, with yellow turban over one eye and aquiline Arab face, ready for any joke or any adventure and full of an engaging irresponsibility, was – as he told me himself – "less a shaikh than a bedu." They had both befriended MM. Van den Meulen and Von Wissmann on their visit to Wadi 'Amd, and were still full of all that they had done together at that time: 'Ali the Bedawi, that is to say, was full of these recollections, for 'Aluwi had other memories, of eight months spent in England, and talked, as we made towards the western wadi, of the delights of Paddington and Woking.

We passed al-Qatn and left word that we would stop on the way back to arrange the day for Shabwa. Out in the wadi a caravan from San'a in Yemen was trailing in, with small donkeys gambolling unloaded about the hulking camels. The men were tall, unlike our beduin of the Jōl, bearded and aquiline, and friendly. They came, they said vaguely, from the direction of prayer, "qibli," as they call the north-west beyond which Mekka lies: they cracked their fingers towards its sun-hidden spaces, while their caravan, a hundred camels or so, laden with sacks of millet, waited and lifted their slow heads and blinked in the sun. It spoke of the peace that now lies along these western marches: it was making for Shibam, the "bank" of the Hadhramaut, as Hasan called it. The group of tall men, having told and collected the news, lingered to watch us start – all the leisure of their deserts around them.

We turned now towards the south, along the wide route of our coming a fortnight ago – the headlands dim in mists of sun before us: we waved to the walls of Dhiar al-Buqri where the slaves lounged at their look-out, to show we had no time to stay; and then we turned west from the Do'an route into the Wadi 'Amd.

Here, after a great stretch of barrenness, one comes again to villages and oases, but of a more desert quality than in the great wadi: the 'ilb tree rather than the palm is grown. This is indeed near the beginning of that country which Maqrizi describes, where they sow "relying on the rain," and where there are "very many *nebk* ('ilb) trees, so that one tree is a load for five camels and sells for ten mithqals of gold, and if there is lack of rain, the trees wither and no sowing remains. . . . " And these people, Maqrizi adds, have the extraordinary power of changing themselves into wolves. In fact the Hadhramis were credited with magic powers, and the "men among them fly by night in the air from Hadhramaut and change into the form of birds such as the rakhma and the huda'a till they come to India"; so that their travelling instincts may be inherited after all. The country so described by Maqrizi is north-west of 'Amd, among the Se'ar: and beyond, near the Ahqāf (in the southern desert sands), lie lands where "there is no water at all," but if it rains there are great harvests: "and then a tribe descends into it . . . and stays there with its camels and its women for four months and needs no water . . . but lives on milk."

The Wadi 'Amd is nothing like this; it is scattered with small villages and plantations: but yet the nearness of the desert is on it, with a certain arid cleanness and hardness. It is a beduin valley, divided between the tribes of Nahd and Al Ja'da, under the authority of the 'Attas Sayyids in their town of Huraidha. In old days it must have been more populous than now, for the ruin-fields south of Huraidha are, according to M. Van den Meulen, the largest known in Hadhramaut; and opposite to Huraidha, 18° by my compass from Sayyid 'Aluwi's house, lies 'Andal "the first town of Hadhramaut." The highroad of traffic must have passed here, both in ancient and mediæval times; and the Wadi 'Amd would be well worth more careful investigation. Except for MM. Van den Meulen and Von Wissmann, and Herr Helfritz, it has not, I think, been visited by Europeans (since Von Wrede's account of this part of his journey is obviously not genuine).

We lingered at the opening of the wadi in the shadow of an 'ilb tree among sand-dunes. Three shepherdesses, in black with silver girdles, came up when Sayyid 'Aluwi called them, for we were now in the 'Attas country, and they knew him. They were young things, but all widows, their husbands killed in the war between Dhiar al-Buqri and the town under the cliff. Their own town, Sayyid 'Aluwi told me, was the boldest of all the little fighting towns, and its inhabitants were busily digging trenches there now, so as to be ready for the end of the truce which fell in two months' time. The little widows, meanwhile, pulled the leaves from the 'ilb trees with their long poles and offered us berries from small round baskets. They looked at me, intrigued and timid, for they had never seen a European woman before: but they presently came up and sat beside us, fingering with curiosity the stuff my clothes were made of.

"We are democratic here," Sayyid 'Aluwi said, obviously glad to be back after the metropolitan luxuries of the great wadi. "In the Wadi Hadhramaut you will have to pay five hundred thalers or so for your wife's dowry: but here in Wadi 'Amd, twelve (eighteen shillings) is the maximum."

The sun was climbing and we wished to make Huraidha before noon. We left the shepherdesses and continued westward, keeping among stony debris under the cliff, which here juts out like a snout into the valley and has at its top the ancient well, the Bir Ghumdan, down which Von Wissmann and our Bedawi Sayyid climbed. He told me about it until the inequalities of the road jolted us out of conversation. 'Ali the Berber could make a car do almost anything: we entered the dry ditch of a stream and took it like a wave: on its farther side the town of Huraidha leaned against the cliff at the turn of the valley, surrounded by stony open spaces. Its cemetery lay before it with a few white domes, and a well-house carved and white: its two white minarets rose airily against the rocky wall: the town lay brown between, blistered in sunlight. And the ibex horns that decorated its roofs and curved against the sky showed us that here we were again in the old-fashioned Hadhramaut, among the uninterrupted traditions of Arabia.

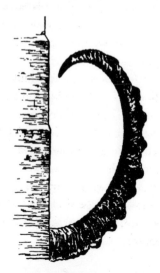

22

Huraidha in 'Amd

*"The watchers will not keep his death from the lord of Marib, nor the
    strongholds that ring him about,
It will climb up to him after the night's first sleep by a linen ladder
    tightly twisted."*

('Alqama.)

Sayyid 'Aluwi was not expected in his house at the edge of the
town. There was a great deal of welcoming and explanation,
and the carpets, which had been put away during his absence, had
to be pulled out again.

He busied himself for my comfort, thinking of all that one is
accustomed to in the district of Paddington and supplying me with
it in the kindness of his heart. There was a great deal, for the
Hadhramaut must be among the world's chief consumers of tinned
fruit, milk, biscuits, and such things, and there was never any
stint in the hospitality with which they were offered everywhere.
I accepted gratefully, and watched the Sayyid as he struggled with
his housekeeping, and interrupted himself at intervals to explain
how useless women are, and how incapable of imagining what a
European might require.

But Jamila helped him. She was sent for, and came to look after me, dressed in beduin black with a key at her girdle – a middle-aged woman with an independent mind and kind and charming face – the long, large-mouthed, high cheek-boned type of the Hadhramaut where it is untouched by mixtures from Java. She walked about the house unveiled and free, a friend rather than a servant, as much a part of the family structure as the walls, and quite as much of a support in her own way: for here we were back in the feudal country, with all its loyalties.

The old architecture of Do'an was here again too, the doors carved in seven bands or so above the lintel, their heavy latches pulled by a chain which ran through one story after another to the top of the house: the rooms had the dark wainscoting and beautiful carved pillars of the old Hadhramaut, and Sayyid 'Aluwi apologized for them as he sat on the ground and saw to the cleanliness of plates and spoons as they were placed before me, and sent for water in an earthen bowl sprinkled with frankincense to make it pure. "We are democratic in Wadi 'Amd," he said at intervals: then added: "It is better than the luxury of Hadhramaut," for he was proud of his valley and pleased when I told him that I liked it: and expressed his feelings by turning to labour at the opening of yet another tin.

I should have been very happy with all this friendliness, but I now began to feel terribly ill. Jamila shooed out an invasion of ladies and left me to rest alone. Indescribable paroxysms shook me: I looked through all the diseases described in that most valuable book, the Royal Geographical Society's *Hints to Travellers*, and wondered what mine could be. I came to the conclusion it must be malaria. The symptoms of a dilated heart are unaccountably not mentioned in the book, and nothing but malaria seemed to fit even remotely what I felt. Simple malaria, the little book added, is never fatal: I hoped that mine was simple. I looked out over the sunlit, empty stones of Wadi 'Amd stretching southward, the ancient highroad to the sea, and doubted for the first time if I should ever be strong enough to leave this desert-locked land. The house stood high; its fortress walls were, in their smaller way, an imitation of the wall of rock behind them: the gutters stuck out and poured themselves on to the hill-side below: there was one under each window, so that I could throw my bath water out of the drawing-room without troubling to open the shutters. The valley below was dead under the midday sun, shadowless and peaceful, for we had reached Huraidha at eleven, three hours nearly from Shibam. I lay down and tried to rest; then the door opened slowly, and the head of a small boy peeped through. He had crept past Jamila's guard to look at me: hesitated as one might at the open door of the lion house in the Zoo; saw me smile, and came and squatted beside me.

"From where did they fetch *you?*" he asked, and opened out his little hands to show plainly how remarkable he thought me.

His name was Ja'far, and he was almost sure that he was seven years old. He went to school and did his lessons on a wooden slate instead of a copy-book. He wrecked whatever sleep I might have had, for Jamila, hearing voices, now let in the ladies of the harim.

They wore lovely clothes of the Hajarain pattern, and red and black cotton kerchiefs round their heads brought by an Indian pedlar. Traffic now comes up by Wadi 'Amd owing to the fact that goods are no longer plundered at Bir 'Ali and the customs there are lower than those of Makalla: but the safety of the upper wadi is not yet very great, so that most of the trade turns eastward to Do'an and so to Shibam, over the Jōl instead of by the valley. It is one more proof of how the ancient and convenient routes in this country remain fundamentally the same, though shifted for temporary reasons of security.

The ladies were not interested in these matters. What they were hoping for was to be allowed a little drive in our car, up and down the valley bottom: this had been promised once before, when a car came to Huraidha, but nothing had come of it and they had never sat in a motor in their lives. I was asked to do my best for them, and mentioned it to the Sayyid — who smiled in an indulgent way. But when I enquired next day, I found that the promised treat had not been granted after all. "Trifles," he said: "the things that women think of." The harim and I looked at each other regretfully, but we knew our places well enough to say no more about it.

I was too ill to go to the ruin-field visited by Von Wissmann, a mile or more above the town: but I wandered round the streets of Huraidha, its three mosques and library, and brown houses crumbling to the cliff. The most ancient mosque is high up, with square minaret like that of Hajarain – and below it, not far inside the threshold, two Himyaritic slabs:

It is tantalising to know so little as we do about this Himyaritic Script: its ancestors are unknown, though the first alphabet of the world, as we understand the alphabet, is probably among them: for so momentous an invention alone, the south Arabian past is worth investigation. But the last days of the Himyaritic writing and its supercession by Arabic are almost equally obscure. An inscription of the second century A.D. *(Nova Acta Eruditorum* 1773) mentions a certain M. Ulpius Castoras *Librarius Arabicus,* which goes to prove that Arabic texts of some sort were known at this early date. But in the sixteenth century, Hamdani still mentions Himyar as spoken in various districts. Conder, in his *Arabia* says, without giving his authority, that "When the Koran appeared in the Cufic character the inhabitants of Yemen were unable to read it" (p. 42).

The fact that the Himyaritic writing was still known in the Hadhramaut at the beginning of Islam is proved by the story of Qaisaba ibn Kulthum, who became a Muslim and took part in the conquest of Egypt. It is told by Faraj ba 'd esh-Shidda (Partl., p. 130) on the authority of Ibn al Kalbi, how Qaisaba was captured by the Banu 'Uqail (probably in the neighbourhood of Bishe) when on his way to the pilgrimage before the days of Islam, and was kept a prisoner for three years, his people believing that the Jinn had made away with him. But he wrote a message in the Himyar script (Musnad) with his knife on the saddle of a passing camel, and the message eventually reached his tribe in Hadhramaut. He was set free by means of an expedition of the tribes Sakun and Kinda.

The modern mosque of Huraidha was built with beautiful and elaborate workmanship by the uncle of the present Mansab, the religious head of the town. It is large and imposing, and has water running out of taps, and on its roof a library of 10,000 volumes, they told me, kept under the white dome: only a long and careful investigation could tell if anything of value yet unknown lies there amid its theological volumes. As we visited it, the children of Huraidha, let loose from school, pounded on the door outside: they were friendly, for my little Ja'far, small but evidently influential, was among them and had certainly told them that I was human, but they wished to see as much of me as they could: to go into the streets among them was like descending into an arena with the Bedawi Sayyid and his stick in the gladiator's part, and I, in all but my feelings, in the role of the Christian martyr. We were glad to return to our house, whose parapets and ibex horns now shone on their slope in the evening sun.

I had made a mistake in Huraidha, and should have gone to stay with the Mansab there, Sayyid Muhammad ibn Salim al 'Attas. We had seen his house being redecorated in the lower town, with masons, suspended on platforms along its outer walls, picking out with delicate dove-grey the little portholes round the roof by which the harim looks down upon the street below. No one, however, had told me that here was the chief of Huraidha, until Sayyid Muhammad himself and his brother came to call. There was some little feeling about the matter, not with me but with my host, for the guest is supposed to go to the chief of the clan. But my fatigue was sufficient to let me stay where I was for the night. The two brothers sat and talked for a while about books: they were friendly and charming, and in looks like some Van Dyck picture, noblemen with long and delicate faces and slender hands. They are the old aristocracy of the Hadhramaut, descendants of that Sayyid Ahmed ibn 'Isa who came from Basra and whose tomb we saw on the road to Tarim. I promised to lunch with them next day, and they left me and sent a mattress from their own house to increase my comfort for the night.

When they had gone, the harim came down again with many other ladies from the town. They brought a drum to entertain me with music, and asked me to sing Ferangi songs. All I wished for that night was to die quickly if such were to be my fate and, if possible, alone – but I was the first European woman they had ever seen and some response had to be made to all this effort: I sang such nursery songs as I remembered while the ladies seethed about, and changed places now and then to see my features from a different angle. A small child left her mother suddenly and came and nested her tiny body in my lap; she was dressed gaily in pink silk with green skirt Java fashioned, fastened with a safety-pin; and as the language we depend on is not that of words, my misery was soothed by the human contact of that small affectionate creature. An old woman was there, too, with hennaed yellow hair; she seemed incredibly old, toothless and with blue eyes rare in that country, light and watery with age, with so much compassionate kindness in them as she held my hand and gazed at me, that from her, too, a spirit of comfort crept into my heart; for the fact is that, being so ill, and gazed at like a creature from a zoo, made me feel desolately lonely. And presently Sayyid 'Aluwi came down, hospitable and anxious, and – shooing the ladies and their drum away with a wave of his hand – left me to get through the night as well as I could on the Mansab's mattress in one corner of the carved and pillared room.

The fact of lying down probably did some good, for I woke in the morning with renewed courage, though shaken, and with the conviction that, if this were malaria, I should have a day or two's respite to get back to Shibam before the next attack. I felt this to be the more prudent thing to do, though I wished I could stay longer in Huraidha, and perhaps get well in its clean air of rock and sunlight. "Here," Sayyid 'Aluwi said, "we have no sickness; we are well or we die."

He came with a tumbler foaming with camel's milk which I drank and then climbed to the top of the house to take a compass bearing on the village of 'Andal. Every lady of the harim had an apartment of her own up here, and kept it locked with a wooden key at her girdle: all the little pegs had to be fitted into their appropriate holes, and it was a matter of time to open a way from story to story to the upper whitewashed terrace where the ibex horns curve out over the town below.

Here Sayyid 'Aluwi in his dressing-gown strolled in the morning sun. The goats in the wadi below were pattering out to pasture in a black and white line; their little tails curled jauntily over their buttocks, their neat-ankled feet picked out the way with competent daintiness: beyond them the wadi stretched open and shallow and brown. The Sayyid's authority wanes there as one goes to the south: it is still strong in the small townships, but the enclosing beduin hang over it, and the progressive, anti-Sayyid party, the Irshād from Java, begin to spread their propaganda among the tribesmen.

This is the burning topic of Wadi 'Amd, as the road is that of Tarim: I heard later about the Irshād, as we sat with the Mansab and his brother after visiting their school, and they told me the history of their family.

Their ancestor was al-Faqih al-Muqaddam Muhammad 'Ali, descended, like all the Hadhramaut Sayyids, from the Basra apostle Ahmad ibn 'Isa, and the first institutor of the rule that no Sayyid should go armed. After him, about three hundred years ago, Sayyid 'Omar 'Abd-ar-Rahman al-'Attas came to Huraidha, built the first mosque there – he built fourteen altogether – and died A.H. 1074 (A.D. 1663–4), after concluding seventeen peace treaties with the surrounding tribes. From him and his three sons the 'Attas of

Huraidha are descended. One of them, 'Ali ibn Hasan, settled in
Meshed in A.H. 1172 (A.D. 1758–9), and the families are still closely
connected; another became a king in Malay.

In the Wadi 'Amd this family remained, and gathered in their
hands and guarded through many vicissitudes all civilization that
the valley contained. Just so, in the Dark Ages of Europe, the
lamp of learning was fed – a feeble flicker, yet sufficient to light
a greater flame when the general illumination of the Renaissance
ushered in the modern world. How many obscure heroisms, what
invincible patience and hope must have gone to carry through those
bloodstained ages the mild treasure of wisdom! Psychologists tell us
that the impulse of sex is the fundamental mover of this world, and
we are perhaps getting a little tired of hearing it so often. But there
are two impulses stronger than desire, deeper than love of man or
woman, and independent of it – the human hunger for truth and
liberty. For these two, greater sacrifices are made than for any love
of person; against them nothing can prevail, since love and life itself
have proved themselves light in the balance; and the creature man
is ever ready to refute the Matter-of-fact Realist and his statistics by
sacrificing all he has for some abstract idea of wisdom or freedom,
unprofitable in every mercenary scale.

What with popular lectures, compulsory instruction and the
belief that one is educated if one can read and write, we sometimes
forget that this hunger of our soul exists: but in the Wadi 'Amd it is
difficult to satisfy, and therefore more easily recognized for what it
is, and the two Sayyids were not surprised to find that I should travel
from Europe to the Hadhramaut in pursuit of their ancient learning.
They were waiting on their threshold when I went to them, their
cashmere shawls on their shoulders, dressed in white immaculate
gowns. They led me up the steps of their mosque to where the
10,000 volumes lie in peace under the white dome. "Here you must
come for months," they said, "to study."

The children of Huraidha were at school in a room close by:
about forty of their eighty pupils were there. They sat on mats in
rows, high-spirited little beduin mostly, with brighter eyes and less

submissive manners than in the schools of Makalla. The sunlight slanted in on them in shafts, across a blackboard at the far end of the room. Sayyid Muhammad's brother, who was teacher there, handed the following qasida to one small scholar, which he read out in the emphatic voice of poetry, while his fellows fixed on me their rows of quick brown eyes and kept them there unwinking all through the ceremony:

QASIDA

"Peace be on you, and the mercy of God and his blessings." And afterwards:

"On the occasion of the arrival of the free and respected one, and of her honouring the court of our excellent school, I rise to welcome her happy visit to the abode of the noble Sharifs, the country of Al Ahqaf, the place of residence of our venerated ancestors and that where our forebears were born. Her spirit and firm courage are shown to us inasmuch as she is the first woman to visit the province of Hadhramaut alone, without any companion of her own sex or associate of her people, and that in her wandering and moving from place to place she travels entirely by herself.

"We are not told by history that since Hadhramaut became a land, any woman of Western race has come to it in this manner; she is the first woman who has trodden its soil and succeeded in travelling there. Therefore we thank the nation that has produced this noble lady, and do tribute to her lofty enterprise and her aspiring soul.

"And I, the writer, stand forth to represent my brothers the pupils of the educational school, asking the Lord that she may have a happy journey and a fortunate return, and that peace accompany her when she alights and proceeds, and in conclusion I offer the heartiest greeting."

When this was finished, they all sang: the sudden onslaught nearly knocked me over: the Sayyid had just told them that, as I was the first Ferangi woman to come to Huraidha, a half holiday would celebrate the occasion, and so perhaps a special strength of enthusiasm had crept into their song. They had been learning by heart, that morning,

the four different ways in which one is allowed to wash oneself –
a necessary but not enthralling subject; and now there was a great
closing of books; a pause for photographs; a couplet of welcome to
be written out on the blackboard by the Sayyid's brother:

"*By your arrival our eyes were refreshed and we obtained our desire,*
   Freya Stark – welcome as to your home, greeting!
"*Two lines to you from the headmaster of the educational and*
   instructional school of Huraidha!"

He wrote and rhymed it extempore, for he was an excellent
poet; and then the school of Huraidha, with whoops of joy, rushed
out into the sunlight, where they no doubt soon got dusty enough
to put the Rules for Ablution to a test. The Sayyids and I returned
to lunch at the Mansab's house.

It was a beautiful house inside, white and shiny and clean. The
diwan below was hung like Meshed with drums and standard poles
and ornamental spears for use in processions: upstairs was a carpeted
room with pillars, and here we sat, and looked at very old books,
and discussed the route to Shabwa, for which the Mansab's uncle had
written out an itinerary which disagreed with every other account
I had seen, but which I have copied at the end of this volume. They
also had a genealogy of the 'Amd Sayyids written in exquisite script
by the Mansab himself.

"Here," he said, "you will see how the Imam of the Yemen, and
the mosque of Azhar in Cairo have written to confirm our titles: but
these young men in Java, they will not give us our names: anyone,
they say, may be called Sayyid, or Sharifa (if it is a woman) or
Habīb (if it is a child), irrespective of whether they descend from
the Prophet or not: but here we have the proof that our titles come
to us by right of descent, and all authorities admit it."

The Irshād quarrel of the young men in Java started in 1918 over
a school in Singapore. The Sayyids who had endowed it suggested
that all should contribute a quota towards it: this being refused, they
decided to keep the school for Sayyids only: hence the feud. The
name of Irshād came from a newspaper in which the Sayyids were

attacked by the great 'ālim Muhammad ibn 'Aqsh, a friend of the
Imam of Yemen, and so influential and anti-British that – according
to Hasan, from whom all this information came – if he had lived,
the Yemen treaty would still be unsigned.

This the Sayyids corroborated, and spread before me the doc-
uments with their signatures and seals, and the book where the
names of the Sayyids were written in black and red. Far into the
past they went – no doubt with the same long and delicate faces,
the eyebrows slightly raised at the outer temple, the soft and charming eyes, full sensitive lips, the long fingers and little tuft under the
chin: such as they probably were when, as nobles of Qoraish, they
rode to join the Prophet's banner.

"Our power is threatened now," the Mansab said. "But who will
take our place here in this valley? Who else could live unarmed as
we among the beduin? And what will happen when all power falls
into their hands? Our schools and our books – will they care for
them? All will be spent in war one against the other." And indeed the
Wadi 'Amd, which lives more or less the life of England in the time
of Alfred, is not yet ripe for the Suppression of the Monasteries.

Meanwhile we had had our lunch, and yet we did not go. Ill or
well, I meant to see 'Andal before returning to Shibam, and I knew
that in Arabia what is begun in the afternoon stands little chance of
being completed that same day. Hasan, sitting in stout Olympian
calm on the carpet opposite, answered enquiries about the car with:
"It will come;" but he did nothing. Sayyid 'Aluwi, who was coming
back with us, had things in his house to see to, and the Bedawi
Sayyid, who was also coming, had to say good-bye to one of his
wives.

"I am coming with you to Shabwa," he said.

"Anything that is new, I like," he explained. "And a Sayyida like
you – travelling in our country – we should not let you go alone. I
know the beduin, and I will come."

It was he who finally collected the car. The Mansab and his
brother came to their doorstep and packed us in. They brought me
a gown of brocade, for Hasan had told them how much I liked these

vanities, and six earthen bowls for the two Sayyids in the dicky: the little boys of Huraidha devoted this part of their half holiday to sending us off with cheers and dances. Just as we were starting, the Mansab's brother came with a last request – would I send him the letters of the Himyaritic alphabet and their Arabic translation, so that he might read the stone slabs found in the neighbourhood? I promised, touched and delighted, and thought of the monks of Jarrow who copied out their manuscripts for remoter brethren in the darkness of England: and of that King of Yemen who, in the fourteenth century, sent envoys to Afghanistan for a commentary of the Quran: this was the tradition of the Mansabs of Huraidha. As we jolted away and I looked back, their little town, with the beduin and the cliffs like a Damocles' sword above it and the treeless fields below, seemed as it were a symbol of the dignity of learning – a little brown place where, still building in the future, surrounded by deserts and wan, lives a faith more disinterested than most religions, a more sublime passion than most terrestrial loves.

23

'Andal

*"The sons of Cush . . . Seba and Havilah, and Sabtah (Shabwa) . . .
And Joktan begat . . . Hazarmaveth and Jerah, and Hadoram, and
Uzal (old name of San'a) . . . and Sheba, and Ophir and
Havilah . . . And their dwelling was from Mesha as thou goest unto
Sephar (Dhufar?), a mount of the East."*

(Genesis x. 6–21.)

When we had passed under the headland of Bir Ghumdan, where the Wadi 'Amd turns towards the East, we saw that a strip of sand-dunes lay between us and 'Andal on the northern slope, about a mile and a half away beyond a village called Lakhūm. None of my party had the slightest wish to go there, and had hoped no doubt that, considering the lateness of the hour, this caprice of mine might be forgotten: but they made no protest, and I wondered if an English chauffeur would have turned his car so amiably on to the unknown sand without a murmur.

'Ali the Berber, however, enjoyed taking risks. He added to them by keeping his loaded gun beside him, so that its six cartridges would go off underneath us if we crashed: it was an American gun — a thing called, I believe, a Remington repeater — and far more tenderly treated than most children: it was last in and first out of the car always; and though 'Ali the Berber was a silent man, and never spoke except to convey some information, so that his feelings remained unexpressed, one could see a gentleness come upon his face when the precious object was handled.

He now looked at the sand-drifts before us, remarked that they had not yet been crossed by a car, and went straight into them. If we could reach the opposite side of the wadi all would be well, for the softest ground is always in the middle: 'Ali steered like an expert, taking advantage of every hard ridge and going fast over the yellow bits where the sand is soft. We had to stop once and prospect, but there was no mishap, and it was still early in the afternoon when we reached the few mud huts to which 'Andal, the "first town of Hadhramaut" has dwindled.

The old site is east of the present village and its debris fill a bay in the cliff; they lie in hillocks of stones over five acres or so. Sprenger considers it to be the home of the Antidalei mentioned by Pliny: it is referred to by Bakri and Yaqut (both quoting from Hamdani); by Ibn Khordadbah, who describes it as nine stages from Marib; and probably by Ibn Mujawir, who speaks of 'Antar, nine farsahs from Shibam on the way to Aden, as a place "inhabited and prosperous in old days, now a wilderness." Imru' l-Qais, the Prince of Kinda, witnessed raids here, as we have seen.

The inhabitants now are Ba Jabir beduin, of a "mashayakh" tribe, one, that is to say, that does not carry arms. They poured towards us out of their low huts, almost naked. Many of them looked as if they belonged to the small dark race of the South, so different from the Semitic Arab. The contrast between the two is noticed in an amusing account of the men of Kinda in the earliest days of Islam given by the historian Tabari (p. 1220). Four hundred men of Sakūn (a tribe of Kinda) fought, he says, in the Persian war under their leaders Mu'awiya ibn Hudaij and Husain ibn Numair, in the army of Sa'id ibn Waqqās. This army was reviewed by the Caliph 'Omar and, says the historian: "behold there were among them youths *black and lank-haired* with Mu'awiya ibn Hudaij, and he (the Caliph) turned away from them, and he turned away, and he turned away, until it was asked of him: 'What have you against these people?' He said: 'I am in doubt concerning them, and no people of the Arabs has passed before me whom I mislike more.'" (Which shows, among other things, that there was not very much intercourse between Mekka and the Hadhramaut at that time.)

And again there is the story of Qais ibn Kulaib, who was chamberlain to 'Amr ibn al 'As the conqueror of Egypt. The poet Abd al Mus'ab al Balawī wrote, mocking him: "Qais has no noble female ancestors; but only wretched little women of Hadhramaut" (the word ﺷﺮ being translated in the French dictionary *chétif et traité de dédain à cause de la chétive apparence*). And, to conclude this subject, we may record Muqaddasi (Bib. Geog. Ar. 111, 87 and 103), who mentions the men of Hadhramaut as lovers of learning, fierce zealots, and *very swarthy*.

But to return to the people of 'Andal; they were now rushing out towards our car, and greeted us with a matter-of-course composure explained by the fact that most of them had travelled in Somaliland or Eritrea and had seen Europeans before. Not so the women. They gathered in a group of beduin black, and sent a messenger to ask if I would go up to them and let myself be looked at: one of them, coming too near the car, saw her own image in its shiny varnish and leaped away shrieking: "There is a veiled woman here."

The headman came out; he showed his dignity among the half-naked flock by a complete dress and a yellow turban: he had a sparse white beard and shrewd and wrinkled eyes. He hunted round desperately to find something to wrap his hand in before contaminating it with the touch of mine; grabbed at the nearest loin-cloth – found it inadequate – and, making the best of a bad business, shook hands and smiled. In a little procession from their twenty houses or so, the beduin took us over the ruins. They lie on three small knolls, and there is little enough to see except a piece or two of wall, a small cistern, three by five feet, and three wells, like the Meshed one but smaller, one in the hollow by the town and two on the two nearer hillocks: the third and farthest hillock has no well.

On the nearest of the hillocks, the beduin told me they had found a jug filled with golden jewels and beads, and had sold it in Do'an: they had come upon it as they dug under the ruined wall. The whole place was covered with fragments of pottery, mostly very rough, and difficult to identify as to date. Two small lustre shards belong to the ninth or tenth century and a green glaze resembles the output of the kilns found by Sir Aurel Stein on the coast of Makran. There were many pieces of greenish glass: no trace of anything definitely earlier than Mediæval Islam; and the ruin-fields fitted with what the meagre literary references suggest – an early Islamic town flourishing somewhere about the ninth and tenth centuries A.D. A single Chinese fragment belonged at earliest to the fifteenth century – too slight a clue to go upon.[1] I found a cornelian bead, and a small pearl with a hole to thread it, such as the girls wear in their nose rings: but there was little more; what treasures 'Andal holds must be underground, and the afternoon was going.

I thanked the old headman.

"You must come again," he said. "You must come and stay and we will dig for you."

"And if there is gold," I said, "you shall keep it: and if there is brass, you will give it to me."

This suggestion was approved with enthusiasm: we left 'Andal and made east along the northern wadi shore, towards the opening into Wadi Hadhramaut.

It was too late to reach Shibam, and we decided to spend the night in the old town of Henin, on the north side of the great wadi. Two brothers, Ibn Martak, live there, and had invited me some time ago. They had been to 'Andal in a car a day or two before, and we were now able to follow their tracks and save ourselves much trouble.

We turned the north-west corner of the wadi, towards the width of the Hadhramaut valley, under the walls of Lukhmas and Sheriuf, "the most famous of the fighting towns," Sayyid 'Aluwi told me.

---

[1] This data is due to the courtesy of Mr. Hobson at the British Museum.

Trenches were being dug here: the eight months' truce in honour of the Sultan of Makalla's visit had nearly expired, and everyone was busy preparing for the next war. A covered way and towers already existed at Lukhmas, and showed against the cliff like an old painting of a mediæval town: in the dunes about us were watch-towers and trenches. It was men of Lukhmas who had killed the three husbands of the pretty shepherdesses who gave us 'ilb tree berries on our way out. Sayyid 'Aluwi smiled in his placid way: "No soldiers, no arms," he remarked. "What can we do about it?" He was a philosopher and the Inevitable did not disturb his kind and quiet temper.

We left Dhiar al-Buqri and our friends from Java on our right, and shot between them and the town under the cliff, their enemy, into the open sand-dunes of the Wadi Hadhramaut itself. As 'Ali the Berber took a soft yellow slope sideways on two wheels, the door of the car opened and deposited me gently on the ground. I thought the car was coming too, and crawled away with quite a collected mind to get clear. When I stood up, 'Ali the Berber had recovered himself and stopped. Hasan had leaped out to support me in his arms, and the two agitated Sayyids, much impeded, were trying to climb out of the dicky.

The only harm done was the loss of my little 'Andal pearl, which I had been holding in my hand for safety and dropped as I fell: that, and the severe shock to the feelings of everyone concerned except myself. The Bedawi Sayyid and Hasan, what with relief for my safety, sorrow over the pearl, and surprise over the calm and expert way in which I fell out of cars, uttered exclamations as they groped about the ground; but Sayyid 'Aluwi, after the first excitement, regained his placid calm and suggested that we look on the pearl as a ransom and leave it to the Jinn of the sand-dunes. The evening already was throwing a mantle of yellow light upon us; the edges of the cliffs were clear and sharp in the sunset. We climbed again into the car, and followed Ibn Martaks's tracks to his town of Henin, under the northern wall.

Here in the evening light a Shabwa caravan was camping, its camels couched before the houses in the sand. A desert peace lay on the dunes of the valley, for Henin is the last village but one, towards the west, and over its few houses and stunted palms there is a feeling of wider spaces and stronger forces than their own: by day, its western cliffs, dwindling in openness and distance, fade there in the heat of the sky. The older town and some of the modern too, is in a bay of the cliff behind: but Ibn Martak's two square houses stand forth almost alone under their precipice, which rises sheer, and at night grows strange in darkness behind the illuminated façades, when an electric lamp shines above the Martak door.

These Ibn Martak are four brothers, whose fortune comes from Batavia. Two of them live out there, while two stay at home, and these now made us cheerfully welcome, and led me into a guest-room painted Batavian fashion in many colours, with five windows and two doors. They had so many guests, they explained, on this station of the western road, that they had built this house for the purpose, and kept their harim in the other square building close by.

"Would she mind," they asked my Sayyids, "coming down into the diwan? The beduin would like to look at her?"

"They have no easy time," Hasan explained as I got into my shoes again," these Ibn Martaks; they are the only rich house here, and the beduin all about them. At any time they could sweep down and rob: they have to buy the beduin off with presents and be polite to them always, even when they do not feel inclined."

And indeed, as I stepped into the diwan, and wished peace to the tribesmen cross-legged round its three walls, I could not help feeling that perhaps this was one of the occasions on which the two gay young men might have preferred not to have to be so polite. The beduin belonged to the Nahd tribe, and sat about with an air of truculence very different from the Ba Surra's receptions in Do'an: here there was no Head to symbolize Authority – the abyss that divides the nomad from the townsman was visible to all. The gathering, I thought, was rather like one in a French chateau during the Revolution, with a nervous landowner receiving the sans-culottes.

A swashbuckling Nahdi heaved himself up and came to sit beside me. He was pock-marked and repulsive: his enormous naked stomach seemed insecurely buttressed by the dagger in his sash: he talked in a loud and blustering voice, very unlike the ordinary courtesy of the tribesman. I disliked him, and began to think that I, at any rate, need not be polite at all costs, especially as he wished to show off his wit in baiting me with questions before the audience of his tribe.

"Are you a prince?" I asked him, when I thought I had answered enough. He was taken aback for a moment, for he was half slave-bred, and some of the listeners laughed.

"Why do you ask that?" he said.

"You walk in as if this house were yours, you come to sit beside me – I thought you must be a prince or a king: perhaps one of the royal house of Kinda?"

There was a general laugh now, and I left the assembly with only one enemy, and a chastened one at that. The young man, my host, took me back with a relieved air to my room.

It was he who had been the bridegroom at Hajarain when I passed through, and had his bride at home now in the house next door. She had ridden on a camel, according to the marriage custom, but he had come by car. I climbed up to see her, and found a radiant child of fourteen, decked bridally with all her necklaces and ear-rings and much petted in her new harim by the other ladies.

"She is a charming bride," I said to my host as we came away.

He smiled and shrugged his shoulders slightly.

"What can you do with them as young as that?" he said. "Our women give us no peace till we marry."

After supper, he told me, we would listen-in to the wireless, the only one in Hadhramaut, and hear the news from London.

The wireless was set up on the terrace which opened from my room. The beduin, who had to be allowed in because they wanted to hear, were already squatting there in a half circle when I went out: their indigo shoulders scarce showed in the darkness – only a bracelet or a dagger gleamed here and there among them. The two brothers fiddled with the box, trying to pick out London among the wandering noises of the world. Below us a blur of embers and faint gurgling of camel showed where the caravan from Shabwa slept.

The voice from London came startlingly through the Arabian quiet. As it was Sunday evening, it was the service in some church or cathedral. A blurred sentence, then words solemn and clear. "The Lord keep and preserve you, in body and in soul." Those were all I heard: after them, strange noises swallowed everything, and left only a vague sound of prayer: but I sat shaken, moved by the comfort of those words and filled with loneliness. As it was quite dark, and I was exhausted, I wept. The wireless continued to make hideous noises.

"If those are prayers," said one of the beduin, "ours are better."

Ibn Martak twisted the knob about, trying to find something articulate in the capitals of Europe: horrible discords rent the Arabian night. I begged him to stop, and retired to the painted cheerfulness of my room: the electric engine died down soon after, as I was opening the bullet-proof shutters of one of the five windows: the illuminated façade of the harim sank back into one darkness with the cliff behind it: the sleeping camels from Shabwa, couched in a circle below, lay brown and soft under their stars: and, beyond them, sandy billows blown hither by desert winds lay also soft and brown.

24

Breakdown in Shibam

نزلت على اهل المهلّب شاتياً   غريباً عن الاوطان في زمن محْلِ
ما زال بي إكرامهم واقتفاؤهم   والطائهم حتّى حسبتهم أَهْلي

"In winter I descended upon the family of Al Muhallab,
In time of dearth, far from my home;
The honour they did me, their courtesy and kindness,
Were such that I thought them my kindred."

(Hamasa.)

In spite of the problem of the beduin, the two young men of Henin were careless, gay and delightful hosts, and lived as cheerfully as people who inhabit the sides of volcanoes or other potentially explosive sites. They asked me to return, and I said I would sleep here on my way to Shabwa, for I still thought my disease to be malaria, and hoped for improvement. A lean emaciated man, the Hadhrami prototype of a club bore, invited us to his village nearby: he liked to talk of learned things and was collecting, he told me, the English names of diseases: this seemed to me at that time a peculiarly depressing form of research, but I enriched his vocabulary with the word for measles, and discovered that he had no idea that quinine was good for malaria: his interest was independent of anything to do with cures.

We left them all at eight in the morning, and skirted eastward among sand-dunes along the wadi edge. All here used to be palm trees about sixty years ago; the sand, encouraged by local battles of the past, has blotted them out. It comes down the wadi from the western deserts like waves that forerun the tide, reddish and finer in texture than any sand I had ever seen, so that it did not grit at all between one's fingers: a tribal fort of the Nahd was buried in it to the shot-holes: distorted leafless 'ilb trees stood dying at its edge.

Presently the clean yellow ribs began to look more solid: bright green rāk or hamdh bushes (*Salvadora Persica*) grew on it, good for camels; and each bush, collecting the sand beneath it, formed a small hillock of its own. The twigs of these bushes are broken off, splintered at the end, and used for toothbrushes. In the shelter of one of them, three birds which they called quail, but which looked to me like plover, were hiding, very quiet on their long legs: but when 'Ali the Berber pulled out his gun they flew away at once on speckled wings.

"Their song," said Sayyid 'Aluwi, "is sweeter than that of any other bird in the Hadhramaut."

We had some slight trouble with the engine, and while 'Ali the Berber attended to it I wandered off to a lonely house in a walled palm garden nearby. The wall was dilapidated, and I walked in. The palms were young and pleasant, with bars of sunlight stabbing them like swords. The house itself was a fortress, buttresses at every corner, and windows and shot-holes particularly high up. Another building, very like it, stood close by, but they were both shut away by a wall.

Hasan, rather nervous, now came. With the air of a grown-up who says that matches are not to be played with, he assured me there was no way in: but I had just discovered a small postern, and went through it to take a photograph.

Heads appeared like Jack-in-the-Boxes at the lattice work of the windows. "Come up," they shouted.

I was just hesitating when the Bedawi Sayyid, also very nervous, came in through the door, shouted a polite negative to the windows above, and begged me to hurry to the car. As we left the outer garden, a returning beduin met us, who seemed surprised and asked what we were doing, and seemed even more surprised when I gave him my hand.

"Have you come to take our treasures?" he asked, and again seemed surprised when I laughed.

I told him I had taken the picture of his house.

"You must pay to do that," he said.

"*You* should pay," I remarked. "Do you not give rewards to those who make you famous?"

The beduin looked uncertain. Another young lad, his hair in shocks over naked shoulders, was standing by the car, which 'Ali the Berber had just got going again. He, also, when I shook hands with him, looked first at his hands and then at me, as if in two minds about it, omitting to answer my greeting of peace. This is always a bad sign, and I began to see that my Sayyids were very anxious to be off. We were in the car and away before the two beduin had come to any conclusion about us.

"You should not have gone in," the Bedawi Sayyid reproached me as soon as we were well away. "These people are known. They live by robbing those who pass through the sand-dunes alone. If it had not been for us and because we are Sayyids, you would not have got away."

I thought our success more probably due to the beduins' surprise at my appearance and the fact that I shook hands with them: a hand-shake carries great weight, and is the preliminary to friendly relations among all castes in the Hadhramaut. But I did not contest the point, and 'Ali the Berber contributed a third theory: the two neighbouring houses, parts of the same fortress, had now fallen out among themselves, he said, and were busy besieging each other, so that they had no time for passing strangers. The name of the place is Juwa.

"What would have happened if we had gone in?" I asked.

"They would have taken money. But not so *very* much," the Sayyids told me.

We now cut across the dunes and reached Qatn on the south side, with no further incident except a meeting with a barefoot runner, his loin-cloth trimly girt, a long staff in one hand, a letter held up to us in the other. The letter was not for us, but for Henin. The man went, his plum-coloured shoulders glistening in the sun. In this manner, the postal affairs of the district are carried on, nor did I hear of any letter going astray – though it would be difficult to send a very secret message by this means. After the runner had gone, we spent quite a long time wondering why Sewun should be writing to Henin, and *what* could they have said?

When we reached al-Qatn, we were welcomed as friends.

"Anistu, you please us by coming."

The steward smiled; a retainer stood to shake our hand on every landing; the Sultan himself gave shy and dignified greetings to all: 'Ali the Berber, having put away the car, joined us and kissed his hand.

The beduin for Shabwa, the Sultan said, were ready. They would wait five days till I felt better; they were asking for too much money, and it would do them good to hang about and become reasonable. From Shabwa, said the Sultan of Qatn, they would take me either into Yemen or to Aden – about a month's journey altogether – as I preferred. I suggested that I might follow the more northerly route to Najran; a letter had just come to the Sultan from Ibn Saud's wakil to say that it was safe, and it lies through unknown country: the beduin there hold partly for Ibn Saud, partly for the Imam of Yemen, and only the recent peace has brought quiet to that desert fringe.

"There is still a *little* fear," said the Sultan. "You cannot go there."

Quiet and friendly, his word was final, and I wondered what the gift of authority is, that makes one man's words mean so much more than those of another: an inner deffiniteness, perhaps, the courage to face and accept responsibility and therefore to come to decisions in one's own self? It is a quality which even animals understand and obey. We left the matter of the road beyond Shabwa and talked theoretically only of those western sands.

A great mixture of religions, the Sultan told me, is to be found among the tribes between Hadhramaut and Najran. Some Ja'feris or Ismailians are up there – remnants of the time when the chief of the Assassins, the Old Man of the Mountain, sent propagandists to Yemen. The Puritan 'Ibadhis also are still to be found.

The 'Ibadhis have a history in the Hadhramaut. Their name is derived from an obscure ninth century 'Abdalla ibn 'Ibadh, and their sect now chiefly exists in N. Africa and in 'Oman, moderately puritan and apparently related to the Kharijite tenets. In the eighth century, 129 A.H., one of their followers, believing he had a mission, took counsel with the heads of the sect in Basra, and came to the Hadhramaut. His name was 'Abdulla ibn Iahya, better known as Tālib al-Haqq, the Seeker after Right. He and his lieutenant, Abu Hamza, got possession of all south-west Arabia to Medina and Wadi Qura, where they fought a battle and were defeated by 4000 men under Ibn 'Atiya, sent against them by the Caliph Marwan. Tālib al-Haqq and Abu Hamza were killed in the battle: the 'Ibadhis were hunted and massacred, and those that were able escaped to the Hadhramaut and took refuge with Tālib al-Haqq's governor, who still remained in power. Ibn 'Atiya pursued them. The rebels marched out to meet him four stages from Hadhramaut, probably not far from Shabwa, for that was the main road; but Ibn 'Atiya circumvented them by a night march, and took Shibam behind them, and all their stores. He was busy pacifying the province, when an urgent order from the Caliph forced him to go north in haste with only a few companions, and there some of the Murad tribe in Jauf, who still roam about that ruined land, murdered him to avenge one of their kinsmen.

The 'Ibadhis mentioned by the Sultan of Qatn must probably be descended from these rebels of twelve hundred years ago, for there is still an extraordinary immobility in this Arabian land. Motor cars have not yet changed it, and the ancient geographers lead one more competently than modern map-makers. In Henin the Martak brothers had spent their evening copying out of my Hamdani a reference to their family made nearly a thousand years ago. The Sultan of Qatn told me that when his own ancestors came from their Yafi'i highlands four hundred years ago, they first settled in Lakhūm close to 'Andal – so treating 'Andal as the "first town of Hadhramaut," even as their ancestors had done before them. The Ja'da tribe, he told me, which now inhabits Wadi 'Amd, is very modern; it had come from Yemen only two centuries before.

I left the Sultan with the hope of returning in five days' time. "Your sickness will go now," Hasan told me; "there is nothing so good for fevers as a sudden shock like falling from a car."

That incident, I noticed, was never mentioned abroad. I had admitted that it had been my fault, for not attending more carefully to the door, and this amused them, and the Bedawi Sayyid referred to it in frequent exclamations – but only when we were alone; we kept the regrettable secret to ourselves. In spite of it and its medicinal value, I collapsed as soon as I reached Shibam.

Hasan left me there. He belonged to the Kathiri, and every moment in the Qe'eti domains amid their rival comforts was pain to him. He looked round at the airy and quiet pleasantness of my bungalow as if it were a place of ambush. "Uncivilized," he said, and snatched my face towel to wipe my tumbler. My hosts, Husain and Sa'id, easy-going and friendly, bore him in silence. My two Sayyids decided to take him on to Sewun before he made trouble. They would all come back in a few days. They left, and wrote from Sewun a friendly testimonial, which I treasure.

"*This is a certificate to Miss Freya Stark, English, a traveller in Hadhramaut, that she is conversant with laws and guided by religion, and of an honourable house, and is the first woman to travel from England to Hadhramaut alone – and is mistress of endurance and fortitude in travel and in the suffering of terrors and danger. We thank her greatly, very greatly.*"

"Sayyid 'Ali al 'Attas al Bedawi."

Meanwhile Husain and Sa'id, relieved, surrounded me with cordiality and kindness. "Are we not British?" they said, whenever I thanked them. "We are born in Singapore. Your King is ours."

Every day they came to see me in my bungalow, where I now lay getting rapidly worse. I had discovered at last that my disease was not malaria and that something was very wrong with the heart. At intervals I treated it with coramine injections, and lay quite still; but it weakened gradually.

My hosts gave me Husain's own body-servant, Iuslim. They had been brought up together as the Hadhramaut fashion is, and when he spoke of what he had seen or done, it was never "I" but always "I and Husain." He was devoted to him, and was gay, affectionate, unreliable and charming; brown, with quick and pretty movements like a cat, a large mouth, a way of putting his head on one side when he talked, and soft eyes which lit up if he heard a shot or a cry in the wadi; he would then rush to the terrace and hope for a battle. He had a pleasant voice, too, more like a European than an Arab, and would sing as he washed himself or my dinner-plates in the pool below my window. He always served the guests that came to the bungalow, he told me, and the British airmen who have fairly often alighted on the landing-ground of Shibam. He approved of them, "though they do not know how to speak correctly when they mention the Prophets or the Messenger of God (Muhammad)."

"Sometimes," I said, "they may not have been very religiously educated."

"That is so," said Iuslim. "'Anbar, the black slave downstairs, keeps out of their sight when they come, because he is afraid of losing his religion. But he does not mind you," he added. "You neither drink nor smoke, and you never speak of the Messenger of God without saying 'praise be upon him'."

On the third day, when I grew very ill, another servant called Salim was sent to help. They lay wrapped in a blanket outside my door, and fed me with coffee at intervals through the night.

I was losing my strength. I could not see my watch, but listened to a tiny pulse in my ear like a wave of life breaking on some unmapped shore, and waited for it to cease: when it did so, I should no longer be there to know: the thought was terrifying and strange, as every new venture must be. It was not my sins that I regretted at that time; but rather the many things undone – even those indiscretions which one might have committed and had not. I was not troubled with repentance or sorrow, but rather, in a quiet light, saw the map of my life as it lay, and the beauty of its small forgotten moments: tea on an English lawn in summer, gentians in the hills, hot sweet scents of pinewoods in the south – all small and intimate things whose sweetness belongs to this world. I tried to think of them, for I knew that I must keep my mind as cool and quiet as I could. Salim lifted my head at intervals to feed me, with as much tenderness as any nurse; he was a perfect servant, devoted and understanding. He had a charming ugly face, long with a narrow chin, and the big sensitive mouth common in the Hadhramaut, and a high forehead which the white skull-cap, tilted back to the very verge of his shaved head, made to appear even higher. He looked at me with infinite compassion and moved quietly.

I thought I had little time left. I was afraid, too, of fainting and being buried alive. This sometimes happens, Iuslim had been explaining to me; and only a little while ago some Mulla subject to fainting fits had been so buried; a devoted servant happened to be out at the time, and when he came home and found his master already underground, had insisted on opening the grave, and discovered the Mulla sitting up inside it; there is always room in the Muslim grave, since the dead body has to sit up soon after death to answer the questions of the two angels, but it would be an unpleasant awakening. I told Iuslim to see that they waited half a day before doing anything with me, and taught him how to inject the coramine in case I fainted; I was incapable of doing it myself any longer.

This was a very painful performance, which only Iuslim enjoyed. "Now," he remarked with unconscious irony, after jabbing what felt like a skewer into my arm," I may say I am like a doctor."

He held my writing block for me and guided my hand from line to line; I wrote a short note and, lying back exhausted, saw him staring at it in perplexity.

"I gave you the wrong side," he said. "This is blotting-paper: you must do it over again." He was like a butterfly at a deathbed, pleasant but irrelevant.

Towards morning I slept for three hours, and woke from happy dreams; I had been with my father in some Mediterranean city, luminous in the opal sea; my firiend came laughing towards me in a firelit room; I woke with these companionships still upon me and saw the sun on the spiky palm leaves light against the window. There was a twittering of birds; a pleasant air came from the garden and dangled the crochet mats on our small tables; it was the earliest, charming hour after dawn. For a second I forgot that I was ill; and then realized that this was indeed my last day, unless Mahmud the chemist arrived from Tarim with some new medicine. My own methods had failed one by one; the heart was now so faint that I could feel no pulse. The whole affair seemed unreasonable, monstrous, and inevitable, with the world around me and my own mind so pleasantly alive; so it must seem on their appointed day to men condemned to die.

I was saved, I believe, by Mahmud.

The difficulties of intercourse between the two Sultanates and the fact that a wedding was going on in Tarim and that Hasan had gone off in a huff, explained the three days' delay which nearly killed me, but a last S.O.S. had made them all realize how urgent the matter was. My host, Sa'id himself, after this terrible night, set out for Sewun in his car and met the rescue party, and at about nine o'clock, when I had given up all thought of it, Iuslim came to me with shining eyes to say he heard a car: he stood at the window and told me that he saw it – a speck drawing swiftly near, trailing the wadi dust.

Soon they came – my two hosts, and the Sayyids of 'Amd, Hasan weeping, with Mahmud. He, good man, felt what pulse there was, remarked that it was angina pectoris and dyspepsia, a combination which surprised me, and proceeded to inject loconol in my vein; it had a swift effect and seemed to send an elixir of life once more to the exhausted heart.

Mahmud took over the direction of affairs, which had lain on my shoulders almost as heavily as my illness, and I turned gratefully to sleep. My two hosts said they would show their friendship by staying in the bungalow until I was better, and ordered a feast to be prepared downstairs for all the party: and soon the jovial sounds that floated up made me feel that I and the world about me, whatever else might be the matter with us, were at any rate not dead.

25

Visitors

*"And yet I quickly might arrive
Where my extended soul is fixed,
But Fate does iron wedges drive
And always crowds itself betwixt."*

(ANDREW MARVELL.)

I was better for a day, and then relapsed. In the stress of the crisis I wrote to my friends in Aden and asked for a doctor to be sent if any R.A.F. planes happened to be coming to a Hadhramaut landing-ground: a flight, they told me, was expected in Shibam and the chance was too good to miss. The great 'Id, the yearly Feast of Sacrifice, was now approaching: it would last for a week and no runners would be going to the coast during that time: and in any case a letter must take anything between a fortnight and six weeks to reach Aden. Such as it was, I took the chance and wrote, and my hosts – I learned afterwards – despatched a telegram on their own account by the same runner with the concise message: "Please send aeroplane." This was to be handed to any ship with wireless that happened to pass: I am thankful to say that no chance came to send it, and the Royal Air Force were spared the surprise it might have caused.

I, meanwhile, was nursed by Mahmud, and lay untroubled, with nothing to think about at last. He hunted through a book he had, filled with every conceivable disease, in which I refused to take an interest. He had been with a doctor in Aden for two years, through an epidemic of plague, and this experience, and his own earnest and intelligent nature, enabled him to help me. He sat downstairs through the night, not sleeping, "praying," he told me, "that Allah may save you." On the third day after his coming I was definitely better, and a little later he left me to return only at intervals from Sewun.

One day, while I lay very ill, a beduin from Qatn came to see me. He walked in alone one afternoon through my open door and gave me his greeting of Peace. He was a tall Aulaki from the hills, dressed in sacking, a cartridge belt round his waist, and he leaned on a rifle: but apart from these things, he might have been the figure of Christ in some old picture – the broad and level brow and curling auburn beard, straight features, quiet eyes and noble carriage.

Twice, he said, he had been denied permission to enter: but he waited till no one was below, and now he came to say farewell. He and his comrades could wait no longer: they were going to their own home.

"I cannot come," I said sorrowfully, "I am ill."

"Allah heal you; Allah restore you and bestow good upon you. No good comes but from Allah, may he be praised and exalted."

It was a beautiful blessing, and said so earnestly, it brought with it a serene acceptance, an atmosphere of brave and spacious life. And when the man asked for a gift because of his days of useless waiting, his word even for that was noble – "ikrām," a thing "given to honour." I was unable to give him anything, for I could not rise, and my hosts told me that the Sultan of Qatn would do this for me and let me know: but when the time came, he never allowed me to repay the debt, and all I could do was to leave him my copy of Hamdani. But throughout this day I remained pleased and comforted by the visit of the beduin, and thought as I lay that the magic of Arabia, which so many have felt, is due perhaps less to the sun-wrinkled arid land itself than to the innate peculiar nobility and charm of its people.

It was at this time, before I was able to leave my bed at all, that they brought me word of the German traveller to Shabwa.

He was a young man who had been in the country before, had written two books about it, and taken beautiful photographs: but he made himself disliked by printing a report that the Se'ar beduin were cannibals. This, of course, is an idiotic thing to say of any Arab tribe, and roused a great deal of feeling in the wadi which had treated him with hospitality. He had other crimes also to answer for as a traveller, for, having actually been to the gates of Shabwa, from which a beduin had turned him away, he increased the distance from Shibam to seven days instead of four; reported himself as the first European in Do'an at a time when that whole valley was talking of the visit of MM. Van den Meulen and Von Wissmann; appeared never to have heard of the Bents; and seemed to have got himself threatened with shooting and death more often than was reasonable even for the most tactless tourist.

When he presented himself, all unsuspecting, to the al-Kaf Sayyids in Tarim, they were embarrassed to know what to do with him: the young men of the wadi wished to express their feelings plainly, and the old-fashioned and religious party were equally incensed. For he had offended them by saying that the school of Robāt, the religious centre of learning in the Hadhramaut, provides its students with 'eine Frau' together with other amenities.

The book existed in Sewun, and I was asked to translate the objectionable passage, to which the learned men listened speechless with indignation. They taxed the young German with his words when he came; and he explained that 'eine Frau' in this instance meant little girls who were allowed to attend the school (not that even little girls are allowed, as a matter of fact.)

Hasan and Mahmud both came to me after this with the book in their hand, to ask if the interpretation were plausible: perhaps, they said hopefully, I did not know German very well: the word Frau might possibly mean a small child of uncompromising age?

But I refused to perjure myself for an unknown German: a Frau, I said, was a Frau and nothing but a Frau. And when my two hosts and a large circle of Sayyids hastened to call and tell me that the young man was on his way to Shabwa before me, and to express the friendly hope that something in the manner of an accident or sudden death might yet happen to him by the way . . . my feelings were such that I merely smiled at the idea.

Someone now came to bring me news of him every day, while I lay and chafed. He had gone to Sewun, he was staying with Sayyid Abu Bekr. He would not move, they said, till after the great feast, for it is the time when everyone is celebrating weddings, the beduin marry off their daughters during this week, and there is practically no travelling. By the time the feast was over, I might be able to ride again, and Sayyid Abu Bekr sent me word that he would see to it that I got a clear start. He would do his best to keep the German quiet. I soothed my conscience by remembering his sins, and Iuslim, pretending to scatter food with his long fingers to imaginary dogs, explained that this was what would happen to the unconscious young man if he were to visit the offended inhabitants of Shibam. "Cannibals," he muttered at intervals, as he dusted my room with a palm-leaf.

Then the news came that, feast or no feast, the young German was starting. He had picked up a beduin in the market place of Sewun, and had arranged to be taken straightaway, in spite of Sayyid Abu Bekr's efforts at dissuasion. I admired his promptitude, and then heard from Mahmud that it was due to Hasan, who had told him to hurry, or I might yet set off before him.

What actually happened I never came to know, and am still loath to think ill of Hasan. He had been devoted and most faithful till illness threw me into the care of Mahmud, whom he disliked: his hatred of Mahmud, or possibly merely the love of conversation, may have led him to speak: it is a depressing fact that the East, on the whole, is more steadfast in its hatreds than in its loves: yet I would give him the benefit of the doubt. But the Wadi Hadhramaut was rent with discord: I lay helpless, my journey crumbling like cardhouses around me; and I felt ashamed that I should mind if others reached my city before me – for this matter of being first is not really a very creditable passion. Iuslim, darting gay and graceful about my room, would put one finger and thumb delicately round his neck, would point to the ceiling, open his hand to show that all is over, and with his usual drastic point of view in the matter of justice for others, would observe that people who betray their friends ought to be hung, so.

The German reached Qatn and went on. Word came from the Sultan there to say that he had passed, but that his beduin, though they would reach the modern village, would not be able to take him to the site of the ancient city, a day's ride farther on: this I took to be mere kindness on the Sultan's part, but it turned out to be true.

Months afterwards, when I had already left for Europe, I had a letter from Husain in Shibam:

"The German," he said, "came back from Shabwa and we met him at Qatn in the palace of the Sultan, and we asked him about the ruins there, and he said there is a mine and oil and gold to be found: and he brought the picture of an idol from there: and he was not happy there, he had a half day only, because the tribes struck at him: and he has now come and gone to the coast; and he went to the suburbs of Shabwa but they did not let him enter into the whole of it."

The Sultan had been right in his surmise: the ancient city and its sixty temples still await the traveller.

26

Shabwa Renounced

"What if I live no more those kingly days?
Their night sleeps with me still.
I dream my feet upon the starry ways ;
My heart rests in the hill.
I may not grudge the little left undone;
I hold the heights, I keep the dreams I won."

("April and Rain," G. W. YOUNG).

Now made what plans I could for when the feast should be over. I decided to be carried in a litter to the coast, as had been done with my host the year before, when he was ill: it would take eight days or more according to the length of our stages, and relays of six men would carry me for fifteen thalers each; the food problem would be solved by the purchase of three goats, who were to have the rather exhausting task of trotting alongside and providing milk at intervals. Everyone was optimistic about this project, though I could not help thinking of the last pages of the Bents' book, which ends tragically with just such a litter-journey. But the hot weather was coming soon, and I must leave the valley somehow.

I lay now through a weary quiescent period, enlivened chiefly by Iuslim's conversations. He would come in to gossip in the evening, while Salim, saying little, embracing his knees on one of the velvet chairs at the foot of my bed, nodded his brown head from time to time.

They suggested that I should try the Hadhramaut fashion of medicine and offered to bring a wise man to see me. If I had not just been through so much, I might have accepted: as it was, I listened to Iuslim's rather drastic list of cures. Honey and antimony, he told me, are mixed and eaten for dysentery. Wind, "which attacks one half of you all the way down," is discouraged by a fortnight spent in total darkness, "where nothing grows" – usually in a cavern in the hills; light food only is allowed, and probably explains the success of the cure. Snake bites, he said, are dealt with by a circle of men who sing round the patient while one of them sucks out the poison; and scorpion bites are cured by the pressing of a thaler on the wound. "As for the cough which comes after measles, you are lucky to be rid of it, for it often gives one a choking in the throat and one dies: over one hundred people have died these two last months in Shibam."

From my window I could see Shibam and its five hundred houses clustered like one fortress above a filigree of palms. On the dusty space in the foreground, camels were treading out the corn. They dragged a palm log in a circle round and round: the men, as they gathered up the straw in sheaves, sang a song together.

Everything in the Hadhramaut is done with singing. The houses are built with songs from the first mixing of mud and straw for their bricks to the last touch of whitewash to their cornice. Even the camel has its special song; the beduin croons it gently as he bobs to and fro: the camel pads along and turns its head contentedly from side to side; and the two together make such a picture of domestic happiness as they jog through the sunlit solitude of their lives, that I have often wondered how many married couples understand each other as intimately as they do.

As I lay and looked out on it all, Iuslim, wandering by the window, would give me bits of gossip here and there. Shibam was going to have a war, he told me, "with those houses over there" – a small and inoffensive-looking hamlet across the wadi whose particular truce was ending in a month's time.

Shibam had a garrison of about sixty slave soldiers, though the Sultan of Qatn had many more Yafi'i of his own apart from the Government of Makalla. Even now in peace time, the city gates were shut from 8 p.m. to dawn (two o'clock Arabic time to Fajr). Iuslim, who wished to go to a wedding one evening after dark, asked for my torch. The battery had come to an end, and I suggested a lantern.

"That would be no use. They would shoot me," said Iuslim.

"Who would shoot?"

"Why, the soldiers at the gate."

They used to show two lights there through the night, and one other small candle-gleam shone alone and apart among the buildings: otherwise the town stood like a crowd of shadows with heads pressed close together, and the wadi and the cliffs lay black around it, until the moon, rising above the eastern wall, made the outlines velvety and deep under her vague solitary sweetness, and made the barren thorns and palm bushes on the sandy patches look gentle and familiar as a western moor.

When the moon sank, the night lay dark as ink again, till morning broke swiftly, striding over the wadi walls from the Incense land: ten minutes were all that lay between darkness and dawn. Through my southern window, light then shone like a halo behind the cliff that overhung us, and caught the square watch tower, and showed the four boulders put there to look like ambushed men when the beduin had been shooting towards Shibam below. From the western window, the houses of Shibam reappeared in sunlight above their ditch, in which, said Iuslim, harlots, riding with shaved heads on an ass, are beaten round the town.

The methods of justice are simple. There is an old well in the middle of the town where, the worst offenders are put and their food is let down to them from above. For theft, a hand is cut off. Iuslim approved of justice, and told me with admiration the story of

Ibn Saud's judge and the man who lost a box of flour. The man went to claim it after a year and found it in the police station: the judge ordered it to be opened before him; one of the soldiers had pushed his finger through the keyhole to see what the box contained and the impress was still there in the flour for all to see: the soldiers' fingers were laid along it, and when the guilty one was found, it was cut off.

Iuslim, himself far too easygoing to hurt a fly, approved of this severity. But there is little reason for it in the Hadhramaut. Crimes arc committed, but usually by beduin, who go quickly back to their Jōl out of reach – such as the men who carried off a donkey from the garden suburb of 'Uqda in sight of our bungalow – an event which relieved the monotony of housekeeping and kept Iuslim amused and happy for some hours.

Slaves sometimes will be seized by the beduin when they get the chance, and be sold to new masters, and the slaves of the wadis, even when freed, will not venture on the Jōl alone, for fear of being so kidnapped and taken to some distant region to be sold.

Mahmud told me how two boys from Calcutta had recently been enticed with the promise of a job by Arabian sailors from Sur in 'Oman. When they landed, the Arabs sold them for 700 thalers to Se'ar beduin who took them to the north-west, and kept them to draw water for two years: at the end of this time, the master happened to bring them to Sewun on some business and they escaped and asked the townsmen if there were any Indian or British subject there. They were sent to Mahmud, who told the story to Sayyid Abu Bekr, and the beduin master was asked for. One of the two slaves had escaped, but the other one was bought by the Sayyid for 500 thalers (£38) (the beduin had asked for 1100); and was then sent to his home. This was ten months before my visit.

Children are sometimes kidnapped and sold. Sayyid Abu Bekr, to whose goodness no one appeals in vain, bought one of these small boys for 400 thalers (£30): he took the trouble to find out where he came from and wrote to his parents far away in Najd, but the boy would not return to them, and I saw him among those who waited on me in the household of Tarim.

As I listened to these stories, and the days passed quietly, our wadi and its traffic began to seem in my eyes, as it did in those of its inhabitants, a little island of peace and pleasant living.

I used to lie on a mattress on my terrace and read the works of Virgil, under perfect circumstances – my enjoyment of the classics being of that weak-kneed kind apt to be distracted if anything more easily readable lies anywhere around.

Virgil is one of the most restful of the classics to be ill with. No other poet that I know has so many or such lovely images of sleep, of the quiet of night and the resting earth. And I found, too, something greatly inspiriting in his disinterested, pagan fortitude of death.

> *Stat sua cuique dies, breve et irreparabile tempus omnibus est vitœ; sed famam extendere factis, hoc virtutis opus.*

or

> *Quo fata trahunt retrahuntque sequamur;*
> *Quidquid erit, superanda omnis fortuna ferendo.*

Who would not be encouraged by such words? Their majestic cadence sang itself in my ears with the sleepy creaking noise of wells, of which there were three in the neighbourhood. One or other was always working, and I could look down from my window and see our swimming-pool being refilled every two days or so. I could see the leather buckets rise slowly from their depth, hang a second or two suspended, then sink on to the trough, bend over their fat oozing sides, and pour out water: the swish of the water went on all day, dwindling and increasing as the buckets came or went: the wells were pleasant places under trees, speckled with shadows; and that was the only *running* water in the land.

From my mattress under the whitewashed wall I looked up into a light blue sky with clouds in it like thin folded veils. Small birds with black cravats and flat-topped black heads looked down at me from the roof-edge. There were hoopoes amid the pomegranates in flower. The pomegranates in Shibam had fruit, already quite big, and flowers, at the same time: they had been greatly encouraged by Squadron-Leader Rickards, who showed Iuslim how they ought to be pruned, and whose name is since mentioned with praise whenever the pomegranates are admired. His and Colonel Boscawen's are much-loved names in the wadi. There were many other birds there, of which I only recognized a wagtail, a white and brown eagle or kite, doves flocking in the cliffs, filling all with their sleepy voices, and the crows or ravens "that come and go with the corn and the dates."

At five by my watch (no longer very reliable) the sun went down. The sky grew yellow and green like the sky of Aden. The cliffs, jutting into the wadi, glowed like still fire; they stood like a fleet at anchor, one behind the other, alike and parallel, and each threw its shadow diagonally across the one behind into the farthest distance, where the wadi turned,

Maioresque cadunt altis de montibus umbrae.

A blue and green mistiness rose from their bays and inlets, till only the flat Jōl-edge gleamed and grew dull and died. Another long night was upon us.

27

Flight from the Valley

"I'll put a girdle round about the earth
In forty minutes." —

("A Midsummer Night's Dream.")

"And I said, O that I had wings like a dove! For then would I fly away,
and be at rest." — (53rd Psalm.)

The feast was the most elusive I have ever known.

Everyone was preparing for it, everyone was talking about it, but when it was actually to begin no one could say: some said two days and some said twelve. But the signs of its approach began to multiply at last. The beduin began to fire welcoming rifles as they approached Shibam – an expensive form of greeting, for every four shots cost them a thaler, and the government has now forbidden this amusement in the narrow streets of the town.

Then Salim asked leave of absence. He had a wife; he had paid sixty thalers (£4 10s.) for her, being a virgin (otherwise the price would have been only thirty); and he was also a butcher by trade, and would be needed to slaughter hundreds of sheep for the Friday:

these two reasons were sufficient, and Salim left me for a day or two, while Iuslim came at intervals, and the black slave 'Anbar stayed on guard below.

The Feast began on Tuesday. The first and second are the children's days, and people buy toys. The third is Zulfat al-Kubār, on which the dish called 'asi is eaten, a mixture of dates and corn and haidowān seed from the Jōl, cooked together for five hours. The fourth day is Friday, day of the Hajj, and they eat harīsa, the gruel of flour and meat I tasted in Do'an. On the fifth day, they visit al-Hauta of Shibam, the tomb of Ahmad ibn Husain bn Ahmad, outside the town beyond our bungalow: And on the sixth, there is a visit to Shaikha Sultana, the female saint beyond Sewun whose tomb we had passed there by the way.

I asked Iuslim why she was a saint, and he explained that it was because she had never married.

"Then," I said, "if I had died here the other day, and you had buried me as you promised you would, beside the landing-ground under a white dome, I would have been a saint too, and had a day for visitors?"

Iuslim looked non-committal.

"It is a good thing you did not die," he observed, "because what should we have done with your things? All the time, when you were so pale, that was what I was wondering. I decided to lock up everything at once, and then no one could ever think that *I* took anything myself."

Iuslim knew all the feasts in the country, and there are a great many. One of the chief round about here is at Qatn, on the 12th of the month Rabi' al Akhir, a five days' visit to the tomb of al-Habib 'Omar al-Hadhdhar. But the beduin, he said, really pay attention only to the Great Feast: even the one at the end of Ramadhan, here called Shurbat al-Ma', they scarcely observe.

By the 14th of March, the third day of the feast, when I had lain over a fortnight in my room, I thought I felt strong enough to walk a little in the sunshine. There was nobody about the bungalow, except the black slave 'Anbar, who came with me, and a lean dog with whom I had made friends – so lean that flies settled on him, which they never do when they are fat, said the slave.

We went along gently and sat by a siqaya by the roadside under palms. It was like the road to Camelot, and I – after a fortnight's prison – felt not unlike the Lady of Shalott looking with unaccustomed eyes on the traffic as it padded in the dust; peasants on donkeys, sitting on produce or with a sheep stretched across the saddle; Sayyids flowingly and immaculately white; beduins and camels; women flapping their blue trains behind them, a small jug or basket balanced on their head; negro soldiers, naked but for their loin-cloth and cartridge belt and gun; people carrying oil or samn in little leather bottles; donkeys invisible under a dragging load of reeds dried for fodder. Beside our little dome the animals stopped to drink: their drivers ladled the water out for them through the whitewashed lattice work of the siqaya into a shallow trough.

The people from the fields around came up to greet me and enquire, for they had heard about my illness, and gossiped about prices as country people do. It must be difficult to trade in the valley, for every town has weights and measures of its own. Shibam has an okīa, the weight of a thaler; the rotl, which is twelve thalers' weight; and the musra' which is twenty-nine; but in Ghurfa the musra' is more and in Sewun it is less than in Shibam. The prices have varied, too, with the world crisis: Shabwa salt, of which one used to buy sixty musra' for a thaler four years ago, rose to only four musra' to the thaler, and has now descended again to thirty.

Sa'id, my host, now came riding along on a small white ass and carpet saddle, and got off when he saw me and walked back with me to the bungalow. He brought me a phial of Indian sandalwood essence and talked about ambergris, which is still found along the shores of Shihr. When he left, I lay on my mattress in the shade of the terrace and read the Aeneid. I was thinking with regret that, having exhausted everything else, I would now have to begin the dull part, after the seventh book, when a buzzing sound, which had been gradually growing louder, at last drew my attention. In the sky, coming from the south-east and spanning all the valley, were four R.A.F. bomber planes, their aluminium shining in the sun, more beautiful to my eyes than any aeroplanes that I had ever seen.

They circled and landed east of the city walls: the notables hurried out like a row of ants to meet them: and out of one of the cockpits stepped Dr. Haythorne Thwayte and made his way towards my bungalow.

He found me too ill to move through the heated bumpy air of the afternoon, and we waited for the next dawn. In that early hour they strapped me into a stretcher and laid me crosswise in Sa'id's car and drove to the landing-ground near-by.

I could not turn my head, which was strapped down, but I could see the top of the cliff: it shone like a red sword in the sun.

The faces of Sa'id and Husain, the old Governor, Iuslim, and others, appeared one after the other over my cockpit horizon to say good-bye. I was in some kindly, improbable dream. Thoughtful and capable hands had taken the burden of decision from me. We rose: the walls of the wadi, that lime and sandstone prison, dropped away: as we flew, the doctor told me what lay below; in my mind I saw the Jōl and its shining paths made smooth by their millennial traffic, and the long massive watershed of Kor Saiban.

We refuelled at Fuwa, and here again friendly faces from Makalla climbed up to greet me where I lay. Flight-Lieutenant Guest, who piloted our machine, kept it high and steady in the cooler upper air; in five and a half hours altogether, we were in Aden.

> *It doesn't do to wander*
> *Too far from sober men,*
> *But there's an Island yonder,*
> [in sands if not in seas]
> *I think of it again.*

Appendix

Notes on the Southern Incense Route of Arabia

* The first number of the references refer to books that are
  listed from page 265.

† See map of Incense Routes.

Anyone who travels in South Arabia with an interest in historical geography will carry with him, it may be presumed, both Hamdani's *Jazirat al-'Arab* and Sprengers' *Alte Geographie Arabiens*.

Apart from these, however, a good deal of information exists, fragmentarily scattered, derived chiefly from more recent travellers, and from ancient inscriptions that have come to light. I had hoped to compare some of this with what clues I might collect in the country itself, especially along that stretch of the Incense Road which led from Shabwa to the sea. I was prevented by illness, and these notes are nothing but the summary of such information as I had gathered for my own use – a sort of skeleton to be clothed by local investigation. A satisfactory study of the ancient trade route of Arabia, the Incense Road which carried the spices of the southern coasts and the goods of India to the Mediterranean, requires far more historical knowledge than I can profess to have. Apart from the monuments hitherto recovered from the ancient Arabian empires, which must be studied, there is probably pre-historic material waiting for the student in half-obliterated mounds beside the way: and since this route must have been a desert route for most of its length ever since the termination of the pluvial period in Arabian geography – a route therefore defined by physical necessities of water – it is also well to follow its history as far as one can right through Mediæval Islam and modern time for, in its rough outline, it is likely to have remained unaltered.

We know from inscriptions that the southern empires had colonies or outposts to the north along the road which followed more or less the Hajj, the pilgrim route, building as it went Doughty's tomb city of Hejr (Madain Salih) and other monuments probably buried in the sand. No European has followed it from Syria to Mekka except that engaging adventurer, Ludovico de Varthema, in the early sixteenth century (i)*. One branch of it went by Petra, "where many Romans and strangers reside" (Strabo, xvi, iv, 21); and there was an easterly branch towards Syria, where the caravans came in from Gerra on the Persian Gulf: in 1900 B.C. "Asiatics of the Desert" brought antinomy to Egypt from Carmania (5. p. 192). The oasis of Taima, the Thaim of Ptolemy's map and Tema of Job, known in the days just before Islam as one of the places where Jews found it worth while to trade and settle, (2. p. 54), was a very old station on this Syrian branch, *"carrefour des routes de Syrie et du Héjaz"* (2. p. 314). Byzance used to keep small native outposts on it, and oil, corn and wine were exported to Arabia (2. p. 309).

The main Incense Road appears not to have passed through Mekka, which lies west of the direct way (3. p. 127). It touched Tabāla, where there was a famous temple to the Venus-God, Dhu-l-Halasa (4. p. 232), and thence reached the centres of the pre-Islamic empires of Arabia, an interesting and practically unknown portion of the great trade route.

The most northerly and most ancient of the empires known to us is the Minean, and its capital at Ma'in was visited by Joseph Halévy in 1870, in danger and in disguise, and by no European before or since. He collected a number of inscriptions which bear out Pliny's account of the Mineans as the oldest known commercial people in

South Arabia, holders of the Incense Route and monopolizers of the trade in myrrh and frankincense (5. p. 105). Pliny also gives an interesting reference which relates them with the Mineans of Crete, but this is by the way (5. p. 105).

The Minean king-lists, so far as they have been scheduled at present, lead us back approximately to the fourteenth century B.C., but there is no doubt that very much older records still await discovery in South Arabia. Whether or no they will connect with the Euphrates delta still remains to be seen: the Sumerian name of Magan used for the Persian Gulf may be related to Ma'in (4. p. 65); many words and names of the Hammurabi dynasty in Babilonia are South Arabian (4. pp. 61–2); and the coins found in South Arabia use symbols "that trace back to a very remote Babilonian antiquity" (6. p. 27): it is possible that there may be some foundation in local legends such as that quoted by Maqrizi, who makes 'Ad ibn Qahtan rule over the Babilonians and his brother Hadhramaut over the Habashi (of Dhufar) (5. p. 142); or in the Oman tradition (25) that some of the descendents of Shem, escaping from the Deluge, settled in Hadhramaut and thence spread into Arabia.

This is only one of the directions in which a study of ancient South Arabia will lead us. Trade with India and with Africa open up two other histories of which the scanty records we now have show only the later stages.

That the Indian trade was long established at the time of our Minean inscriptions may be inferred in various ways. The use of teak wood in the ancient Yemen buildings shows the intercourse with India (3. p. 157); and the Dravidian alphabet is supposed to be of Himyaritic[1] origin (5. p. 210): Lieutenant Speke, when he explored the Nile, found that the Hindu texts were his best geographical authority, owing to an ancient commerce with Abyssinia (5. p. 230).

---

[1] The words Himyaritic and Sabæan must often be used in a generic sense because there is no other single word to include the whole of South Arabian antiquity.

It is still an open question whether the "Land of Punt" to which the eighteenth dynasty Pharaohs sent their fleets, is to be located on the Arabian or African coast. On the Deir el-Bahri reliefs which illustrate these expeditions in the fifteenth century B.C., both the incense trees and the cattle are of the Arabian and not the African varieties (5. pp. 218, 270). An Egyptian tale of the eighteenth century B.C. speaks of Paanch, the island of the King of the Incense Land, the Panchaia of Virgil (Georg. I. 213), probably the island of Socotra and legendary home of the phoenix, that lays itself to die on "a nest of cinnamon and sprigs of incense" (Pliny, x. 2.) (5. pp. 133–7).

Whatever the exact location of the "Land of Punt" may be, there is no doubt as to the antiquity of its trade. The first known Egyptian expedition for incense was in the twenty-eighth century B.C. (5. p. 120), and even then the land must have been long "heard of from mouth to mouth by hearsay of the ancestors. The marvels brought thence . . . were brought from one to another . . . as a return for many payments," even as Richard Burton describes the trade from the heart of Africa to Egypt, handed from tribe to tribe.

There is also no doubt as to the early and close connection between the Arabian and African incense regions. Arabian names were taken over by colonists to Africa: the Ascitæ or Asachæ of the *Periplus*, of Stephanus of Byzantium and Bion crossed probably from Hāsik on the coast beyond Dhufar (5. p. 62); the Habashi, whose name developed into that of Abyssinia, the Hbsti of the Egyptian inscriptions came to Africa from the "lands of the Abaseni" east of Hadhramaut (5. p. 62). Josephus says that the capital of Ethiopia was called Saba till Kambyses changed it to Merce (7. II. p. 9).

The colonizing and trading activity of the Arabs along the African coasts has continued from the days of the south Arabian empires to modern times. In the first century A.D. the *Periplus* describes the coast towards Zanzibar as being "under some ancient right which subjects it to the sovereignty of the state that is become first in Arabia," which "sends many large ships, using Arab captains and agents who are familiar with the natives and intermarry with them" (5. p. 28).

Of all these colonizers and traders, the Habashi are the most interesting. Attacked by Hadhramaut from the north, they left their home along the Mahra coast towards the beginning of our era; built the city of Axum, and founded the kingdom of Abyssinia which perpetuates their name (5. p. 9). Their later alliance with Rome, which permitted the entry of a western power into the Red Sea and the Indian Ocean, and the substitution of a sea for a land route, finally was the cause of destruction to the south Arabian supremacy.

In the age just before Islam, Arab enterprise by sea seems to have declined, and the vessels mentioned as trading from the port of So'aiba near Mekka (for Jidda came later), are all Abyssinian (2. p. 15). But at the time of the *Periplus,* six centuries before, Muza (Mauza') and Ocelis (near Perim) were busy roadsteads "crowded with Arab shipowners and seafaring men" (5. p. 30). The ancient empires came down to the sea at these points. A Minean inscription has been found at Ta'izz and Abyan in Yemen (8. p. 70); and San'a mentioned as a "capital" in a pre-Islamic poem – (8. p. 8), was possibly the Uzal of Genesis x. 21: but the chief Incense Road passed through the hinterland farther east, and there seem to be no ancient vestiges on the western side of the Yemen watershed (9. pp. 7, 144) nor, in the days of the Hejra, were any Jews settled in this region (2. p. 154), at a time when most of the profitable trade was in their hands. The most westerly traces of the ancient empires were left by Himyar, whose capital was Tzafar near Yerim; and this westerly location is due to the shifting of trade towards the sea route, which gradually superseded the inland caravans.

From the centres of the Minean empire – Ma'in, Yatil (later Baraqish), Karnan (later as-Sauda), etc., which lie round the Wadi Kharīd in the region of Najran and Jauf (4. p. 15) – the great trade route entered the lands of Saba.

The Sabæans, mentioned in the book of Job, may possibly have come down from north Arabia. A Minean inscription mentions

them as attacking a north-going caravan to Egypt (4. p. 65). They
send tribute to Sargon in Assyria, and a Sabæan king is mentioned
under Sennacherib, in 685 B.C. (4. p. 75). They rose as the Mineans
declined, and their capital at Marib is the best known of all the
ancient capitals, owing chiefly to the destruction of its great dam in
the sixth century A.D., a catastrophe seized upon by Islamic legend
to mark what was no doubt in reality the very gradual breaking
up of old prosperity. The dam has an inscription dated A.D. 542–
3, and was repaired in A.D. 449–50 (4. pp. 105–6), so that its
destruction must have occurred only just before Islam. That this
affected the prosperity of the region as greatly as Arab fantasy and
later authorities have taken for granted is I believe very doubtful.
In his expedition to Arabia long before this date, Aelius Gallus the
Roman commander reached Mariaba (Marib) and there turned back
for lack of water – a conclusive proof that the region was not so
flowing with streams and honey as later writers profess. Indeed, I
believe that the whole of this great route was created, not by the
fertility of the lands through which it passed, but by the extremely
profitable nature of its trade – an argument which explains its sudden
decline as soon as that trade was deviated to the Red Sea.

The march of Aelius Gallus is interesting as a further corrobora-
tion of the old route, for he touched neither Mekka nor San'a but
marched east through Najran and other places in the Minean lands
(10. p. 389), and turned back at Caripeta – possibly Kharibat-Sa'ud,
where Katabanian inscriptions have been found (6. p. 20).

Marib is described by Pliny as a town six miles in circumference.
It has been visited by Arnaud (11.), Halévy (12.), and Glaser (13.),
to whom we owe most of the inscriptions and a plan of the great
dam, and of the Haram Bilqis, a temple built in that elliptical form
which, according to MM. Rathjens and VonWissmann (9. p. 212)
existed before the Mineans and other Semites displaced it with the
rectangular style which can be seen in the mosques of Hadhramaut
and Yemen to-day.

From Marib the route led, as it does now, to Harib and thence
to the Wadi Baihān.

Harib was the mint of the Katabanians, whose capital Tamna' lies somewhere in Baihān, though yet unidentified. Their descendants, the tribe Kitban, existed in the twelfth century as a sub-tribe of Dzu-Ru'ain (Sam'ani) whose origin was in Sarw-Madhij, south-east of Baihān (Hamdani. 90.).

What little is known about the Katabanians is due chiefly to Carlo Landberg (Arabica V.) and to Glaser (13. p. 24), who collected about 100 Katabanian inscriptions from beduin (4. pp. 23, 59 ff.). They were sovereigns in their time over their tract of the Incense Road; before and after the sixth century B.C. they warred with Saba, which engulfed them finally in 115 B.C., and celebrated the event by adding the title Dhu Raidan to that of Saba (4. pp. 87–8). Katabanian coins, however, continued to be struck (4. p. 94). Strabo describes them as extending to the straits of Bab el-Mandeb over the later lands of Himyar (6. p. 1).

The Gebanites, the Gebanitæ of Pliny, who ousted and succeeded the Katabanians in Tamna', also went down to the sea at Muza and Ocelis (8. p. 76). The track whichWyman Bury mentions as made in the eleventh century from Hadhramaut to the Tihama by way of Ibb (19. p. 15) possibly followed the line of the older highway. It was a branching off from the main Incense Route in favour of the African imports, on which custom dues were gathered. Pliny, when he speaks of myrrh (XII. p. 35) – which is now no longer grown for export in Arabia, but was still found in the Hadhramaut by the Bents (15. p. 89) – describes the Minean kind, which includes "that of Ansaritis in the kingdom of the Gebanitæ." And: "The growers pay the fourth part to the King of the Gebanitæ" (see also 5. p. 31).

Tamna' indeed, which Pliny describes as a city with sixty-five temples was one of the key positions on the Incense Road. The description of the traffic is interesting.

"The incense, after being collected, is carried on camels' backs to Sabota (Shabwa), of which place a single gate is left open for its admission. To deviate from the highroad while carrying it, the laws have made a capital offence. At this place the priests take by measure and not by weight, a tenth part in honour of their god, whom they call Sabis; indeed, it is not allowable to dispose of it before this has been done; out of this tenth the public expenses are defrayed for the divinity generously entertains all those strangers who have made a certain number of days' journey in coming thither. The incense *can only be exported through the country of the Gebanitæ,* and for this reason it is that a certain tax is paid to their king as well" (XII. p. 32).

Indeed the enormous length of the road, and the passing from one people to another, must have entailed a great deal of very delicate diplomacy and many distant relationships. The Mineans for instance appear as friends in Hadhramaut in early days, with a colony there (4.) and as friends of the Gebanitæ also (8. p. 75). The whole of the trade was an immense machine, delicately adjusted.

"There are certain portions also of frankincense which are given to the priests and king's secretaries: and in addition to these, the keepers of it, as well as the soldiers who guard it, the gate-keepers and various other employees, have their share as well. And then besides all along the route, there is at one place water to pay for, at another fodder, lodging of the stations, and various taxes and imposts besides; the consequence of which is, that the expense for each camel before it arrives at the shore of our sea [the Mediterranean], is 688 denarii. . . .

The Wadi Baihān, the highway between Tamna' and Shabwa, must have been a prosperous and populous region: the quantities of statues and inscriptions which are brought and reported from there testify to this apart from other evidence.

South of it, between Kataban and the sea, the kingdom of Ausan existed: we have two inscriptions only (4. p. 60 ff.), but it gave its name to the Ausanitic coast of East Africa (5. p. 74), and to the place near Zeila which the Somalis call Ausal. The only accounts I know of this region are, in Mediæval writers, Ibn Mujawir, who gives a route Aden-Shibam by Abyan, Dathina, Baihān, and 'Antar ('Andal?) (3. p. 144), and in modern times Wyman Bury's "Land of

Uz," where the existence of ruins round Nisab and Dathina suggest that in ancient, as in modern days, a number of tracks led up from the coast over the difficult watershed of the Kōr to feed and come into the great road somewhere south of Harib. Many ancient places here lasted on from the times of paganism into Islam, and Muller gives a list of such names: Dhu-l Qail, al-Qamar (between Sarw and Dathina), Hasa, Shammar, al-Baidha, al-Hajaira, "all castles . . . in Sarw and Radman, of pagan times" (8. p. 44). Even in the fourteenth century, Sarw Madhij sent out 20,000 men to fight and the Banu Wahas are mentioned "in a fort from the times of paganism" (14. III. 4. pp. 139, 247). The Yafi'i and Aulaki hillmen still frequent these tracks, by which the Turks, entrenched at Lahaj during the Great War, were able to get supplies, avoiding the coast. Idrisi's route from San'a to Hadhramaut and Dhufar, follows a roundabout way through this southern country by Sauma' and thence presumably by Nisab (3. p. 148); his eastern distances are very wild.

There must have been tracks to the sea from these populous highlands; but the testimony of the ancients, the geography of the country and the location of such finds as have already been made, all point to the fact that the main Incense Road, continuing by the Wadi Baihān to Shabwa, did not come to the sea until it reached a point more or less south of that city, where the *Periplus* mentions Cana (5. p. 32), the Canneh probably of Ezekiel, xxvii. 23, as the first port east of Aden.

To Shabwa "all the frankincense . . . in the country is brought . . . to be stored" – an indication which shows it to be in a key position west both of the incense forests and of the main road from the coast. The position of Shabwa is known, since a village of the name exists near the ancient site, and its salt quarries are as famous in the country now as they have been right through the Middle Ages. One of the British Museum bronze tablets dedicated to the god Almaqah is from Shabwa. Bakri describes the place as being reached from Marib by way of the small market place of Namra . . . through a sandy plain to the Sengar spring, and then by sandy dangerous lands belonging to the Banu Harith ibn Ka'b to Shabwa. This is the first town of Hadhramaut, and one sells there a camel load of fruit for one dirhem' – so that it must still have been a fertile spot in the eleventh century A.D. Its eastern approaches, now desert, must also have been fertile at that time, since Bakri continues to say that from Shabwa, "one village touches another to Jarima [?], the most blessed spot in Hadhramaut, surrounded by gardens" (3. p. 139). It is probably along this route that Husain ibn Salama, the great Ziadite Wazir in Yemen, built mosques and minarets in A.H. 409, one mosque at every stage, with wells and milestones, along the sixty stages between Tarim and Mekka (27. p. 236; 9).

The "sandy dangerous lands" west of Shabwa, were the south-east continuation of that wilderness of Saihad (called Dhahyal by Yaqut) which "divides between the inner lands of Yemen . . . and Hadhramaut, by four or five stages between Najran and Baihān," and "ends not far from Marib." (Hamdani). Hamdani, cited by Bakri (615.), mentions the loss of a caravan 270 miles from Najran in Saihad in his time. "Behold the desert of Saihad is an empty desert, a wilderness where the winds blow in all directions, a country where the crows are king." (Ibn Rusta, Bib. Geog. Ar. vii. p. 113.)

It was probably more of a wilderness in the days of Islam than earlier, for the sands have been encroaching in this desert corner. Hamdani, followed by Yaqut, (iv. 434) describes two roads, one along the Wadi Baihān and one north of it across Saihad. This northern road is a short cut to the Minean lands. It still exists and is used by caravans between Hadhramaut and Yemen whenever there is a condition of comparative tranquillity along that wild border. I was in the Wadi Hadhramaut at such a time, and met one or two of these caravans coming by way of 'Abr and Shabwa. The following itinerary for this route was written down by the grandfather of the present 'Attas Sayyids of Huraidha in Wadi 'Amd, and I copied it from his MSS. in Huraidha: he collected the names from beduin, and I give it for what it may be worth. No European has been along this way.

'Arudh – 'Ain (border of Hadhramaut) – 'Abr (marked on maps) – Mlais (tiny hamlet) – Mishainīq (spring) – Shirā (wadi,

good water) – Hadhbar Al Ja'aid (hill in wilderness with water) –
Khalaifa (little water) – Najran: 8 days altogether.

*   *   *

Practically nothing is known about the country through which this
northerly route travels; but the fact that, in spite of being shorter,
it does not seem to have interfered with the supremacy of the main
Incense Road south of it points either to a want of security or
to desert conditions (or probably to both) which would make its
use less satisfactory than the longer way. Another route which the
Bents mention (15. p. 129): (20. p. 220), in Wadi Ser, marked by a
Himyaritic signpost, was said by the beduin to have been abandoned
500 years before, because of encroaching sands. The fact seems to be
that the desert, though it has encroached sufficiently to destroy the
fertility of the Marib-Baihān-Shabwa fringe (assisted by the decline
of trade and external prosperity), was probably never, even in old
and prosperous days, *very* far from its present boundaries.

As for the main road, Marib – Shabwa – Hadhramaut, it is further
referred to by Ibn Khordadbah (Bib. Geog. Ar. v. 143) as nine sikak,
or post-houses, between Marib and 'Andal – proof that a post route
existed in the ninth century A.D.: by Ibn Rusta (ditto, vii. p. 113) as
three stages Shibam – Hadhramaut – Saba (i.e. Marib) – inaccurate,
but he makes an interesting reference to gold mines at Marib and
to the fact that the Shaikh's palace there dated from before Islam:
by Yaqut (iv. 434) who also wrongly makes Shabwa (i.e. J. Milh)
three days from Marib: by Ibn Mujawir, eight days, and, coming
to later times, by Niebuhr (26. p. 130), who gives Shibam-Marib,
with his usual accuracy, as ten days. This route is still the one most
generally followed by caravans from San'a.

We now reach Shabwa and the two main routes, south to the
port of Cana on the coast, and cast to the incense forests and Dhufar.

Shabwa, described by Pliny as a city with sixty temples, by the
Periplus (5. p. 32) as "the metropolis Sabbatha in which the King
lives" was the focus for both these streams of traffic, and its power
and importance is shown down to the early days of Islam, when

the Hadhrami present at the conquest of Egypt were first known as al-Ashbā ('Abd al-Hakam 47B, and Hamdani, p. 98). The name of a national dance in the Hadhramaut, the Shabwani, still perpetuates the name of Shabwa.

There can be little doubt that the main route between Shabwa and the coast lay along the Wadi 'Amd, the easiest and most direct way, full of ancient ruin-fields and signs of a once dense population (16. pp. 199–200). A way into Hadhramaut long continued to pass by 'Andal at the northern end of this wadi; the name 'Andal seems indeed to have been used as a synonym for Hadhramaut: "from Marib to 'Andal, which is Hadhramaut" (3. p. 143) (see also Hamdani, 85,26: Bakri and Yaqut merely quote from him).

It is probable that a parallel way led to the coast, as it does now, by the large and important ruin-field of Meshed to Do'an, Pliny's city of the Toani, and Ptolemy's Doan, and thence by the route taken by VonWrede in 1843 from Khuraiba in Wadi Do'an to meet the 'Amd route in Wadi Hajar: here the ruins of Obne corroborate the geographic arguments in favour of the ancient highway (17. p. 82). Von Wrede is no authority for the Wadi 'Amd, where all his statements are incorrect, but seems excellent for the piece between Do'an and the sea, which he alone has travelled. The Van den Meulen party travelled from 'Amd to the sea, but in too harassed a manner for historical research. The argument that from Do'an the route went south-west to Cana rather than south-east to Makalla is strengthened by the fact that there seem to be no Himyaritic ruins between Do'an (or Wadi Thiqbe close by), (16. p. 58) and Makalla; and Makalla itself cannot be traced back beyond a mention by Ibn Mujawir in the thirteenth century, and an unconfirmed remark by Hirsch, that it was founded in A.D. 1035 by a Yafi'i Ahmad ibn Mejim al Kesad (18. p. 12).

It is likely, therefore, that caravans went from Cana north, either by 'Amd or Do'an as they do now, while another route north-west from Cana led by the ruins of Naqb al-Hajar and Maifa'a, either into 'Amd along the Wadi Jardān or direct to Shabwa across the highlands of Madhij. These three routes, by which all the traffic from

Cana must have travelled, have never been properly investigated. The actual site of Cana itself is not located. The bay of Bir 'Ali fits with the description of the *Periplus* (5. pp. 32, 115); but Colonel Lake, one of the few people who have actually visited the region, suggests a natural harbour slightly farther east, nearer Ras al-Kalb. The place is, at any rate, in this immediate neighbourhood.

This important "market town by the shore," the Kane Emporium of Ptolemy, unfortunately lies in country as unhealthy now as ever it used to be when the frankincense "was gathered by the King's slaves and those who are sent to this service for punishment. For these places are very unhealthy, and pestilential even to those sailing along the coast" (5. p. 33), and this fact, and the uncertain temper of the tribes, has hitherto prevented research.

We now come to the frankincense land itself.

At this time it included the lands of Hadhramaut and Shihr (5. p. 117) as well as the modern incense regions of Dhufar. Indeed the Chatramotitæ, the "Hadhramautis," are the only people shown in the incense lands of Arabia on Eratosthenes' map, 220 B.C.

Incense still grows in the Hadhramaut valleys; I found it used all over the country, both in small earthenware braziers, or floating on drinking water "to make it pure," and always locally grown; and the Bents and M. Van den Meulen both found it: but the volume of trade declined with the substitution of burial for cremation and the disuse of sacrificial fires, and there is now no export west of Saihūt, though Muqaddasi (87.), Maqrizi (21. p. 28), Marco Polo, and Niebuhr in the eighteenth century (26. p. 202), still mention the export of frankincense from Shihr. Its great value when the trade was flourishing must have ensured its cultivation wherever it would grow, and the Hadhramaut seems to have been one of the best incense regions, second only to that of the Habashi in Dhufar.

The first King of Hadhramaut we hear of is a relative of the Minean Abi-Yadi'a Yatu (4. p. 102). Inscriptions are rare; most of them probably await discovery round Shabwa, the capital. The early spelling of the country is HDRMT (the omission of the waw (w) does away with the favourite Arab etymology of Hadhramaut from

maut, death). It is the Hazarmaveth of Genesis (x.), the Atramitæ of
Pliny and Chatramotitæ of Strabo, Eratosthenes, and Stephanus of
Byzantium. It must have been this incense that the Romans referred
to when Aelius Gallus turned back "two days from the incense land" –
an understatement in any case. (20. p. 12). Pliny (xii. 30), says:

"Almost in the very centre of that [frankincense] region are
the Atramitæ, a community of the Sabaei, the capital of whose
kingdom is Sabota, a place situate on a lofty mountain. [The cliffs
of these Wadis are referred to as 'Mountains' by other writers
also.] At a distance of eight stations from this is the incense-bearing
region . . . inaccessible because of rocks on every side, while it is
bounded on the right by the sea, from which it is shut out by
tremendously high cliffs. The forests extend eighty miles in length
and forty in breadth."

This description fits the Wadi Hadhramaut far better than Dhufar.
The incense was probably in the gullies of the Jōl as it is to-day;
it would take a few days to bring into the wadi, and four days
from Shibam to Shabwa, so that eight days altogether is reasonable.
About the end of the first century B.C., when the Habashi migrated
to found Abyssinia, Hadhramaut took over their lands of Mahra,
Socotra, etc., and became "King of the Incense Country" in its
entirety as far as Arabia is concerned (5. p. 119) until by the third
century A.D. it was engulfed in the Himyaritic kingdom of Saba (4.
p. 114).

With so rich a traffic in its borders, it is not surprising that the
Wadi Hadhramaut should be strewn with ancient ruins throughout
its inhabited length. The places where such ruins can be found
branching off the main valley are probably the lines of the old route
to the coast. Two such may be looked for east of Wadi Kasr – Do'an:
one in the Wadi ibn 'Ali, where the Bents found inscribed stones,
incense still flourishing in the gullies, villages, and a track "much
used and apparently ancient," leading across to the Wadi 'Adm (15.
pp. 161–9): and the other in the Wadi 'Adm itself, where there are

the important ruins of Sūne, visited by the Van den Meulen party (16. p. 145). Two inscriptions from there were kindly given to me by Sayyid Abu Bekr al-Kaf and are now in the Ashmolean. These ruins are on the present main way to Tarim from Shihr on the coast: their existence and the ease of the route itself suggest an ancient outlet to the sea, though no evidence of this has come to light at Shihr.

The town of Shihr replaced Cana in the Middle Ages. Marco Polo mentions it, and so does Ibn Batuta. Though it has an easy inland route behind it, it is an open beach with no natural protection or facility for landing, and its unimportance is easy to understand in the days when Cana was flourishing and safe. Shihr (the same word as Sahil – coast), presents many difficulties, for the name was used by the writers of Islam indiscriminately for the town, for the sea-coast of Hadhramaut, and as a synonym for that and Mahra together (22.). We have to deal with this when we come to the problem of routes between Hadhramaut and Dhufar, the most difficult part of all the Incense Road to trace.

That there was a close connection between Hadhramaut and Dhafur is obvious from the necessities of the incense trade and from the scattered evidence: but in what proportion the intercourse was carried on by land, and by what route, is far more difficult to gauge. So far as I know, no pre-Islamic inscriptions have yet been found in Dhufar: of the only two investigators, Mr. Bertram Thomas (23.) does not corroborate the Sabæan findings of the Bents (15. p. 240 ff.) who preceded him. That some trace of the ancient empires must exist there, is practically certain, but for the present the earliest historical evidence we have is that of classic times.

The Saphar of Genesis, "the mountain of the East," mentioned with Hazarmaveth and Hadoram'may, may well be Dhufar rather than the Tzafar of Himyar. The *Periplus* (5. pp. 33, 133) tells us of a fort and storehouse for frankincense at Ras Fartak, and then brings us to the port of Moscha, in eastern Dhufar (p. 140), the "harbour of the Abaseni" of Stephanus of Byzantium and Abyssapolis of Ptolemy. Frankincense "lies in heaps" over all this country and can be loaded on ship-board only by the King's orders. This state of things continued through the Middle Ages; it is described by Marco Polo, who mentions the Prince's profits on the sale of white incense as 600 per cent. According to the Marasid al-Ittila,' a geographical dictionary of this period, incense could be taken only to Dhufar (5. p. 144). All this points to sea-borne traffic along the Arabian coast. Throughout the Middle Ages, Dhufar was a port for Indian merchants, who were well treated and encouraged (Ibn Batuta). It is mentioned as a good port by Varthema in the sixteenth century (1.). It had a fleet of its own, used in the piratical raids to the Aden coast which led to the Rasulid conquest in the fourteenth century (22.).

A road along the actual coast is described by Ibn Mujawir (3. p. 144), but the journey was probably mostly done by sea: Ibn Batuta (I. 194) merely says that it took a month to go to Aden "over desert" – which suggests an inland way. The coast seems to have been difficult and full of obstacles (as any one who now looks at it from the sea can well imagine): the Rasulid advancing army in A.D. 1276 found it so (14. III. 3; 208 ff.), and the coast road to Oman on the east was just as bad (22.). Ships probably touched at Moscha (Dhufar), Syagrus (Ras Fartak), and Cana, and left a wild country in between, much as now, or as when Ibn Batuta, speaking of Dhufar, mentions it as "a city in a desert" with no villages near. The Bents give a vague rumour of an inscription near Mosaina'a and an equally vague legend that the basalt coast of Qosair is built up "of the ashes of infidel towns" (15. pp. 215–6); but they found "no ancient traces along the coast" as far as they went (15. p. 91): the land route to Hadhramaut probably passed behind the coastal ranges and declined with the decline of trade and the general wildness of the Mahra tribes. When the Bents visited the Qara hills, they declared that there was no communication with the interior (15. p. 270).

Hirsch mentions a land way from Dhufar to Hadhramaut, but gives no details (18. p. 80). The evidence for such a route in mediæval and modern times is meagre enough. Ibn Mujawir gives the stages between Shibam and Dhufar: they follow the Wadi Masīla from Tarim to Qabr Hud, and then become mere names denoting palm trees, ravines, and the fact that the last bit of the way at that time (thirteenth century) was well watered but little populated (Fol. 128B, B. Mus. MSS.). The incense regions, he says, are twenty farsah (eighty miles) from Dhufar. There are still many ancient traces as far east as Qabr Hud (16. p. 152), and the ruins of a dam farther down the wadi, known by the people of Hadhramaut and marked in Squadron-Leader Rickard's map from the air. Mr. and Mrs. Ingrams, who are the only Europeans to have followed the wadi to its estuary at Saihūt, saw no further traces of ruins: this however is not conclusive evidence against the existence of the ancient route, for the lower wadi is much silted up, and we have seen in any case that the Incense Road took long uninhabited stretches in its stride.

The mediæval writers become tantalizingly reticent and vague when they reach the stretch Hadhramaut-Dhufar. Bakri, from his Jarima in Hadhramaut makes it "three days through a sandy desert inhabited by Mahras to Ashfah on the sea-border of Oman, and then Raisut" (3. p. 140). During the Rasulid invasion from Yemen, one division marched from San'a and reached Raisut in five months' time, fighting all the way; the conqueror of Dhufar then made his way to Shibam, taking one month about it, but again with no details of the route (22.). Ibn Batuta remarks that Qabr Hud is in the Ahqaf, "half a day [sic] from Dhufar" (I. 197), an absurd underestimating of the distance; but it rather suggests that people were in the habit of making the journey, as the Arabs would otherwise have told Ibn Batuta that it was months away and inaccessible. Ibn Khordadbah and Qodama make the coast road, Oman-Mekka, go inland from "Shihr to the Incense land and Kinda (i.e. Hadhramaut), and then through Madhij to the coast at Aden" (3. p. 141). Kindi (Bib. Geog. Ar. I. 27) says: "The people of Hadhramaut and Mahra traverse the whole of their country until they reach the road between Aden and Mekka, and their distance is between twenty and fifty stages." The difference of thirty stages between Hadhramaut and Dhufar is reasonable if it is all overland, and this statement has about it a less vague appearance than most.

Our troubles are much increased by the fact that the word Shihr and Mahra are interchangeable, and used in the vaguest way, Shihr being as we have seen (22.), either the town itself, or that part of the coast which corresponds to Hadhramaut north of it, or the whole of the Hadhramaut and Mahra coasts to Oman; while on the other hand Mahra can be extended west to include "Asar, a port of places in Wadi Do'an" (Hamdani). The quotation from Kindi given above, however, mentions thirty stages between its western and eastern points of departure; the journey from Hadhramaut to Dhufar as done now, by the W. Masīla to Saihut and then by sea, takes sixteen days (3. p. 143), and this is what Ptolemy gives: we may take it that if Kindi is correct at all, he is speaking of a longer overland route through the mountains, which takes fifty days from Dhufar and twenty from Shabwa to reach the Mekka road – a reasonable estimate.

Another clue is given by Ibn Mujawir (Fol. 129B, B. Mus. MSS.), when he describes the terraces to which the ancient 'Adites used to migrate in spring. These terraces, he says, "with their fireplaces still well preserved" lie "between Hadhramaut and the borders of Oman, both along the coast and in the hills." He was told of them in Mekka by a man from Marab, a place half-way between Hadhramaut and Dhufar, along the land-route quoted from him above.

So much for this route. The evidence, meagre as it is, must be taken in conjunction with the geography of the country and the requirements of the ancient trade; when this practically unexplored region is better known, traces of old stations may yet be found making for Dhufar from somewhere in the Wadi Masila between Qabr Hud and the sea.

There is evidence of another inland route which, in the Middle Ages, went direct from Oman to Mekka, to the north both of Dhufar and Hadhramaut. This route is almost impracticable now. Burckhardt mentions it as long ago abandoned, but Sprenger had heard of it (3. p. 14), and Palgrave met two beduin who crossed from Oman to Najran by oases of wild palms, mostly uninhabited. Miles heard of a Nejdi who crossed from Najran to Abu Thabi on the Persian Gulf in fifty-six slow stages. Wyman Bury (19. p. 143), also heard of caravans crossing from the eastern sea by the desert. This may have been the old track found by Mr. Thomas in lat. 18°45′N 52°30′ E (27. p. 152). It was unpopular because of its want of water even in the early Middle Ages, when it is given by Mucaddasi and the Jihan-Nama as twenty-one stages to Mekka, eight of them waterless (3. p. 147). Hamdani (p. 165), describing the land between Yabrin and Hadhramaut calls it "a broad country, not to be crossed." But the Uqail tribe ranged over it (24. I, p. 70) and reached Mahra by a one and a half month's journey "where no other tribes dwelt." Even now the south of these sands are traversed. Mr. Thomas found "never a man in my escorts who had not raided into Hadhramaut": the Se'ar and others used a way along the edge of the southern desert for their raids; and in his camp at Shanna, guests appear "on their way home to the steppes north-east of Hadhramaut." The route has probably become more difficult in modern times. Mr. Thomas says very truly: "This tradition of ancient trade routes should not lightly be dismissed as impossible. South Arabia is held never to have had an ice age, and this very different pluvial climate may have long persisted and made possible a very early civilization" (27.).

It must also be remembered that it is far more the amount of profit at the end of the way, than the discomforts of the journey itself which determine the use of a trade route. When Baghdad was worth going to, the desert was crossed both from Baraqish (ancient Yatil) in Yemen, by Yamama – by the Tariq Radhradh still used in A.H. 649 (14. IV. p. 99) – and from Raisut in Dhufar, where a built-up causeway took the Indian trade to Iraq and beduin, in A.H. 616, brought horses twice a year (Ibn Muj. Fol. 132B). This route went perhaps by Yabrin, where it must have crossed the Oman-Mekka track. The trade in horses, which were shipped from Dhufar to India, must have kept open the desert routes to the north (22.). Distance and difficulty indeed seem to have been extraordinarily little thought of: Ibn Mujawir mentions the tanning industry in Yemen which used to deal with skins from Kerman and send them back to Transoxiana (3. p. 150). It seems probable from what evidence we have, that the desert route Oman-Mekka, under better climatic conditions and more frequented than now, might be open to travellers from Dhufar: but it is not likely that, with a populous and easy region to the south of it, the regular trade can ever have followed that more difficult way: the main traffic must have gone into the Wadi Hadhramaut overland or, most probably, gone to Cana by sea.

To the close connection between Hadhramaut and Dhufar we have many references. Even now the Qara mountain people call themselves Hakalai and derive their origin from Hadhramaut whither, they say, their ancestor's came by sea (23.). The bonds with Hadhramaut appear to be closer than those with Oman; the fashion of ornamented roofs, a very ancient fashion, is that of Hadhramaut and not of Oman, and the Omanis call the tribes of Dhufar, whose language is an old South Arabian dialect, Ahl al-Hadha ra (23.), just as the Hadhrami were called Hadharim by the northern Arabs after the coming of Islam. The contact between the two incense-bearing regions of east and west must have been intimate and prolonged: the routes by which it was maintained may come to light when the inland country between the W. Masīla and the Qara is explored.

List of Books Referred to in Appendix

(1) Ludovico de Varthema: *Itinerario.*

(2) H. Lammens: *L'Arabie Occidentale avant l'Hegire.*

(3) A. Sprenger: *Post und Reiserouten,* 1864.

(4) *Handbuch der Sudarabishcen Alterthumskunde:* ed. by Dr. Ditlef Nielsen.

(5) *The Periplus of the Erythraean Sea:* trans. by Schoff, 1912.

(6) G. F. Hill: *Ancient Coinage of South Arabia.*

(7) Josephus: *Antiquities of the Jews.*

(8) D. H. Muller: *Die Burgen u. Schlosser Sud-Arabiens Hamdani's Iklil.*

(9) Carl Rathjens u. H. v. Wissmann: *Vorislamische Alterthumer* (Hamburg Univ. Bd. 38, 1932).

(10) Jomard, in Mengin: *Histoire de l'Egypte sous Muhammad 'Ali.*

(11) Thos. Jos. Arnaud: *Journ. Soc. Asiat.:* Serie vii, vol. iii.

(12) Joseph Halévy: *Journ. Soc. Asiat.:* Serie vi, vol. xix, 1871.

(13) Edouard Glaser: *Forschungsreisen in Sudarabien.* By Otto Weber: *Alte Orient* ser., Leipzig, 1909.

(14) Al-Khazraji: *History of the Resuli Dynasty of Yemen.* Gibb series.

(15) Theodore and Mrs. Bent: *Southern Arabia.*

(16) Van den Meulen: *Hadhramaut: Some of its Mysteries Unveiled.*

(17) A. Von Wrede: *Reise in Hadhramaut.*

(18) L. Hirsch: *Reisen in Süd-Arabien Mahraland und Hadramūt.*

(19) Wyman Bury: *Arabia Infelix.*

(20) D. H. Hogarth: *The Penetration of Arabia.*

(21) Maqrizi: *Kitab at-Taraf 'arabia min Akhbar Hadhramaut; De Valle Hadhramaut Libellus*. Bonne, 1866.

(22) Rhuvon Guest: *Zufar in the Middle Ages. Islamic Culture:* vol. ix, No. 3.

(23) Bertram Thomas: *Arabia Felix*.

(24) Yaqut.

(25) Wellsted: *Travels in Oman*.

(26) Carsten Niebuhr: *Description de l'Arabie:* vol. I.

(27) Omarah's *History and the Karmathians in Yemen;* translated by H. C. Kay fr. *Kitab as-Suluk of Baha ad-Din al-Janadi*.

Other Books Consulted

The Encyclopaidia of Islam.

Bib. Geog. Ar.

Hamdani: *Jazirat al'Arab.*

Ibn Mujawir: MSS. in British Museum.

Ibn Batuta: *Rihlah.* Egyptian edition.

Carsten Niebuhr: *Reisebeschreibung, 1774.*

A. Sprenger: *Die Alte Geographie Arabiens.* Bern, 1875.

O'Leary: *History of the Fatimite Caliphate.*

Wyman Bury: *The Land of Uz.*

Tritton: *The Imams of San'a.*

H. F. Jacob: *Kings of Arabia.*

Amin Rihani: *Coasts of Arabia.*

O. H. Little: *The Geography and Geology of Makalla.*

Karolus Conti Rossini: *Crestomathia Arabica Meridionalis Epigraphica.* Rome, 1931.

H. St. John Philby: *The Heart of Arabia.*

H. St. John Philby: *The Empty Quarter.*

J. Helfritz: *Chicago der Wuste.*

J. Helfritz: *Land ohne Schatten.*

R. G. S. Journal: *Papers on Hadhramaut.*
   The Austrian Expedition to Southern Arabia and Socotra: Vol. 13, 638.
   J. T. Bent's Expedition: Vol. 4, 315.
   L. Hirsch's Journey: Vol. 3, 196.

Exploration of the Frankincense Country: Southern Arabia: J. Theodore Bent, Vol. 6, 109.

Air Reconnaissance of the Hadhramaut: Hon. R. A. Cockrane, Vol. 77, 209.

Notes on the Hadhramaut: W. H. Lee Warner, Vol. 77, 217.

Treasure of Ophir: C. E. V. Cranfurd, Vol. 75, 545.

Housebuilding in the Hadhramaut: Ingrams, Vol. 85, 370.

Film of the Hadhramaut by Squadron-Leader Rickards shown at the Royal Geographical Society.

Index